THE RUSSIAN ART OF DETERRENCE

DMITRY (DIMA) ADAMSKY

THE RUSSIAN WAY OF DETERRENCE

Strategic Culture, Coercion, and War

STANFORD UNIVERSITY PRESS

STANFORD, CALIFORNIA

Stanford University Press

Stanford, California

© 2024 by Dmitry (Dima) Adamsky. All rights reserved.

Printed in the United States of America on acid-free, archival-quality paper

Library of Congress Cataloging-in-Publication Data

Names: Adamsky, Dima, author.

Title: The Russian way of deterrence : strategic culture, coercion, and war / Dmitry (Dima) Adamsky.

Description: Stanford, California : Stanford University Press, [2024] | Includes bibliographical references and index.

Identifiers: LCCN 2023017225 (print) | LCCN 2023017226 (ebook) | ISBN 9781503630871 (cloth) | ISBN 9781503637825 (paperback) | ISBN 9781503637832 (epub)

Subjects: LCSH: Deterrence (Strategy) | Strategic culture—Russia (Federation) | Russia (Federation)—Military policy.

Classification: LCC UA770 .A33 2024 (print) | LCC UA770 (ebook) | DDC 355/.033547—dc23/eng/20230629

LC record available at https://lccn.loc.gov/2023017225

LC ebook record available at https://lccn.loc.gov/2023017226

Cover design: George Kirkpatrick

Art: Victor Vasnetsov, *Heroes (Bogatyri)*, 1898, oil on canvas, 116.2 in x 14.6 ft, Tretyakov Gallery, Moscow, Russia, with additional photoshop by George Kirkpatrick

Typeset by Newgen in 10.75/15 Adobe Caslon

To BDA

CONTENTS

ACKNOWLEDGMENTS

This work would not have been possible without the generous assistance of several people. I would like to briefly express my debt of gratitude to them.

The initial idea for the book evolved from my conversations about the nexus of strategic culture and art of deterrence with Jacqueline (Jackie) Deal, Andrew (Andy) Marshall, Andrew May, and Stephen Peter Rosen. I owe my gratitude to them for introducing me to the basic research question, for stimulating me to do cross-cultural comparative work on it, and for encouraging me to look deeper into variation of deterrence across strategic communities on both sides of the Atlantic, in Asia, and in the Middle East. Unparalleled opportunities to conduct, present, discuss, and polish my research in summer studies, seminars, and workshops as well as their questions, remarks, and suggestions during the last decade have been indispensable.

I would like to thank the Russia Strategic Initiative (RSI) at U.S. European Command, RSI director Ken Stolworthy, and Senior Strategic Advisor Michael Rouland for supporting an in-depth research endeavor on the Russian way of deterrence. The RSI Project Connect seminars offered the most valuable feedback to this end. I have benefited enormously from the observations, comments, and opportunity to develop knowledge together with Kristin Ven Bruusgaard, Samuel (Sam) Charap, Anya Fink, Michael Kofman, Roger N. McDermott, Andrew Monaghan, Olga (Olya) Oliker, Joe Cheravitch, and Katarzyna Zysk.

Michael Kofman and Andrew Monaghan dedicated to this work more attention that anyone else. Both have been generous with their time and wisdom—Michael Kofman on practical aspects of deterrence in the Russian context, and Andrew Monaghan on the peculiarities of Russian strategic culture. For several years, both skillfully combined collegial encouragement, sharp critique, constructive challenge, and useful advice. I benefited much from these two intellectual-social comrades in arms and would like to thank them.

I would like to thank Uri Bar-Joseph, whose work has informed my thinking on deterrence theory in the nonnuclear realm and assisted to better polish the notion of the culmination point of coercion. I would like to thank Yossi Baidatz, Nehemia Burgin, Keir Giles, Daniel Rakov, Yaacov (Kobi) Falkov, Lukas Milevski, Amr Yussuf, Keir Lieber, Daryl Press, Ariel (Eli) Levite, and Gideon Frank for the insights that highlighted the uniqueness of the Russian case within the broader comparative context.

Over the years I presented my work in several academic and nonacademic conferences, workshops, and seminars in the U.S., Europe, and Asia. I would like to thank Corentin Brustlein, Eliot Cohen, Eric Edelman, Janice Gross Stein, Ahmed Hashim, Beatrice Heuser, Robert (Rob) Johnson, David (Dave) Johnson, Sarunas Liekis, Thomas Mahnken, Kimberley Marten, Lawrence Rubin, Frans Osinga, Jeronim Perovic, Michael Raska, Michael Reynolds, Nicholas Roche, Adam N. Stulberg, Stephan De Spiegeleire, Tim Sweijs; Nicholas (Nik) Taylor and Alex S. Wilner, who invited me to present at these venues, to receive feedback, and to develop my ideas further.

I am indebted to Assaf Moghadam, Eithan Shamir, and James Wirtz for advice on theory and methodology, which they provided to me when I was preparing the book for publication. Two anonymous reviewers reread several versions of the manuscript meticulously and offered constructive and original suggestions, which I much appreciate and which approved the quality of the final product.

Special words of thanks are due to Ruvik Danieli for the superb editorial work and for always being there for me. I wish to acknowledge the professionalism of Alan Harvey and Daniel LoPreto of Stanford University Press, and thank them for their support, patience, and advice along the way.

I dedicate this book to BDA, who taught me about the limits of coercion, about the importance of reassurance, and about the greater significance of other aspects of life.

THE RUSSIAN WAY OF DETERRENCE

INTRODUCTION

THIS BOOK IS ABOUT the Russian approach to coercion and the cultural factors that account for its unique features. Coercion is a form of geopolitical influence. Its aim is to prevent an opponent from engaging in unwanted behavior by threatening to use force, or by its limited employment. Coercion targets the adversarial strategic calculus. By communicating that the costs of a prospective action outweigh the expected benefits, it seeks to convince the adversary to do something against its will. This strategy has two subcategories. Coercing an actor from doing something is called *deterrence*. Coercing an actor to do or stop doing something is called *compellence*.

In each form of influence the mechanism is identical—imposing one's strategic will on the adversary by the use of threat without resolving to massive use of force. Coercion rests on negative incentives, but it is a strategy of psychological influence, not physical domination. In international politics coercion is one of the main tools of statecraft, along with diplomacy and war. It is also a prominent scholarly concept in the academic world, where it features under the rubric of "deterrence theory."

Deterrence theory was incepted during the first decade of the nuclear era. Since then it has turned into one of the key constructs of international security studies. Until recently, the scholarship implied that the principles of deterrence theory and policy are somewhat generic and universal. However, the more scholars have explored how different actors practice this strategy worldwide, the more they have come to realize that the concept of coercion (both deterrence and compellence) varies across strategic communities. Various international actors conceptualize and practice this strategy differently. The Russian case offers an excellent illustration of a unique approach to deterrence by a non-Western strategic community.

This book dubs the Russian theory and practice of coercion (both deterrence and compellence) as deterrence *à la Russe*. This choice of wording reflects the Russian tendency, evident until recently, to use the term *deterrence* as an umbrella reference to all forms of coercive influence. The book explores the evolution of deterrence *à la Russe* and its intellectual sources, novelties, strengths, weaknesses, and prospective avenues of development. It investigates how and why this concept differs from the Western practice of this strategy and outlines the implications of this singularity for the policy and theory of international security.

The intellectual histories of the Russian and Western approaches to deterrence differ. For various reasons, which this book discusses, Russian deterrence theory is almost five decades younger than its Western equivalent. However, since the Soviet collapse, Russian defense intellectuals and practitioners have not only bridged the knowledge gap with the Western scholarship on this subject, but have also developed a unique and innovative theory of coercion. The Russian conceptualizations seem to be at least as sophisticated as the Western community's take on this matter. Russia is in good shape to deal with the psychological-cognitive dimensions of deterrence; it has demonstrated flexibility in merging different domains, and sophistication in its search for effective calibration of damage and in its effort to tailor its approach to the adversarial strategic culture.

Until the recent splash of interest, for most of the 2000s, Russian scholarship of deterrence left Western theoreticians and practitioners of this strategy somewhat behind. In the West, especially in the U.S., international security studies during the 1990s took what some call a vacation from military thought and strategy. As a result, up to the first decade of the twenty-first century, deterrence largely fell into disfavor in Western academic and defense circles. In the meantime, in Russia, deterrence theory was in full blossom. The new Russian "deterrence" converts have been storming the ivory tower of Western Cold War strategic theory and exploiting the Western intellectual hiatus to catch up. While Western deterrence theory has been in relative stagnation, and its practice has atrophied, the Russian experts have explored, internalized, critically emulated, and adopted certain constructs. Like the mythical Holy Grail, canonized deterrence theory has provided Russian experts with insights as regards two goals: to make better sense of adversarial strategic behavior, and to organize their own strategic behavior in the protracted political-military competition with the West.

MAIN ARGUMENT

This book compares and contrasts the Russian approach to deterrence with the Western conceptualization of this strategy. It argues that deterrence *à la Russe* has a much broader meaning than what Western experts have in mind when they use this term. In Russian parlance, it stands for employing threats, sometimes accompanied by limited use of force, to maintain the status quo, change it, shape the strategic environment within which the interaction occurs, prevent escalation, or de-escalate. Russian discourse uses the term to describe activities toward and during military conflict, and the usage of the term spans all phases of war. Also, deterrence *à la Russe* is not so much about rhetorical threats as it is about an action itself, concrete engagement of the competitor, which Russian experts see as a necessary condition for shaping a situation of coercion.

The official Russian term for the host of coercion activities in various operational domains is "strategic deterrence." At least until recently, Russian strategic thought tended not to differentiate, as is customary in the West, between *coercion*, *deterrence*, and *compellence*. This is one of the book's leitmotifs, and it matters in understanding Russian strategic behavior. The analysis in this book is guided by the argument regarding the peculiar Russian way of conceptualizing the relationship between *deterrence*, *coercion*, and *compellence*. The individual chapters integrate all three concepts rather than treat them separately.

What accounts for the difference between the Russian conceptualizations and the Western version of this strategy? Where does the sophistication of the Russian approach come from, especially considering that their research and development of this concept has been shorter than in the West? The main argument of this book is that cultural and ideational factors account for the peculiarities of the Russian approach. The singularities of deterrence *à la Russe* emanate from Russian strategic culture, national mentality, military customs, and intelligence traditions. The book demonstrates how the latter have been conditioning the former.

The book integrates the concept of coercion with the strategic culture framing, as the main lens to explain it. This nexus is the book's main novelty. To explore the impact of cultural factors on the Russian approach to deterrence, this work leans on several bodies of literature and builds on the author's previous efforts.[1] It offers delta as compared to the author's work and the state of the field. The basic facts about Russian strategic culture and military modernizations, the meta-themes of this book, which the author has been exploring elsewhere, have not changed. They therefore demand revisiting to promote the main argument.

The book itself, however, is a fresh analytical product. The author's previous endeavors were mainly micro-oriented. They are the point of departure for the novel claims and the framing of the macro picture. The book adjusts, expands on, and widens the author's earlier findings and supplements them with new empirical evidence, new linkages and contexts, and innovative theoretical explanations. The comprehensive analysis that the book offers has a synergetic effect—the new framework (i.e., cultural exploration of the Russian approach to coercion) is larger than the sum of its elements (i.e., an expanded earlier work with added, entirely new components).

CONTRIBUTIONS

Why does the Russian approach to deterrence matter for international security theory and policy? *Strategic deterrence*, or what this book calls *deterrence à la Russe*, lies at the heart of the current Russian art of strategy and is one of the main tools of statecraft in the Kremlin's arsenal.

Figuratively speaking, it occupies an intermediate position between classical war (i.e., use of massive brute force) and traditional diplomacy. Exploring the intellectual history of this concept and contrasting it with the equivalent tool in the West is not an arcane exercise, but a necessary condition for understanding the deep mechanics of this Russian stratagem.

Scholars and practitioners on both sides of the Atlantic have been laggard in tracing the evolution of the Russian theory of deterrence, its conceptual apparatus and terminology. With few exceptions, Western observers often lack a suitable framework of analysis to grasp Russian strategic theory and its operational applications. If left unaddressed, this shortcoming may downgrade Western performance in the national security realm. Examining Russian conduct through what some Western experts see as the "universal logic of deterrence" and analyzing it using the terminological apparatus of Western strategic studies is at best unhelpful. At worst, it could result in mirror imaging, intelligence misdiagnosis, and misperceptions, leading to security dilemmas and inadvertent escalations. If investigated properly, however, it can enrich Western strategic thought and improve crisis behavior and military performance.

Theoretically, the book breaks new ground in three subdisciplines of international security studies. First, it contributes to the field of Russian area studies. The book is the first comprehensive intellectual history of the Russian approach to deterrence. It arranges the existing knowledge on the subject, offers novel findings pertaining to the unique mechanism of deterrence *à la Russe*, and makes it accessible to broad audiences. It merges state-of-the-art scholarship on various aspects of the Russian theory and practice of deterrence with Russian strategic culture literature to offer the first-ever discussion of the cultural sources of deterrence *à la Russe*. Scholars can apply this pioneering method to explore other fields of Russian strategic behavior.

Second, the book contributes to the field of international security studies. This is the first systematic effort to merge the literature on deterrence with works on strategic culture, and to utilize the latter to explain the former. As a rule, these two corpora of research have been kept apart in the security studies literature. The literature has employed strategic culture theory to better tailor deterrence programs to the object of influence. This book is among the first comprehensive efforts to do things the other way around—to employ a cultural lens to explain an actor's proclivities when initiating a strategy of coercion. This novelty has potentially broad theoretical implications. The analytical framework that the book introduces aims to open a new avenue of research. Scholars of international security studies can replicate and apply the propositions, research design, and method that this book offers to other empirical cases of coercion.

Finally, this is a trailblazing effort in all three subdisciplines of international security studies (i.e., deterrence, strategic culture, and area studies) to compare and contrast, through a cultural lens, the Russian approach to deterrence to Western strategic theory.

STRUCTURE

The main argument about the nexus between strategic culture and the Russian approach to coercion in the nuclear, conventional, and informational realms knits together the individual chapters. The book sets out to outline the intellectual history of deterrence *à la Russe* and then offer cultural explanations for its traits.

Following this Introduction, the book proceeds as follows: Chapter One introduces the reader to the strategic culture scholarship and deterrence terminology—two key theoretical concepts that frame the book's analysis.

Chapter Two presents the genealogy of deterrence *à la Russe* from Soviet times to the present. It analyzes the various realms of deterrence as well as their cross-domain integration, highlighting the unique characteristics that distinguish deterrence *à la Russe* from the non-Russian, mainly Western approach to this strategy.

Chapter Three explores Russian strategic culture. It traces the peculiarities of deterrence *à la Russe* to unique cultural, ideational, and historical factors pertaining to the Russian style of strategy and military tradition.

Chapter Four critically discusses deterrence *à la Russe* and hypothesizes about the main challenges, which Russian practitioners of this strategy have been facing.

Chapter Five identifies the unknowns pertaining to deterrence *à la Russe*, merges them with the preliminary evidence from the war in Ukraine, and outlines the avenues of future research. The Conclusion summarizes the findings.

A note on terminology is due. Terminological discipline is necessary to study any foreign sphere of strategic activity where the object of analysis, in this case Russia, possesses its own professional vocabulary. This is not a casuistic, but a way to understand the otherness of a strategic other and avoid mirror imaging. Russian and Western experts often mean different things when using the same terms and use different terms to refer to the same things when discussing deterrence. Moreover, even Russian sources differ among themselves. This book sticks to Russian jargon as much as possible. It explicitly mentions when it uses the English terminology and when it introduces its own terms in order to better grasp the Russian concepts. In keeping with this approach, the book uses the non-Russian term "cross-domain coercion" in order to explain and discuss the Russian term "strategic deterrence" and make it accessible to non-Russian audiences.

A note on the sources is also due. The book explores the genealogy of Russian strategic thought and the intellectual climate within which it evolved. The analysis draws on a wide range of primary and secondary sources. Russian authors are affiliated with the establishment to varying degrees and come from different, often competing organizations within and beyond the Russian strategic community. The book seeks to represent this intellectual edifice in its entirety. It covers doctrinal and theoretical debates and competing schools of thought, comprised of active-duty or retired officers and officials, defense intellectuals, and experts from Russian academia and the think-tank industry. The book specifies who is writing what, and the extent to which the writings reflect formal doctrine, policy plans, and strategy.

A note on the analytical approach: the book also pays attention to disconnects between theory and practice—a recurring trait in Russian strategic tradition. Russian holistic theories, as the book demonstrates, do not always cover everything adequately, and often mix descriptive and aspirational arguments. The book seeks to represent the Russian discourse as a coherent whole, but also highlights its internal incoherence.

Deterrence *à la Russe*, like any other strategic theory, is constantly evolving. Deterrence as a subject of study is not a passing fashion but one of the main themes in the Russian international security discipline. In this regard, the Russian expert community is far-flung and vibrant. In the foreseeable future, this milieu is more likely than not to double down on its efforts to refine this tool of strategy and open new avenues of exploration. For Russia watchers in the West, then, it is essential to systematize knowledge about deterrence *à la Russe* and closely follow its evolution. This book does exactly that, but it certainly is not the conclusive statement on the matter. Rather, it delves into the intellectual history of the concept and outlines a prospective research program.

The book was completed and went into production several months prior to the Russian invasion of Ukraine. As of this writing, the war continues to unfold and the big picture is still emerging. Until the initial fog of war fades away, probably after the first cessation of massive fighting, any conclusions are premature. The chapter outlining the known unknowns and the future avenues of research offers some preliminary insights pertaining to Russian coercion prior to and during the war. However, the book's main contribution lies in providing the framework for a systemic examination of the Russian approach, once sufficient data has been accumulated from the battlefields of Ukraine. The book describes the genealogy of the Russian approach to coercion and highlights the cultural, ideational, and historical factors that have shaped it. This intellectual history makes it possible to understand the sources and style of the Kremlin's prewar and intrawar coercive conduct in Ukraine and to examine the prospective evolution of theory and practice of deterrence *à la Russe*.

CHAPTER 1

STRATEGIC CULTURE
AND DETERRENCE SCHOLARSHIP

THIS CHAPTER OFFERS a brief overview of strategic culture scholarship and a concise outline of the current state of deterrence theory.[1] Both are the main analytical lenses of this book. The subsequent chapters use the terminology associated with both concepts. The conceptual orientation that this chapter offers aims to make the book's main arguments immediately accessible to the reader.

The chapter consists of five sections. The first section defines the strategic culture paradigm and outlines its contributions to the communities of theory and policy. The second section discusses its lexicon. The third section describes the genealogy of the strategic culture concept. The fourth section highlights the current generation of scholarship. The concluding section discusses the current state of the deterrence literature and situates this book within this body of work. In sum, the chapter highlights the book's contribution to both research programs—deterrence and strategic culture.

STRATEGIC CULTURE: DEFINITIONS AND APPLICATIONS

Scholars agree that culture matters in strategy. Some argue that it is among the most important factors shaping national security concepts, military doctrines and organizational structures, weapon systems, styles of war, and almost every other aspect of a state's strategic behavior. There is also a consensus that culture is one of the most challenging factors as regards detecting, describing, and operationalizing it in a scientific way. To that end, the concept of *strategic culture* is used. It is a framework of analysis that utilizes cultural lenses to explain the strategic behavior of states in the international arena.

There is no single scholarly definition of strategic culture. As often happens in the social sciences, competing schools of thought coexist. This book defines *strategic culture* as a set of shared values, norms, beliefs, assumptions, and narratives (written, oral, formal, and informal), which shape and sometimes determine the collective identity, instincts, and modus operandi of a given strategic community in its approach to questions of peace and war (i.e., the appropriate ends, means, and ways of achieving national security objectives).

The style of warfare and tradition of war are central to any *strategic culture*. One can further unpack it into the organizational cultures of specific institutions comprising a given strategic community. The analysis could go even further to trace the subcultures of the military services, as well as those of the intelligence community, national security organs, and defense industry, especially since their impact on *strategic culture* varies from one actor to another.

This book utilizes the expression *strategic community* as an umbrella term for the entirety of institutions that officially and unofficially shape and determine various aspects of national security policy in a given state. Usually the military, intelligence apparatus, organs of executive and legislative power, defense-industrial complex, and think-tank industry are central to strategic communities. The significance of a given organ within the strategic community varies from one state to another. In the course of time, it can also shift in terms of bureaucratic weight and the scale of influence. A strategic community, despite the unique subcultures of the organs comprising it, shares general traits of the strategic culture of a given state.

Strategic culture scholars would argue that the ideational explanations they offer are a useful addition to neorealist rationalizations. The latter see strategic behavior as shaped by material and structural factors. The majority of the scholarship utilizes the strategic culture paradigm to supplement, rather than as a substitute for, the neorealist approach. However, in certain cases strategic culture may offer advantages over the non-ideational approach. Theoreticians and practitioners of international security find the paradigm useful in particular when explaining counter-intuitive and puzzling strategic behavior, which appears dysfunctional, ineffective, and self-defeating if judged by universal realist standards.

Foreign cultures may differ fundamentally from one's own in terms of thinking and actual policy in the national security realm. The strategic culture framework makes it possible to step outside one's ideational milieu, and at times ethnocentric worldview, and grasp the "otherness of the strategic other." Employing this analytical framework can potentially reduce the risk of mirror imaging, misdiagnosis, false assumptions, miscommunication, and inadvertent escalation. Practitioners value the analytical predisposition offered by this paradigm, especially in the realm of coercion. Even if they don't call it by its scholarly name, they employ it when dealing with coercive signaling, be it when trying to shape adversarial strategic behavior or to decipher strategic communications received from a competitor.

Originally the strategic culture paradigm was incepted within the narrow, nuclear context of the Cold War. Incrementally, it has turned into one of the main subdisciplines of international security studies and expanded its scope to a wide range of empirical applications. Scholars and practitioners employ the lenses of strategic culture to explain the ends, means, and ways of the security policy of state, non-state, and multi-state actors, in the conventional, subconventional, and nonconventional realms and at all levels of activity, from strategy to tactics.

CONCEPTUAL PREDISPOSITIONS

Scholars of the field have developed a terminology and concepts, on which they do not necessarily agree but which they widely utilize. Any analyst employing the strategic culture framework, explicitly or implicitly, takes a position on the following three theoretical-methodological questions. First, in the relationship between culture and strategic behavior, is the former a cause or a context of the latter? Is culture an independent variable that explains variations in strategy, or is it a context that somewhat conditions strategic thinking and action? As of this writing, the general tendency within the field has been to move away from bold statements about culture as the sole cause of behavior. The majority of scholars see it as a context, or as an intervening factor, or as one among several equally important independent variables, which in some cases offers better explanations of strategic behavior.[2]

Second, what are the sources of strategic culture? Culture, strategic culture specifically, emanates from the interplay of ideational and material factors. Scholars tend to offer a synthetic description of a cultural mosaic and trace recurring behavior to macro-environmental and non-material sources.[3] Shared national narratives (the elite's and collective beliefs about oneself, others, and the environment) may account for a state's approach to international security. To be considered part of national strategic culture, these mythologies must be common to organs of the strategic community. It does not matter whether or not these beliefs are grounded on facts. What matters is whether they are widely shared and inform an actor's identity.[4]

Third, does strategic culture change over time? The consensus is that the culture of a given actor should manifest more continuity than change over time. The literature agrees that changes in strategic culture are possible, albeit rare, and differentiates between three types. The first is a slow cultural transformation that spans a long period of time. Such a change is not brought about by deliberate effort, but through the accumulation of developments. These incrementally shape the norms and values of the given strategic community, forcing it to change. This change does not imply a total reinvention of the strategic culture, but rather the adaptation of earlier behavioral traits to the changing circumstances.[5] The second type of transformation is an opposite process—a rapid and broad change occurring over a short period of time. It usually involves a deliberate decision to disconnect from the previous culture, reinvent itself, adopt a new set of values, and reform professional behavior. Usually, such a sweeping self-reform of a strategic community occurs in response to a fundamental geopolitical shift.[6] In a third type of change, the overall culture stays intact but the strategic community adopts some new norms and practices. Such a change follows a major operational failure, when the traditional instincts cannot deliver. In such a situation, competing subcultures within the given strategic community emerge. They offer alternative philosophies, values, and modi operandi that eventually become the mainstream, thus changing certain aspects of strategic style. Such a shift is similar to the second ideal type in that it is rapid. It is similar to the first ideal type in that it has limited scope.[7]

GENEALOGY OF STRATEGIC CULTURE

Literature reviews systematize the strategic culture scholarship, breaking it down into four generations of research.[8] The first generation emerged in the late 1970s, when Jack Snyder's pathbreaking work coined the term. Snyder wrestled with the then mainstream "rational actor" model in IR theory, which largely ignored inter-state differences. He illustrated how these variations matter on the core issues of international security and might account for distinct modes of strategic behavior.[9] Subsequent explorations of the superpowers' dynamic resulted in the claim that strategic culture is deeply rooted in a set of beliefs, in a nation's formative experiences and political traditions, and creates a distinct mode of strategic thinking. The notion that different security communities might think in different ways about the same strategic matters began to gain acceptance. Empirically, the literature concentrated mostly on the nuclear strategies of the superpowers and their grand-strategy making.[10]

The second wave came in the 1990s. It sought a methodology to make the discipline less vague. This effort is closely associated with one of the key theoretical debates: whether strategic culture is an independent determinant of security policy, or constitutes a context, the intervening variable, the milieu within which strategy is shaped.[11] The competing schools agreed that even if not ultimately driven by culture, national security policy has deep cultural underpinnings.[12] The research program expanded. Several scholars concentrated on the interrelation between norms, culture, and strategic behavior on the national level;[13] others focused on domestic texture to explain styles in generating military power,[14] explored the role of bureaucratic cultures in military innovations and doctrines,[15] and analyzed cultural isomorphism between militaries.[16]

The third generation picked up from the early 2000s. Methodologically, it took the same path. Empirically, the research program reflected the shifts in international security. Some focus went to the "rogue actors." Academics applied the strategic culture framework to non-state actors, mainly jihadist,[17] and explored various aspects of the Iranian[18] Chinese,[19] Russian,[20] and North Korean[21] strategic cultures. In parallel, works on "multi-actor" strategic cultures, European, Asian,[22] and Nordic,[23] flourished. Against the backdrop of major defense modernizations, studies explored how cultural factors condition the military innovations.[24] The Second Nuclear Age stimulated the application of a cultural lens to the problems of proliferation.[25]

In parallel with the evolution of theory, scholars have been contesting its analytical value. Criticism has focused on insufficient operationalization, the nonfalsifiability of propositions, case selection bias (low-n research and low number of cross-cultural comparisons), and meager attention to the contest of different subcultures (i.e., treating the actor as a cultural monolith).[26] The current, fourth generation of literature is seeking to refine the discipline in response.

One line of endeavor implements a rigorous methodology that combines data and the social sciences.[27] Another stream of work deals with the aggregation and disaggregation of strategic cultures. An extension of the earlier "multi-actor" works, it offers a more coherent picture of the macro-level, supranational, but still distinctive regional collective security identities, mainly in Europe and Asia.[28] The flip side of this scholarship is a tendency to disaggregate monolithic strategic cultures. The culture of the strategic community is dissected into subcultures, which coexist and compete.[29] Organizations whose cultures are best aligned with the dominant strategic culture seek to appropriate resources to their interests.[30] Cultures of intelligence communities are another growing subfield.[31]

Finally, comparative cross-cultural analysis is gathering momentum. This method better highlights variation across the cases and better illustrates the idiosyncrasy of a given strategic actor. The literature compares and contrasts national styles in: insurgency and counterinsurgency,[32] nuclear decision-making,[33] deterrence,[34] peace-keeping,[35] and cyber affairs.[36]

DETERRENCE SCHOLARSHIP AND DISPOSITION OF THIS BOOK

This book lies at the intersection of two bodies of literature: theory of strategic culture and theory of deterrence. The latter explores the phenomenon of coercion in international politics. Coercion is a strategy of preventing unwanted behavior through influencing adversarial cost-benefit considerations by threats. One of its forms is deterrence. It aims to preserve the status quo. The other form is compellence. It aims to change the status quo. The academic literature has explored the conditions, mechanics, and peculiarities of these interrelated forms of influence under the general rubric of "deterrence theory."

The latter is one of the oldest and most thoroughly explored subdisciplines of international security studies. When the first wave of strategic culture scholarship arrived, the academic literature on deterrence was already about three decades old. Presumably, as of this writing, the intellectual energy invested in deterrence theory outweighs that invested in strategic culture exploration. This was obviously the case during the Cold War, both in Western academia and in the world of practice.

Following the Soviet collapse, the academic and policy worlds incrementally began losing interest in deterrence theory. During the 1990s and up to the early 2000s, topics unrelated to deterrence took center stage in international politics. The academic world adjusted the research program of international security studies accordingly. The fall of deterrence into disfavor, as an academic theory and as policy tool, lasted until the second decade of the twenty-first century. The post-9/11 security challenges brought deterrence discourse back from the wilderness into the academic and strategic communities on both sides of the Atlantic.[37]

Since Robert Jervis offered his periodization of the scholarship on the subject, literature reviews on deterrence have tended to dissect the corpus of knowledge along the generational lines. The first three waves of literature had a common denominator—they were state-centric and focused on the strategic dynamic within the military realm. However, a particular focus characterizes each body of work. Roughly speaking, the first wave mainly centered on matters pertaining to nuclear coercion. The subsequent two bodies of scholarship explored the rational (second wave) and the nonrational (third wave) aspects of decision-making in deterrence interactions. Historically, the first three waves originated during the Cold War and in its immediate aftermath. Then interest in the field revived in the early twenty-first century and a new corpus of knowledge emerged.[38]

Scholars dub the body of theoretical work that has emerged since 9/11 as "the fourth wave of deterrence literature." Its empirical focus and conceptual predisposition differentiate this wave of research from the earlier generations of work. In empirical terms, it has shifted the exploration focus from nuclear deterrence among state actors to exploring deterrence models for a wide range of strategic interactions within and beyond the nuclear realm, among both state and non-state actors. This reflects the state of international security politics of the time. Conceptually, constructivist or interpretative approaches to international security left the imprint on the fourth wave.[39]

Russian geopolitical gambits provided another boost. The war in Georgia in 2008 and especially the events of 2014 in Crimea further stimulated the splash of interest in deterrence. Academic and national security establishments in the U.S. and the European Union (EU) doubled down on exploring deterrence theory and its applications vis-à-vis Russian strategic assertiveness. As of this writing, the analytical scrutiny of the subject probably parallels, if it does not exceed, the peak of attention during the Cold War. Deterring prospective Russian conventional, nonconventional, subconventional, and informational aggression has been dominating policy debates and academic explorations for about a decade. Academic works on so-called "cross-domain deterrence"[40] have been conceptually informing the "multi-domain" strategies and doctrines in the NATO communities of practice.

Russian assertiveness gave an additional boost to the preexisting research efforts on deterring asymmetrical actors and terrorism. Building on this earlier stream of work, theoreticians began exploring the deterrence of "hybrid threats" or deterrence in the "gray zone," which emanate from a state actor seeking to operate below the level of a major war. This stream of work generated such significant debates and theoretical activities that scholars even began to argue that a fifth wave of deterrence scholarship is emerging. As of this writing, the demarcation line between these notional "fourth" and "fifth" lines of theory is not particularly clear. Nor there is a consensus on how to characterize it.[41] Theory is eclectic and conceptualization is groping in various directions. Proponents of the fifth wave acknowledge both continuity and change in relation to the previous scholarship. As in the earlier generations, the psychological aspect (i.e., deterrence as an effort to manipulate the strategic calculus of the adversary), the threat of military force (deterrence as prevention of force employment by threatening to retaliate in kind), and the distinction between state and non-state actors (as the primary focus) continue to be central to deterrence.[42]

In parallel, advocates of the new wave note certain novelties, which emanate from the current character of war (i.e., the "hybrid" or "gray zone"), and to which deterrence theory should adjust. First, the era of "weaponizaiton of everything"[43] or "securitization of everything" calls for unprecedented expansion of the scope of deterrence. Advocates of the fifth wave argue that we have entered the era of "deterrence of everything"—deterrence is expected to prevent a wide repertoire of threats, the majority of which are "annoying" rather than "deadly."[44] Second, society in its entirety has become both the subject (means) and the object (aim) of deterrence. This is a somewhat novel idea, in that the previous waves mainly focused on elites and the establishment. Finally, due to this centrality of the collective social dimension, a shift is under way from "deterrence by punishment" to "deterrence by denial and through resilience."[45] Although proponents of the fifth wave define the above characteristics as novelties, they can be seen as a variation on the theme of cross-domain deterrence, which is part of the fourth wave.

In conceptual terms, the current scholarship seeks to be a "contextualized" antipode to the previous generations of theory. Scholars of the fourth wave have called for a shift from "a one-size-fits-all" deterrence concept toward a "context-specific" approach to this strategy. Advocates of the emerging "fifth" wave do accept this claim and take it as their working assumption. Dubbed "tailored deterrence," in a nutshell it means crafting a coercion program in accordance with the strategic culture and mentality of a given opponent in a particular context. In a way, this call for "tailored deterrence" is old wine in a new bottle. It reemphasized a classical albeit seldom applied postulate of the previous generations of theory.[46] The simultaneous emergence of new symmetrical and asymmetrical challenges from both state and non-state actors across various operational domains further made this a prime time for the tailored approach to coercion.[47]

The quest for thinking about coercion in the context of a specific actor pushed the deterrence and strategic culture research programs closer to each other. Prior to that moment, these two bodies of theoretical work had been evolving in parallel, with no major intersections. Now scholars and practitioners started to combine the tailored approach to coercion with strategic culture theory. The literature called for utilizing the latter framework for better execution of the former.[48]

This book accepts this conceptual predisposition. However, it utilizes the strategic culture framework in a different way and makes a distinctive argument. *The Russian Way of Deterrence* argues that in order to understand the coercion strategy of a given actor, one must filter it through the lens of strategic culture. In other words, the book calls for a tailored, idiosyncratic approach not only in formulating deterrence strategy, but also in exploring the deterrence policies of different actors. The main assumption of this book is that strategic thinking evolves differently in various ideational realms. Thus, cultural factors condition the approach to coercion strategy and account for differences in this regard across the cases. This is the main argument of this book.

This argument is not novel. Earlier scholarly findings have established that when actors engage in coercion, ideational and cultural factors condition their "theories of victory."[49] Coercion, like any other strategy, has national characteristics, and it may differ from the postulates of Western strategic theory. Even prior to the fourth wave of deterrence literature, scholars accepted that the Cold War dynamics demonstrated that the superpowers—the U.S., the USSR and China—had different approaches to coercion and the assessment of each other's deterrence strategies.[50]

However, as of this writing, the nexus of deterrence and strategic culture from the perspective presented in this book has drawn meager attention. During the last decade, a growing but still limited number of works has explored the ideational-cultural imprint on the coercion strategies of various actors. Evidence from non-Western strategic communities that have invested significant energy in the exploration and practice of deterrence—most notably the Japanese, Chinese,[51] Iranian,[52] and Israeli[53] cases—indicates that the conceptualization of coercion varies across states under the imprint of ideational-cultural factors. *The Russian Way of Deterrence* is part of this research program. Exploring the Russian case study, it shows how the strategic culture of a given actor conditions the conceptualization and practice of coercion. As such, this book contributes to the fourth wave of deterrence theory and to the fourth generation of strategic culture scholarship. It brings these corpora of work together and takes them forward, contributing to international security literature and to Russia area studies.

CHAPTER 2

GENEALOGY OF DETERRENCE *À LA RUSSE*

THIS CHAPTER UNPACKS the main phenomenon that the book seeks to explain—the Russian approach to deterrence in the nuclear, conventional, and informational realms. The chapter outlines the genealogy of this concept in Russia, from its almost total rejection during the Soviet era to its avid embracement in today's Russia, and highlights the unique characteristics and mechanisms of this strategy.

Since 2014 there has been a wave of the Western state-of-the-art scholarship on various aspects of the Russian theory and practice of deterrence. This research endeavor has produced a solid corpus of knowledge, especially as compared to the earlier state of the field.[1] This chapter builds on these works and advances the discussion further.

As compared to the intellectual history of the deterrence concept in the West, that of deterrence *à la Russe* has been relatively short and uneven, in terms of the attention this subject has drawn over time. One possible way to arrange an excursus into the evolution of this concept would be to divide it into three historical periods. Each stage of attention has focused on a different aspect of deterrence, although there have been overlaps. Theory development during the Soviet and early post-Soviet era predominantly concentrated on the nuclear aspects; then, in the early twenty-first century came the focus on the nonnuclear aspects of deterrence, first conventional, and then informational. Each wave reflected the Russian threat perception, views on the character of war, and the military modernization during a given period.

Following the introduction the chapter consists of three major parts. This chapter first scrutinizes the nuclear and conventional aspects of deterrence *à la Russe*, and the unique mechanism employed to bring them to bear, and then unpacks the Russian theory and practice of informational deterrence.

NUCLEAR AND CONVENTIONAL DIMENSIONS OF DETERRENCE *À LA RUSSE*
The Soviet Rejection of Deterrence

To grasp the current state of the Russian theory and practice of deterrence, one need understand the conceptual odyssey of this term in Soviet military affairs and the paradigmatic shift, which occurred immediately following the Soviet collapse. In contrast to the West—where mainly the U.S. and UK strategic and expert communities incepted, developed, and distributed the concept of deterrence since the early Cold War, turning it into the main organizing logic of strategic interaction with the Soviet Union—deterrence was not a central notion in Soviet strategic thinking and military art due to Moscow's dichotomous attitude toward nuclear war.[2]

Intuitively, the Soviet leadership acted upon the logic of MAD (mutual assured destruction) and internalized the facts of life under it. Moscow's military policy was aimed at discouraging the U.S. from initiating a nuclear strike by ensuring that nuclear aggression would not remain unanswered. However, unlike their U.S. counterparts, throughout the Cold War, with a few small exceptions in the final years of the superpower standoff, "the Soviets did not develop an elaborate doctrine of deterrence enhanced by various strategies of nuclear use, selective targeting," and escalation dominance, and did not explore the options for intermediate levels of nuclear warfare, relying instead on the threat of massive retaliation. The Soviet political-military leadership "neither embraced nor ever really accepted the possibility of fighting a limited nuclear war, or of managing a nuclear war by climbing a ladder of escalation."[3]

Soviet strategic thought imposed a professional ban on researching the theory of "limited nuclear war."[4] The logic of flexible response was rejected up front,[5] the notions of "escalation dominance" and "control" were rebuffed, and the view of tactical nuclear weapons (TNW) as a limited tool of war was perceived as doctrinal nonsense.[6] The "bargaining" concept was disregarded as being based on false metaphysics and an invalid worldview. Suggestions along the lines of U.S. deterrence theory were considered a "monstrous heresy."[7] Operating within a different ideational-professional setting, Soviet military strategists, in contrast to their counterparts in the North Atlantic Treaty Organization (NATO), never abandoned the aim of victory in war and had a coherent nuclear war fighting strategy, which did not differentiate between conventional and nuclear war.[8] Even when, in the late 1970s, the Soviet political leadership qualified nuclear war as unwinnable, the military brass somehow reconciled these conflicting demands and continued to prepare to fight and win a nuclear conflict.[9] Soviet military theory saw fighting a regional war with tactical nuclear munitions as an operational activity that did not require a separate conceptual outline. All nuclear and conventional efforts, of all services, on all levels and in all theaters of operations, were seen as interconnected and aimed at producing victory.[10]

Formal rejection of the fundament of deterrence theory and its absence from the canonical military literature did not mean nonacceptance. Declassified materials, doctrinal publications, and the then-programmatic speeches of the political leadership clearly indicate that the Soviet decision makers, military brass, and civilian expert community shared the logic of MAD. However, despite the fact that the U.S. idea of nuclear weapons as a means of deterrence was acknowledged in Soviet military doctrine, the mission of equalizing conventional capabilities that Russian nuclear weapons were assigned in the late 1990s was nonexistent in the Soviet corpus of knowledge. In describing operational and strategic procedures, the doctrinal literature, of which the 1985 edition of the Soviet military encyclopedia is indicative, lacked the term *deterrence*. The Strategic Mission Missile Troops (RVSN), the title of the corps from Soviet times, were dubbed "forces of strategic deterrence" (*sili strategicheskogo sderazhivania*) only toward the late 1990s, a euphemism that was formally codified in doctrinal literature only in the early 2000s.

In post-Soviet Russia, the attitude toward deterrence radically changed. Not only did deterrence cease to be anathema, but in less than a decade this concept would become almost the Holy Grail of the Russian military brass. However, this transition from rejection to embracement of deterrence was a protracted and bumpy journey, accompanied by a significant crisis of knowledge and intensive learning endeavor of the expert community. Since the early 1990s, against the backdrop of acute conventional military inferiority vis-à-vis the West, and in some regards also vis-à-vis China, the Russian political leadership has sought an immediate remedy if war should come tomorrow. There was nothing handy in the Russian inventory back then but the nuclear arsenal. Almost overnight, the military brass realized that the political leadership had changed the role of the nuclear arsenal from fighting a war to supporting deterrence.

This paradigm shift threw the Russian military brass into a state of "knowledge crisis." On the one hand, military experts realized that the political leadership had assigned to the nuclear arsenal a new role (i.e., deterrence of nuclear and conventional war), but lacked a theory for turning nuclear use into an extension of politics. Confused, they qualified their state of knowledge regarding nuclear deterrence of conventional aggression as "the first steps in conceptualization of the newly emerging problem."[11] Indeed, they lacked an indigenous corpus of knowledge to lean upon if and when the need arose to de-escalate a conventional regional conflict by means of nuclear coercion. The Soviet military thought offered the Russian strategic studies discipline poor guidance on deterrence theory and limited nuclear use. To fill this conceptual deficit, for perhaps the first time they seriously took a look at the Western body of deterrence thought, which was for them, back then still brainchildren of the Soviet epoch, more often than not terra incognita.[12]

Conversion to Deterrence and Nuclear Equalizer
The following stage of knowledge development related to deterrence theory and practice lasted from the Soviet collapse until roughly the

early 2000s. It focused on the notion of deterring potential aggression, both conventional and nonconventional, by nuclear means, both strategic and nonstrategic, in a regional conventional war. When the notion of limited nuclear war and the missions associated with it started to appear in Russian official publications in the late 1990s to early 2000s,[13] Russian experts began to develop the requisite knowledge to inform a "regional nuclear deterrence" posture and nonstrategic nuclear weapons missions from scratch.[14] A wave of publications on various aspects of deterrence emerged in the late 1990s, gathering momentum toward the end of the first decade of the 2000s. Senior and midcareer General Staff and Ministry of Defense (MoD) officers, along with experts from government-affiliated think tanks, were the authors.[15] In developing deterrence theory, they adapted the terminology from U.S. strategic theory, and introduced doctrinal novelties that emulated theoretical postulates from the international relations literature about limited nuclear war.[16] The topics, which may sound like déjà vu to veterans of the Cold War, included basic conditions for establishing a deterrence regime, the mechanism of deterrence realization, escalation dominance, signaling credibility, the role of rationality in calculating unacceptable and minimal damage, and procedures of deterrence management.[17]

The overall tone of the publications at the time was one of exploration and recommendation—introducing a new theory and terminology, and establishing novel practices. For about a decade, professional periodicals debated the role of nonstrategic nuclear weapons in deterring and de-escalating regional conventional aggression. This debate generated ample assumptions and terminology, which migrated from one source to another.[18] The tone of the discussion at the time was interpretative, speculative, and hypothetical, and its conclusions fragmented and often mutually exclusive. The debate remained inconclusive about the theaters, missions, and types of nuclear weapons for deterring conventional aggression. Senior Russian experts' constant call for the formulation of theory for nuclear deterrence operations demonstrates a conceptual deficit and not just a lack of administrative power to translate existing theory into an actual posture.[19] The causal mechanism underlying the Russian deterrence approach, which was later defined in the West as "regional nuclear deterrence" or "escalate to de-escalate," was not officially elaborated back then. However, the concept rested on the widespread premise in the Russian strategic community that "regional conventional wars would not involve values for which the adversary would tolerate the risk of even a single nuclear strike. Consequently, limited nuclear use would deter or terminate conventional hostilities, without escalation to a massive nuclear exchange."[20] This was a temporary remedy, both theoretically and practically, as long as conventional military modernization was beyond Moscow's capacity.

The dominant motif and the main focus of that phase of deterrence knowledge generation was on the nuclear dimension. However, toward the end of the first decade of the twenty-first century, the variations on the nonnuclear aspects of deterrence started to appear in the Russian discourse. This initial thinking naturally was underdeveloped as compared to the level of conceptualization, which the next wave would bring. Besides, the consensus within the Russian senior brass and defense intellectuals was that although thinking about nonnuclear tools of coercion might be a useful intellectual exercise, in terms of strategy it was unrealistic, as in their estimate the procurement of a sufficient arsenal of advanced conventional munitions to enable nonnuclear forms of strategic influence was beyond Russian capacity and therefore any discussion aimed at operationalizing them as usable tools would be somewhat premature. Back then, a majority of experts envisioned this type of deterrence as a desirable but somewhat distant prospect and saw no nonnuclear alternative to deterring conventional aggression.[21]

By the end of the first decade of the twenty-first century, almost two decades of steadily intensifying debate and exploration had familiarized the core Russian expert community with the postulates of general deterrence theory and produced the contours of a widely agreed and applicable (i.e., operational) notion of deterrence. Deterrence *à la Russe* coalesced into the threat of nuclear use to prevent conventional aggression, and if deterrence should fail then limited use to de-escalate the fighting by nuclear means. This widely shared conventional wisdom migrated not only between the pages of doctrinal publications and professional journals but also into the operational practices of the Russian military, as annual exercises of that period demonstrated. Still, at that time the Russian deterrence concept was less coherent, monolithic, and elegant than in Western strategic studies, but possibly already comparable in many regards to the state of deterrence in the Western communities of practice during the early–mid Cold War. The level of coherence and synchronization between theoretical debates, official policy, and actual posture would rise during the next stage.

The Holy Grail of Strategic Deterrence

For the sake of analytical clarity, the stage of Russian deterrence theory development that is associated with the nonnuclear and nonmilitary aspects of deterrence can be correlated with the conventional modernization of the military, which gathered momentum following the 2008 Georgia war. Modernization efforts since then have aimed at turning the Russian military into a reconnaissance-strike complex of the IT-RMA (Information Technology Revolution in Military Affairs) era. The main focus has been on expanding the arsenal of standoff precision guided munitions (PGM), upgrading C4ISR capabilities, and training the military to wage combined arms network centric warfare (NCW)-type operations. In addition, this wave of development coincided with the splash of conceptual activity around the Western notion of hybrid warfare (HW) and the comparable Russian conceptualization of the changing character of war under the umbrella term of new-generation warfare (NGW). In a nutshell, both terms refer to an amalgamation of hard and nonkinetic tools across various domains, namely the coordinated application of military, diplomatic, and economic means. NGW, in the Russian view, is a type of warfare the aim of which is regime change brought about by exploitation of externally instigated internal protests, capitalization on indirect action, informational subversion, and private military organizations, backed by sophisticated conventional and nuclear capabilities.[22]

There is no monolithic Russian view on the current character of war. However, some generalizations are possible. Current Russian military science envisions contemporary warfare as an amalgam of *large-scale war* (aka "symmetrical," "traditional," and "classical") and *low-scale war* (aka "asymmetrical," "hybrid," or "mutiny").[23] Russian theoretical writings,

annual exercises, planning of combat operations, and commentaries by
the Russian military brass on how contemporary warfare has been and
should be waged all reflect these two types of warfare. Chief of the General Staff (GS) Valery Gerasimov has emphasized a fusion of these two
types of operations and sees proficiency in waging them separately and
simultaneously as a hallmark of excellence in contemporary warfare.[24]
Another Russian perspective, although nonofficial, views contemporary
war as an amalgam of *kinetic*, *cybernetic*, and *cognitive* segments.[25] *Information warfare* (IW) is a euphemism for the latter two elements. The
recent notion of *mental war* refers to the *cognitive* aspect of this
classification.[26]

A feeling of being more potent in terms of arsenal of capabilities,
coupled with a sense of Russia's rising from her knees geopolitically and
a perception of intensifying confrontation with the West, stimulated the
expansion of deterrence theory to a wide diapason of domains beyond
the nuclear, ranging from the conventional to the informational (cyber)
realms and beyond the military sphere per se. The notion of *"pre-nuclear"*
(*pred-iadernoe*)[27] or *conventional*[28] deterrence and the concept of informational (cyber) deterrence were seen as a prelude to the nuclear form of
coercive influence.[29] The merger of these tools into one system sought to
improve the credibility of Russian coercion by increasing escalation levels, through the threat of launching long-range conventional precision
guided strikes, selective or massive, and by signaling through other, less
devastating nonkinetic forms of engagement. Selective damage to the
military and civilian infrastructure should signal the last warning before
limited low-yield nuclear use, and as such has expanded Russian options
on the escalation ladder.[30] Believing that nonnuclear means (precision
weapons, and ballistic and cruise missiles) and informational (cyber) capabilities generate battlefield and deterrence effects comparable to those
of nuclear weapons, Russian experts, more than before, emphasized deterrence as a function of nonnuclear, hard and soft instruments.[31] The
2014 doctrine codified these thoughts circulating in the Russian expert
community into a nonnuclear deterrence system—a complex "of foreign
policy, military and nonmilitary measures aimed at preventing aggression by nonnuclear means." Within the repertoire of nonnuclear means,

the doctrine singled out precision conventional munitions as one of the main forceful tools of deterrence.[32]

The main feature of this wave of development, progressing beyond the nuclear realm, was a tendency to merge all the emerging tools of coercive influence into one unified system. Nonnuclear deterrence was not a substitute for but rather a complement to its nuclear analogue, as part of the "forceful measures" of strategic deterrence—a system of interconnected measures of both a forceful (nuclear and nonnuclear) and nonforceful nature. In Russian references this type of deterrence might include force demonstration to prevent escalation, and even the limited use of force as a radical hostilities de-escalation measure.[33] This amalgamation of various forms of military and nonmilitary coercive influence into one synthetic system of activity across several domains acquired—initially in public discourse and eventually in official documents—the title of strategic deterrence (*strategicheskoe sderzhivanie*).[34] In line with earlier Russian variations on the theme, *strategic deterrence* implies not only a demonstration of capability and the resolve to use it, but also the actual employment of limited force to signal to the adversary, to restrain it from more aggressive moves, to halt its current course of action, to shape the strategic environment within which interaction takes place, and to prevent escalation or de-escalation during the actual military conflict. Thus, it spans several phases of war, and also includes efforts of strategic influence at the softest end of the continuum, such as dissuasion (*razubezhdenie*) and propagandistic efforts (*raziasnenie pozitsii*).

Although *strategic deterrence* is an indigenous Russian term, some scholars, seeking to convey the logic of this Russian concept to Western audiences, use the non-Russian term *cross-domain coercion*. As the Russian term *strategic deterrence* also refers to compellence, generally preventing a threat from materializing, deterrence in peacetime and the use of force during wartime to shape the battlefield by military (nuclear and nonnuclear) and nonmilitary means, and since in all these cases this is not a brute force strategy but coercion aimed at manipulating the adversary's perception and influencing its strategic behavior, some scholars think that the notion of cross-domain coercion better captures the multifaceted logic of the Russian term.[35]

NUCLEAR AND CONVENTIONAL DETERRENCE *À LA RUSSE*: MECHANISM AND UNIQUENESS

Why do Russian experts and their Western colleagues often mean different things when using the same terms and use different terms to refer to the same things when discussing deterrence theory and practice? In part, the mishmash among the Russian experts is because the Russian theorizing of deterrence is relatively young and has been evolving through the debates of various schools of thought, frequently lacking official codification and a consistent terminological apparatus. More importantly, however, it is due to the unique etymology, internal logic, typology, and terminology, which differ, in several regards rather significantly, from their Western equivalents. In the course of catching up, the Russian expert community has been adopting certain terms from the Western, or what it calls Anglo-Saxon, lexicon. It has given them a Russian cultural reading and interpretation.[36] The end result is a unique Russian terminology, meanings, and approach to deterrence, which differs from the Western conceptualization.

This section compares and contrasts the Russian approach to deterrence to the Western practice of this art, in order to highlight the unique etymological, logical, and terminological characteristics of deterrence *à la Russe*.

In a nutshell, deterrence *à la Russe* is similar to its Western analogue—it is about the manipulation of negative incentives, threats aimed at shaping the strategic calculus, choices, and behavior of the adversary. However, beyond that, the Russian approach exhibits dissimilarities to its Western equivalent. Three differences, *etymological*, *logical*, and *typological*, loom large. These are not linguistic semantics, but rather a different strategic philosophy, which produces conceptual and operational variations. Moreover, as regards theorizing deterrence, in two specific aspects the Russian and Western approaches converge: both seek to be "cross-domain" and "tailored." Even though Russia is a relative latecomer to the world community of theory and practice of deterrence, where the Russian and Western approaches converge Russian conduct has been at least as good as, and maybe even has outperformed, its Western analogue. The paragraphs below unpack this argument.

Etymological and Logical Difference

The English term *deterrence* is usually translated to Russian as *sderzhivanie*. But although these two words, *deterrence* and *sderzhivanie*, apparently refer to the same term in the strategic studies discipline, they have completely different etymologies and thus somewhat different logics. Linguistic variance matters for practical reasons—it underlies different strategic philosophies. Etymologically, the English word *deterrence* is derived from the root terror, *fear*, and implies the infliction of apprehension to shape an adversary's choices and actions. Not the actual use of force but fear, emanating from the threat of prospective use of force, is the key rationale in classical Western deterrence theory. The Russian word *sderzhivanie*, by contrast, does not derive from the word *fear*. In colloquial Russian *sderzhivanie* relates to a concrete effort to hold back, restrain, or contain something (or someone) that is in motion or about to blow up, such as one's emotions, tears, horses, a crowd, pressure, or military aggression. Although, like the Western logic, it does imply the threat of making a particular choice of the adversary not worthwhile in cost-benefit terms, as it appears in the calculations of the other side, the figurative meaning of the word in Russian implies a somewhat different mechanism to achieve this end. The most important linguistic feature of *sderzhivanie*, in terms of the lexicographic association that it produces in the Russian mind, is the notion of a preemptive and proactive move, the concentration of energy, physical or emotional, directed toward a specific object to create the desired effect. The connotation of concentrated effort, proactive endeavor, and preemptive action, which underlies the meaning of Russian *sderzhivanie*, is more straightforward, embedded, and explicit than in the case of English *deterrence*, where fear is the central motif; in the latter the threat of the use of force is implicit rather than explicit, almost spelled out, as it is in *sderzhivanie*. The meaning of the Russian term, as well as the actual Russian approach (on which more below), implies to a lesser extent an expression of the threat to act, but rather an action itself, concrete engagement of the competitor, as a necessary condition for shaping a situation of deterrence. In short, *sderzhivanie* is not only about signaling by vocalizing the threat, as it is in the classical Western approach, but mostly about signaling by actual engagement (on which more below).

Besides *sderzhivanie*, several other words are used to translate the Western term *deterrence* in the Russian strategic lexicon. The Russian word *ustrashenie*, intimidation, which derives from the root *fear* (*strakh*), is the closest approximation to *terror* in English. However, apparently for practical-normative reasons this term has been used more seldom, as compared to *sderzhivanie*. During the Cold War, when the Soviet strategic community followed the Western discourse on deterrence, the word intimidation, *ustrashenie*, was almost by default employed to describe how the collective West was trying to coerce the USSR by using military threats.[37] In keeping with that tradition, in the current Russian discourse, intimidation is used more often than not either along the same lines—to describe Western coercive policies aimed at the Kremlin—or in order to translate one of the two deterrence strategies—*deterrence by punishment* (*sderzhivanie ustrasheniem*).[38] Contemporary Russian experts seldom use this term to describe Russian actions, as in the Russian cultural context intimidation has a negative connotation, implying a forceful, offensive, and aggressive act. Following their natural instincts, Russian experts dealing with deterrence theory define Moscow as operating from a position of defense and "counter-coercion" (*kontrsderzhivanie*),[39] which makes the usage of the term *intimidation* inappropriate.[40] Moreover, in contrast to the Western lexicon, in Russian usage the term *sderzhivanie* is applied beyond the general military-strategic dimension to concrete historical strategies on the grand level. For example, the term *containment*—the grand strategy of the U.S. Cold War policy, which aimed at erecting a geopolitical cordon sanitaire restraining the spread of Soviet influence worldwide—has often been translated to Russian in the same way as deterrence—*sderzhivanie*. In English parlance the two terms are different as they apply to different spheres of interaction— military strategy versus geopolitics—but from the Russian perceptive they are similar since both aim at forcing restraint on the strategic behavior of the adversary—in that case the Soviet Union.[41]

Broader Rationale and Scope

The above etymological dissimilarities correspond with different rationales and the different scope of deterrence application across the cases.

In terms of internal logic, the interpretation of this concept in the Russian strategic lexicon is much broader than the meaning that Western experts have in mind. Deterrence *à la Russe* stands for the use of threats, sometimes accompanied by limited use of force, to preserve the status quo ("to *deter,*" in Western parlance), to change it ("to *compel,*" in Western parlance), to shape the strategic environment within which the interaction occurs, to prevent escalation and to de-escalate during actual fighting. In Western usage, the term *deterrence* implies a more reactive modus operandi, while the term *compellence* has a more proactive connotation.[42] The Russian discourse uses the term *deterrence* to refer to both, although there is a clear line between them in the Western lexicon and terminology. The term *prinuzhdenie*, literally translated as *compellence* (i.e., changing the status quo), features rarely in Russian discourse. Since the word has a somewhat negative normative connotation, the attitude toward it and its usage is similar to the Russian stance toward the term *intimidation*—usually to qualify what the West is doing to Moscow. Still, in the professional circles dealing with peacekeeping operations, which are somewhat secondary in the Russian expert community and in the mainstream of deterrence literature, the term compellence (*prinuzhdenie*) is an established professional concept for peace-enforcement operations. On several occasions, this term has migrated to the center of the strategic lexicon and been employed to describe Russian military practice. One prominent example of usage of this term as a euphemism for deterrence and coercion was the 2008 Russian operation in Georgia, which the Russian president and military brass dubbed an "operation of compelling to peace" (*operatsiia po prinuzhdeniiu k miru*). As of this writing, usage of the term has been growing incrementally, but *prinuzhdenie* (compellence) still features in the Russian discourse more seldom than *sderzhivanie* (deterrence). In the run-up to the war in Ukraine there was a spike in usage of the term.

Finally, regarding the scope and place of deterrence within any strategic interaction, the term is used to describe signaling and activities both toward and during military conflict (i.e., *peacetime* and *wartime*), and it spans all phases of war (*threatening, initial, main,* and *final periods* of war). Thus, deterrence in Russian parlance encapsulates at once several types of the "Western" deterrence taxonomy: not only to prevent hostilities (*broad deterrence*), but also to prevent specific moves within hostilities (*narrow deterrence*). As such, the Russian interpretation of deterrence is closer to the Western conceptualization of "coercion," in its prewar and intrawar forms.[43] That said, there is no established expression or consensual translation for *coercion*, as an umbrella term for both *deterrence* and *compellence*. The Russian discourse often utilizes the term *deterrence* and more seldom the term *compellence* (*prinuzhdenie*) to express a concept similar to the Western term *coercion*. The context usually indicates which form of influence the authors are referring to. The common denominator is that it is about an effort to impose your strategic will on the other side by activities below the threshold of major military activity or the use of brute force.[44]

Varying Typologies: Punishment and Denial vs. Forceful and Nonforceful Deterrence

There are typological differences as well. In the nuclear and conventional realms, Russian thinking about the nomenclature of deterrence types does not parallel the Western conceptualization in this matter. The conceptual dichotomy of *denial* and *punishment* strategies of deterrence, which is widespread in the West, does not really frame the Russian operational art of deterrence, except in the informational realm (on which more below). Classical Western IR literature distinguishes between two types of deterrence—*denial* and *punishment*. Both types share the same logic of coercion—persuasion by a threat of negative incentives—but their means differ. *Deterrence by punishment* shapes an adversary's behavior through the prospect of subsequent retaliation in various forms. It influences the strategic calculus of the adversary by the threat of punitive action following a potential move. It is usually associated with offensive means enabling the victim of potential aggression to retaliate at a time, place, and magnitude of its choosing. In contrast, *deterrence by denial* seeks to influence an adversary's strategic behavior through the prospect of diminishing benefits. This strategy rests on forceful obstacles that hamper the adversarial move or totally deny it combat success. *Deterrence by denial* signals a threat to turn adversarial aggression into a prolonged war of attrition, which is doomed to fail and/or in which the costs of fighting outweigh the expected benefits of the campaign. *Denial* has usually been associated with various kinds of passive and active military defenses, aimed at hardening the target of attack. Although there might be an overlap between these two forms, in the simple language *denial* means "you can not have it, so why bother," and *punishment* means "you might get it but it won't be worth it."[45]

For Russian practitioners, the Western classificatory dichotomy of *punishment* versus *denial* might appear to be irrelevant casuistry—sophisticated but unhelpful reasoning. The Russian discourse tends to focus on the essence of deterrence strategy—regardless of the mechanism (defeating an attack versus retaliating) that the victim of potential aggression employs to manipulate the challenger's perception of the prospective costs and thus prevent detrimental behavior and preserve the status quo. Apparently, the Russian theoretical discourse on the subject implies that since both types of deterrence use different mechanisms to inflict pain, impose costs, and achieve the same goal, they often merge by default and by design; therefore, any purposeful distinction between *punishment* and *denial*, at least along the lines offered in the Western discourse, is apparently meaningless and thus unelaborated. In the Russian case, in the nuclear and conventional military realms, the distinction between the two forms of this strategy has never been as prominent as in the Western lexicon,[46] where both concepts are rather well articulated.

The terms have featured in Russian discourse mainly since the Soviet collapse, when Russian experts began making sense of this Western conceptual dichotomy. Utilizing different terms, the Russians have tried to capture the meanings attributed to *denial* and *punishment* in the Western discourse. The accuracy of translation and the depth of elaboration have been uneven between the two. In contrast to the relatively established translation and understanding of *punishment* as *sderzhivanie nakazaniem* (penalty), *ustrasheniem* (intimidation), and *ugrozoi otveta* (threat of response), *denial* lacks a canonical translation and accepted interpretation. The variety of terms reflects the underconceptualization of this notion in Russian discourse. Although the Russian discourse is replete with several translations of *denial*,[47] Russian practitioners relatively seldom use these terms or even refer to the notion of *denial*. Often they use the generic term *deterrence* and leave it to the context to flesh out the meaning.[48]

Instead, intellectual energy in the Russian discourse has been focused on developing a different nomenclature and coming up with several classifications that are nonexistent in Western thinking. The Russian approach avoids the conceptual-linguistic *denial-punishment* acrobatics, focusing instead on a different taxonomy. Russians perceive strategic interaction holistically, as encapsulating a permanent dialectics between two coercive stratagems: "intimidation" or "fear-inducement" (*ustrashenie*), which refers to declaratory signaling and manifestations of resolve and capability, and "forceful deterrence" (*silovoe sderzhivanie*), which refers to a diapason of limited use of force, on the battlefield and beyond, to coerce the adversary and shape his strategic behavior. Implicitly, both stratagems could and should be employed in tandem during peacetime, the period of threat and wartime. Apparently, since Russians perceive deterrence interaction holistically, the battlefield (which may be beyond the enemy's national territory) and critical infrastructure (which may be within the enemy's territory) are part and parcel of the same adversarial system. Thus, the valuable taxonomy, for Russian experts, is not the *punishment-denial* dichotomy but the distinction between the *forceful* (*silovoe*) and *nonforceful* (*ustrashenie*) aspects of the operational art of deterrence.[49]

Being "Tailored"

The Russian approach to deterrence appears to be at least as "tailored" as the Western one. A quick excursus into history is due to grasp the meaning of being *tailored* in the Western deterrence lexicon. After falling into relative disfavor in the Western international security discipline, in the early 2000s deterrence scholarship returned from the wilderness, under the rubric of "the fourth wave of deterrence literature." This corpus of work has often been referred to as the "tailored" or "contextualized" antipode to the mechanical approach to deterrence, as it shifts from "a one-size-fits-all notion of deterrence," a relic of the Cold War, toward crafting unique, context- and actor-specific and culturally sensitive coercion programs for a wider spectrum of adversaries. During the 2010s, the call by Western defense experts, academics, and practitioners for "tailored deterrence" sounded like "the same old wine in a brand new bottle," since it reemphasized classical but seldom applied postulates of the earlier waves of classical deterrence scholarship. However, operationalizing the principle of being "tailored" in the Western communities of practice was easier said than done. Whatever the level of novelty of tailored deterrence, in concrete military planning terms it boils down to viewing a specific opponent as idiosyncratic, considering a wide spectrum of ideational-cultural variables underlying his rationality, and tailoring military threats to his unique and non-universal values, phobias, perceptions, and interests. The sheer amount of ink that Western academia poured on this subject during the last decade and the empirical evidence from the NATO militaries in the post–Cold War era indicates that it was easier said than introduced into operational planning within the communities of practice on both sides of the Atlantic.[50] Where has the Russian expert community been with regard to this *tailored* Western fashion?

Michael Kofman, Anya Fink, and Jeffrey Edmonds, in what is probably the most fundamental unclassified research so far on Russian deterrence strategy,[51] have devoted meticulous attention to the assessment of threats and damage calibration (i.e., dosage and forms of signaling), which has been ongoing in the Russian professional discourse since the early 2000s. The Russian pursuit, within their discussion on escalation management, of a proper conceptual classification for "deterring damage" (*sderzhivaiuschii uscherb*), as illustrated in the dialectics between the terms "unacceptable" (*nepriemlimyi*), "assigned" (*zadannyi*), and "dosed" (*dozirovannyi*) damage, was not an academic intellectual exercise; waged in large part by uniformed practitioners, it sought to inform and organize the operational targeting procedures of the Russian military.[52] This debate over the most cost-effective way to generate a psychological effect on the adversary, coupled with the calls by Russian practitioners to see the threshold of deterrence pain as subjective, contextualized, and fluctuating, clearly demonstrates how deeply and seriously the Russian approach has adopted what the Western strategic studies lexicon dubs "tailored deterrence." A direct linkage between strategic cultures and deterrence strategies[53] and the centrality of the psychological aspect of coercion, as the main organizing principle for the design of deterrence operations and the force buildup enabling them, have been omnipresent, explicitly and implicitly, in the Russian discourse, especially when Russian sources refer to a "Strategic Operation for the Destruction of Critically Important Targets."[54] Although there are still many questions as to how exactly Russian practitioners operationalize their awareness, as the works of Kofman, Fink, Edmonds, and Clint Reach demonstrate, the significant intellectual and organizational energy that Russia is investing in damage measurement, calibration, and peculiarities and the discussions on these subjects, which are still ongoing in the Russian community of practice, indicate the sensitivity to adversarial strategic culture and the psychological-subjective approach to deterrence. These developments are comparable to Western deterrence theory and practice and efforts to double down on "tailored deterrence" during the last decade. Chapters Four and Five examine the effectiveness of the Russian approach prior and during the war. The Russian efforts have a certain precision to them, but one could argue it has been a false precision, based on a erroneous assumptions. The war in Ukraine demonstrated some of this challenge. The subsequent, postwar research will establish whether Russian tailored approach to coercion has offered genuinely useful, actionable insights.

Being Cross-Domain

An even more significant variation is evident within the quest, common to both the West and Russia, to become *cross-domain*. The term *cross-domain deterrence* entered the professional lexicon of Western strategic studies during the last decade in response to the complex character of current international security, "which contrasts with the bilateral nuclear bargaining context envisioned by classical deterrence theory." In a nutshell, the cross-domain approach to deterrence calls for recognition of the need, and then developing the capacity, to merge various forms of coercive power—military (conventional, nonconventional, subconventional) and nonmilitary—within one integrated program, as well as the need to maneuver from one sphere of engagement to another in accordance with political necessity and strategic circumstances. As of this writing, the work of Lindsay and Gartzke best reflects the state of *cross-domain deterrence* as strategic theory within the Western communities of knowledge and as a tool of strategy among the mainstream of U.S. national security practitioners.[55]

Where has the Russian community of knowledge and practice, under their indigenous rubric of *strategic deterrence*, been with regard to this Western *cross-domain* fashion? In three regards Russian practitioners and theoreticians have come up with at least as sophisticated a conceptualization and execution as their Western colleagues, if not better. First, deterrence *à la Russe* was incepted up front as a cross-domain construct—i.e., in the 1990s influence from the nuclear domain was maneuvered to the conventional sphere to compensate for Russia's strategic-operational inferiority. While Western experts needed to design this feature and introduce it into the art of deterrence, the Russians simply needed to expand this practice, which came naturally to them since the early post-Soviet days, to more domains. Second, as compared to the Russian *strategic deterrence*, the U.S. cross-domain deterrence, at least in its initial state, was compartmentalized and one-dimensional (i.e., tended to isolate one form of deterrence from another). As the writings of Russian military experts and defense intellectuals suggest, the theory of *strategic deterrence* implies that when Russia is maneuvering from one domain to another, all tools of influence should merge and then move as one organic whole into the sphere where the main engagement is taking place. In contrast to this Russian "combined arms" maneuver, and despite a call for combining different military and nonmilitary forms of influence to reach a coercive outcome, cross-domain deterrence, as the U.S. strategic theory and practice illustrates, tends to project one tool of influence from one specific domain into another to gain a competitive advantage.

Finally, when merging domains, the Russian approach has fewer self-imposed normative and psychological restrictions. There is a constant quest for a synergetic effect, so that new domains do not substitute for but complement the existing ones. For example, the focus on the conventional aspects and informational struggle, cognitive-psychological and digital-technological, which gained prominence during the last decade, did not come at the expense of the nuclear capabilities, which not only were not devalued but have been accelerated in parallel. In the Russian case, there has been no tendency—as there has been in the U.S. military community in the post–Cold War era against the backdrop of the IT-RMA excitement and initial monopolization of the precision regime—to isolate the nuclear dimension from all others and preserve it for atomic interaction only. Extended deterrence in the U.S. alliances includes potential first use, Western military planners apparently incorporate nonstrategic nuclear use in their plans, and American scholars also postulate such use of nuclear weapons, as Matthew Kroenig's work exemplifies.[56] That said, as Evan Montgomery's work illustrates, as of this writing the U.S. community of practice lags somewhat behind their Russian counterparts in this regard and is grappling with organizational, conceptual, and cultural obstacles, less present in Russia, when operationalizing the cross-domain form of coercion.[57]

INFORMATIONAL DETERRENCE *À LA RUSSE*
Introduction
Deterrence *à la Russe* is a holistic construct, as it seeks to synthesize nuclear, conventional, and nonkinetic forms of influence within one scheme of *strategic deterrence*. This section singles out the informational aspect from other forms of coercion for analytical purposes only; as of this writing, the repertoire of methods under the rubric of *informational deterrence* has been less elaborated as compared to the Russian conceptualization of nuclear and conventional deterrence. Progress toward coherence, as in the nuclear-conventional realm, and indications of possible major transformations, doctrinal and organizational, in the near future are evident. Still, this relatively novel and constantly emerging conceptual construct, on which the data is fractional, has been underexplored in the West. How do the Russian establishment and expert community define informational coercion (deterrence)? How did Russian thinking about this concept evolve? What is the mechanism of this strategy? This part

addresses these questions and aims to balance the current knowledge on this form of influence with previously discussed Russian forms of coercion. It argues that the philosophy of this strategy differs somewhat from the Russian nuclear and nonnuclear analogues. The main dissimilarity is unlimited use of limited force, psychological and technological, which is central to informational coercion *à la Russe*.

Terminological discipline is particularly important in the case of informational deterrence (coercion), since many basic terms and concepts of the field are still not codified in Russian doctrine. Russian terminology differentiates between *informational space*—all the spheres where societal perception occurs; *information*—the content that shapes perception and decision-making; and *informational infrastructure*—the digital and analog technological expression of the first two, essentially cognitive-perceptional, components. Russian military planners design informational operations as an integrated whole, the aim being to influence the above three components comprising the informational domain that enables and underlies decision-making.[58] The inclusion of *content* within the definition, and the assumption that the *code* is sometimes of equal importance, sometimes secondary, are among the main dissimilarities to the Western approach.[59]

This peculiarity extends to the relationship between psychological and technological forms of influence.[60] Russian discourse differentiates between informational-psychological and informational-technical ways, means, and targets of influence.[61] To better communicate the subtle meanings of the Russian philosophy, this book defines the first type of influence as cognitive-psychological,[62] and the second type as digital-technological, to capture the entire range of systems—cyber (i.e., digital) and radio-electronic (i.e., analog) and their combination. The Russian term *radio-electronic struggle* (REB) refers to offensive and defensive electronic warfare, while the term *cyber warfare* (*kiberneticheskaia* or *kiber voina/bor'ba*) is used in reference to digital computer network offensive and defensive operations. Initially, Western thinking tended to compartmentalize the Russian cognitive-psychological (CP) and digital-technological (DT) capabilities and the countermeasures to them.[63] This book uses the term *informational war* as a rubric for three Russian terms used interchangeably: *informational warfare (voina)*, *struggle (bor'ba)*, and *confrontation (protivoborstvo)*.

There is a consensus among the Russian military brass how central the informational segment of war (be it CP or DT or both) is to contemporary armed struggle.[64] Chief of the Russian General Staff Gerasimov designates it as a leitmotif of new-generation warfare (NGW).[65] Without diminishing the fact that programmatic speeches single out IW as a central effort, as of this writing no evidence suggests that it has turned into a codified *strategic operation*, acquired its own *theater of military operations*, or become a separate *service*. Although there is no such codified concept in the doctrinal taxonomy and planning procedures, since the terms *informational TVD (teatr voennyklh deistvii*—theater of military operations) or *theater of IO* (informational operations) do feature in the Russian professional discourse, this book employs them as a euphemism to group under one category the set of activities employed for the sake of informational struggle (warfare) and coercion. The means of IW, reflecting the phenomenon's dual nature (i.e., technological and cognitive), include radio-electronic, cyber, and psychological operations; they are interwoven into an integrated informational strike on the decision-making and decision-executing elements of the adversary. Such an informational strike is about breaking the internal coherence of the enemy system—not about its physical integral annihilation.[66]

Defining informational coercion *à la Russe* poses a larger terminological challenge than in the nuclear and conventional spheres. This is not unheard-of; the Western discourse on the subject has also been confusing at times.[67] In a narrow sense, by analogy to the nuclear-conventional field, informational coercion implies that the ways, means, and targets of influence are informational. However, formal Russian definitions are broader. In Russian discourse informational deterrence stands for the use of informational tools to shape adversarial behavior in 1) the Russian informational domain, and 2) in the noninformational, military, and nonmilitary realms (for example, to prevent sanctions); and 3) the use of noninformational tools to prevent adversarial influence in Russia's informational domain.[68] As elsewhere, under the Russian approach the same informational sphere is used as a medium to communicate coercive signals pertaining to the nuclear and conventional realms. However, since Russian *strategic deterrence* merges all forms of coercive influence synthetically, at times it is impossible to point to where one form of influence ends and another starts. To complicate things further, the Russian approach merges CP and DT forms of influence under one roof.

This work refers to informational coercion in two regards: when Moscow forces a competitor to do something against its will by threatening to employ informational influence (CP or DT or both); and when Moscow threatens to employ any type of influence to repel malign activities in the informational space. The later Russian discourse sometimes dubs counterdeterrence (*kontr-sderzhivanie*) "incapacitating the enemy to realize deterrence." Counterdeterrence features here as the ability to withstand and repulse adversarial coercion (forceful and non-forceful), by means of mitigating deterrent/coercive damage, which the enemy threatens to inflict.[69] This term is similar to the dyad "strategy vs. counter-strategy of hybrid war."[70] In its logic, informational counterdeterrence in the CP sphere corresponds with the Soviet intelligence term "ideological disarmament of the adversary."[71] An example of counterdeterrence in the DT sphere would be a threat to use force against adversarial C4ISR systems to incapacitate informational superiority and the ability to wage an NCW-type operation.[72]

Informational Deterrence: Genealogy of the Concept
In Russia, as elsewhere, the official doctrine and strategic theory evolve symbiotically. The history of Russian nuclear-conventional deterrence demonstrates that although experts' polemics is not doctrine, it matters. Professional theoretical debates shape doctrinal trajectories, reflect the predispositions of the expert community, and to a certain extent influence the policymakers. The discussion below presents the interwoven evolution of doctrine and the strategic theory of informational deterrence *à la Russe*.

RUSSIAN DISCOURSE: THE PROCESS
On the highest doctrinal level, the topic of *informational coercion* has been under-elaborated as compared to the definition of deterrence in the

nuclear and conventional realms. As of this writing, Russian formal policy papers at the national and ministerial levels have not devoted attention to the topic separately. The CP and DT aspects of the informational sphere have featured in all of the documents, explicitly and implicitly, but none of them was dedicated solely to informational coercion. The stand-alone paragraphs on the subject are not comparable in status and level of elaboration to their nuclear-conventional analogues. Since the early 2000s, when the first references to informational security started to feature in the national-level white papers, for almost two decades the formal treatment of *informational deterrence* has fallen between the doctrinal chairs.

The 2000 *Doctrine of Informational Security* is the first Russian white paper that singled out national policy in the informational sphere as its central matter.[73] It did not touch on the issue of deterrence per se, but differentiated between prevention and repulsion of informational threats.[74] The 2010 *Military Doctrine* paid significant attention to deterrence as a general means of conflict prevention, but did not single out the application of this strategy to the informational realm.[75] The first dedicated examination of informational deterrence appeared in the MoD's 2011 *Conceptual Views on Activities of the Armed Forces of the Russian Federation in the Informational Space*.[76] It offered "ten commandments" on the "deterrence and prevention of conflict in the informational space," which appeared as a separate section of the document. Although the document offered more detailed reference to the subject than the previous and subsequent ones, the elaboration was not comparable to the Russian conceptualizations of nuclear, conventional, and strategic deterrence. Also, there was a discrepancy between the relatively detailed elaboration and the binding doctrinal power; the *Conceptual Views*, albeit an official document, had no legal status as compared to other doctrinal papers, which were all signed by the president.

The first formal reference to deterrence in the informational sphere appeared in the 2014 *Military Doctrine*, which introduced the notion of "the system of nonnuclear deterrence" and implied that informational deterrence would be an element of this system. The wording of this first reference was generic, with no specification of the ways, means, and ends of deterring the CP and DT aspects of aggression. Implicitly, informational deterrence was assigned a stand-alone role under the rubric of "strategic deterrence," in the subcategory of nonnuclear deterrence.[77] The next variation on the theme appeared in the 2016 *Doctrine of Informational Security of the RF*, where deterrence featured as the first among several directions of informational security: "Strategic deterrence and prevention of military conflicts, which might emerge as a result of employment of informational technologies." The document also differentiates between "deterrence," "prevention," and "repulsion" of informational threats, implying that informational security is achieved in different ways in various stages of the confrontation.[78]

Although *informational deterrence* has not been codified as a stand-alone topic in the official unclassified doctrine, from the early 2000s Russian experts have assumed that it may substitute for a nuclear equivalent as the main form of coercion in international politics.[79] Initial allusions appeared in early 2000 when official documents referred to the "informatization of military affairs" and to informational struggle as a form of warfare alongside its political, military, diplomatic, and economic analogues. When the 2010 and 2014 doctrines explicitly urged the development of "tools of informational struggle," the soft and hard aspects of this form of warfare, including the issue of deterrence, began to feature prominently in professional periodicals. What Russian experts qualified as "significant militarization of the informational (cyber) domain" by the U.S., including new organizations, weapons, and concepts,[80] further drove Russian defense intellectuals and the military brass to seek nonnuclear tools to prevent and repel threats for which nuclear deterrence was irrelevant. Deterring threats emanating from the informational space seemed the greatest challenge. Around that time, within the Russian strategic studies community, the notion of "cyber" began to feature as a term to refer to the DT aspect of the informational space.[81]

In sum, several generalizations about the evolution of doctrine and strategic theory are possible. First, until the early 2000s the term *informational deterrence* mainly featured in works dealing with the CP aspects of informational influence, and it accounted for the lion's share of the experts' attention. Starting from the early–mid 2000s, the DT (mainly REB and cyber) aspects of "informational deterrence" have been catching up. Incrementally, this focus has acquired equal status and then taken center stage in the knowledge development efforts. During the last decade there has been a spike in the exploration of the DT aspects of IW, stimulated in part by the cyber hype extending from the U.S. discourse, in doctrinal publications, organizational transformations, and actual operations. In the doctrine, by contrast, the CP and DT aspects are equal, although the former are more elaborated than the latter.

Second, doctrine and theory imply that informational aggression, if unchecked, could materialize into an existential threat to sovereignty and territorial integrity, comparable to the perils emanating from nuclear and conventional aggression. As such, it demands adequate countermeasures—to deter these threats Russian discourse refers not only to informational tools but also to the entire strategic arsenal.

Finally, the maturity of the conceptualization is equivalent to the state of the professional discourse in the nuclear-conventional realm when it was of comparable age, during the first two post-Soviet decades. Doctrinal documents have left many terms, even basic ones like "informational-technological influence," undefined, leaving room for conceptual discussions and an incoherent lexicon.[82] This is especially the case with regard to the CP aspects of informational deterrence. As of this writing, there is no articulated and consensual concept of *informational coercion*, especially in the CP realm, within current Russian strategic studies.[83]

RUSSIAN DISCOURSE: CONTENTS

Still, the evolution of strategic theory, especially within the military community, most markedly during the last decade, is indicative of an effort to crystallize and operationalize a coercion mechanism in the informational sphere.[84] Almost two decades of theoretical dynamic have produced a significant corpus of knowledge and competing schools of thought debating various aspects of the subject. Within this polemics on the mechanisms of informational deterrence, the following five notions are apparently consensual.

First, as a rule, "informational deterrence" has stood in the Russian experts' discourse for the threat, or limited employment, of DT and CP forms of influence against the adversary to attain the political goals. There is a tendency to refer to the CP and DT spheres as separate, but at the same time to hold a combined-arms approach—to aggregate, rather than compartmentalize, in theory, in organizational structures, and in actual force application.

Second, Russian authors have used the terms *informational struggle* and *informational deterrence* interchangeably.[85] According to the Russian discourse, *informational struggle* aimed at preventing and resolving conflicts should enable the attainment of political goals, without resorting to conventional, let alone nuclear, means.[86] Almost synonymously, *informational deterrence* has been perceived as one of the most cost-effective coercion tools due to its ability to produce effects without massive devastation, keeping the damage below the unacceptable level[87] and possibly preventing aggression without direct employment of kinetic force.[88] Since the mid-2000s, when the concept of *strategic deterrence* began gathering momentum, the discourse has tended to conflate the employment of *informational struggle* as a tool of *war* and as a tool of *coercion*.[89] Russian debates on hybrid warfare reflect the same.[90]

Third, another conflation relates to cyber and REB means of IW. Authors tend to blur the distinction between the electronic and cyber forms of informational struggle, to the point of full convergence, presenting them as inseparable against the backdrop of the current character of war. In the discussion, REB, cyber, and fires often feature under the umbrella term *informational strike*. The latter merges various means of influence to attain an informational effect.[91]

Fourth, Russian thinking on *informational deterrence* implies its employment in pure and in cross-domain forms. The latter means threatening to employ informational influence against an adversary not only to prevent informational (CT and/or DT) aggression but also to influence the opponent's behavior in other fields of activity, including kinetic operations. Russian experts believe that "informational pressure" on the adversary, its armed forces, state apparatus, citizens, and world public opinion produces favorable conditions for other forms of coercion.[92]

Fifth, there has been a tendency among Russia authors to assume that the offense-defense distinction is somewhat irrelevant in the informational realm.[93] Although some Russian experts tend to see offense as a stronger mode of conduct in the informational domain, equal attention is still being paid to defensive measures, in both the CP and DT spheres. Despite the view of offense as a stronger form of engagement, and the assumption that this is how things are in the U.S. (whatever the accuracy of this assumption), the Russian offense-defense balance seems to be relatively adjusted. The tendency to disassociate from the offense-defense dichotomy, on the assumption that such a taxonomy is obsolete and not applicable to the informational domain, is an extension from Russian assumptions in other, noninformational fields of contemporary military thought,[94] and has immediate implications for deterrence.[95]

Informational Deterrence: Mechanism and Uniqueness

Three forms of coercion loom largest within the current Russian discourse on informational affairs: deterrence by denial, deterrence by punishment, and deterrence by international regulations.

DENIAL AND PUNISHMENT

The nuclear and conventional streams of the Russian deterrence discourse have tended to disregard the Western *denial-punishment* taxonomy, viewing the categories of "forceful and non-forceful" means of influence as more useful.[96] In the informational realm things differ. Russian experts have been closely following the Western debates surrounding cyber war and cyber deterrence.[97] Among other implications, this has resulted in the penetration of the *denial-punishment* terminology into the Russian lexicon on informational-cyber affairs. *Deterrence by denial* and *deterrence by punishment* are not official Russian doctrinal terms. However, since Russian experts have been employing this terminology,[98] the sections below employ them, too. For the purpose of the analysis here, *deterrence by denial* in the informational domain stands for signaling that one's countermeasures will repel (disrupt or defeat) the prospective aggression in the informational sphere, imposing costs of effort on the perpetrator and denying him the expected benefits. *Deterrence by punishment* stands for discouraging an aggressor by signaling that costly retaliation will follow any informational assault. As in classical deterrence theory, both forms of deterrence imply cost-imposition; the latter form is implicitly based on offensive means, while the former rests on a mix of defensive and offensive measures combined in a potential counterattack.

The logic of "deterrence by denial" and explicit references to defensive measures loom largest where Russian doctrinal documents discuss the ways and means of informational deterrence, especially in the cyber domain. Official documents refer to Russian efforts to create defensive means, which should prevent the infliction of damage by "informational-communicational technologies," in peacetime (i.e., *deterrence*) or in wartime (i.e., *defense*). Similarly, national-level legislation, represented for example by the "Law of the Sovereign Runet" and other initiatives under the rubric of digital sovereignty and substitution of IT imports, refers to various means aimed at sustaining the proper functioning of the Russian national internet, in terms of both the code and the content, including its continuity under scenarios ranging from limited aggression to a strategic blow leading to the disconnection of Russia from the World Wide Web (WWW).[99]

In Russian white papers there are no direct references to *deterrence by punishment* or explicit mentions of the Russian offensive arsenal in the cyber domain. This stands in contrast to the treatment of deterrence in the nuclear-conventional realm: the *Military Doctrine* and the *Foundations of State Nuclear Deterrence Policy* specify conditions for Russian nuclear use, be it for the first or second strike, and imply the offensive arsenal. However, despite being absent from official doctrine, references to *deterrence by punishment* feature in statements by officials and within the professional military discourse. Statements by Russian senior executives have been signaling that informational (cyber) strikes on Russia would result in equivalent and even excessive cyber retaliations.[100] In doctrinal publications "denial" trumps "punishment" and "defense" overshadows "offense," especially in the DT aspects of ID, but this is not the case in the professional military discourse. Military periodicals offer a rather non-abstract analysis of offense-defense dialectics in the DT and CP realms of informational war and the implications for coercion strategy. In stand-alone articles and in its exploration of broader topics, the discourse is replete with analysis of various aspects of offense-oriented DT (radio-electronic-cyber) tools of influence, be it for the purpose of deterrence, counterdeterrence, or fighting a war. Although periodicals pay more attention to repelling adversarial offensive means of informational coercion, Russian means of informational offense, epitomized by the radio-electronic-informational (REI) strike, have drawn significant attention as well.[101]

"INTERNATIONAL INFORMATIONAL SECURITY"

Shaping the norms and regulations of behavior in the informational sphere, which Russian activism seeks to promote, features as a form of informational deterrence in the Russian discourse. Creating favorable "international informational security" sounds more like a state of affairs in arms control than a coercion technique. However, in Russian doctrine, strategic theory, and even policy initiatives, it features as a means of deterrence, which some Russian experts mention next to "denial" and "punishment."[102] Doctrinal documents claim that international norms of CP and DT conduct in the informational sphere can ensure strategic stability and prevent conflict. Russian experts interpret this claim as implying that the "deterrence, prevention, and resolution" of informational conflicts should be conducted "exclusively by peaceful means" and through "formulation of a system of informational international security."[103] Moscow's messaging in forums dealing with "international informational security," like its efforts to elaborate regulations preventing dangerous cyber military activities,[104] illustrates this.[105]

Russian experts even argue that since the early 2000s "deterrence by regulating international informational security" has been the sphere in which the Russian strategic community has invested the most organizational and intellectual energy. According to this view, Moscow has employed this tactic in tandem with other forms of coercion, but sees it as more cost-effective (also in terms of escalation risks) than *denial* and *punishment* for the prevention of cyber conflict.[106] Progress in the field has been slow, given U.S. reluctance to engage with Moscow on the subject matter prior to and especially following the 2014 confrontation.[107] In addition to the geopolitical obstacles, the main bone of contention has been a matter of principle—different definitions of the informational space, with an aversion on the part of the U.S. to regulate content-related and not only code-related behavior, which is central to Moscow, at least to the same extent as code.[108]

This Russian take on informational deterrence somewhat resonates with the Western typology of cyber dissuasion through *entanglement* (the notion that a state's interdependence can dissuade it from aggression to avoid self-inflicted damage) and *delegitimization* (norms and taboos that can restrain a state from aggression for moral and reputational considerations). In the current Western literature, these tactics feature as a means of cyber deterrence next to *punishment* and *denial.*[109] Given that certain Russian experts follow the polemics of Western strategic studies on deterrence by *entanglement* and by *delegitimization*, this conceptualization may have further propelled Russian variations on the theme.[110] The Western and Russian applications of this deterrence technique differ. While the Western categorization implies mainly self-deterrence due to strategic (*entanglement*) or normative (*delegitimization*) considerations, in the Russian case there is a stronger emphasis on formal, legally binding international regulations. Also, the endeavor is more significant in the framework of the Russian than the Western approach, where it is somewhat pedestrian as compared to *denial* and *punishment*. Finally, the CP, soft (noncyber) aspect of informational security is as a rule marginalized in the Western approach, but is central to the Russian approach.

What is the relative weight of each of the above elements in the Russian informational deterrence mechanism? Even knowledgeable Russian scholars, who disaggregate the Russian approach into punishment, denial, and international regulation, differ in their assessments of the actual proportion among the three. Moreover, voices from the Russian military community qualify diplomatic activism in the field of international regulations as a smoke screen (*otvlekaiuschii manevr*), while the genuine Russian interest lies in their interpretation, namely to preserve the current nonregulated regime, as they see DT and CP influence as the most effective tool of Russian coercion for a wide range of scenarios.[111] The latter argument is epitomized by the Russian qualification of the informational arsenal as nonnuclear strategic weapons (NNSW). Indeed, Russian takes on the informational deterrence mechanism may be at times confusing and self-contradictory, including that of such seniors as Andrey Krutskikh, who codifies this policy formally and in parallel formulates informational coercion theory and popularizes it in Russian academic circles.[112] Also, the demarcation between *denial* (i.e., defense against malign CP influence) and punishment (i.e., offensive CP operations) is blurred and subjective.[113]

The coexistence of several epistemic agents is a phenomenon common to the sociology of strategic communities worldwide, and it is not unique to Russia. Because there is no clear division of labor in the sphere of informational struggle, within the intelligence community, and especially within the military, multiple organizations are apparently competing for resources and responsibilities, inter alia through theory development. The forthcoming publications of the fundamental doctrinal documents regarding informational security, in particular regulations on informational deterrence, may expedite the gravitation of these communities of knowledge toward each other. This corpus of doctrinal work that is likely to emerge soon may become the middle ground and common frame of reference for the several communities of knowledge that coexist in Russia today.

RUSSIAN STYLE IN INFORMATIONAL DETERRENCE: CUMULATIVE COERCION

One can see Russian informational deterrence as a two-phase endeavor. First comes the generation of "deterring potential" (*sderzhivaiuschii potentsial*). This is done by means of constant but relatively low-intensity engagement with the adversary. For internal needs, this operational friction *explores* the strategic reality (i.e., examines the adversary, the environment, and oneself), its boundaries, risks, and opportunities. Externally, it fosters a reputation about one's capabilities and resolve, and generates, figuratively speaking, "deterring potential" for prospective employment. The second phase is the leveraging of the preproduced energy according to the needs of the moment. Thus Russian informational deterrence, in its CP and DT forms, involves the serial use of limited force to generate an aggregate effect, which can then be exploited as the occasion demands. For a certain period, uninterrupted friction on informational fronts might not serve any specific goal other than to generate and maintain a generic deterring posture. Eventually, the latter turns into a building block, or even the backbone, of concrete influence leverage when Russian strategists see fit. In sum, persistent operational friction creates a deterring potential, maintains it (i.e., regular recharging), and exploits it to coerce an adversary at the moment of truth.

Arguably, the term *cumulative coercion* well captures the logic of "informational deterrence" *à la Russe*. The term does not exist in the Russian vocabulary; it is an import from the Western deterrence scholarship dealing with conventional and cyber affairs.[114] It is somewhat akin to a merger of what the Western lexicon dubs "general deterrence" and "specific deterrence." The former stands for a generic deterring posture, which is maintained without issuing specific threatening signals. Once the actor exploits this potential at a certain moment (e.g., a crisis), Western scholarship dubs it "specific" or "strategic" deterrence.[115] In the Russian case, the Western categories of *general* or internalized deterrence (i.e., a signal not deliberately crafted) and *strategic* or specific deterrence (i.e., a threat purposely communicated) are apparently commingled. At least in part, and like other actors practicing cumulative coercion, the Russian inclination apparently emanates from a "protracted conflict perception."[116]

Several examples illustrate this modus operandi. During the Syrian campaign, in the CP sphere, the creation and maintenance of an optimal informational background (*polozhitel'nyi informatsionnyi fon*)—by filling the informational space with content favorable to Russia and then exploiting this potential at a moment of operational need—occurred repeatedly.[117] Also, the phases of informational coercion may be compressed in time or their order may change, although the element of friction remains intact.[118] A similar dynamic occurs in the DT realm (i.e., cyber and REB lines of operation). Here, friction for the purpose of learning has been interwoven with efforts to create, maintain, and exploit deterring potentials. In Syria, for example, Moscow tested new

REB weapon systems and the responses of various adversaries to them, and demonstrated by doing so its capabilities and resolve to use them. The same logic of probing, learning, and shaping applies to Russian cyber friction episodes during the last decade aimed at the U.S.[119]

When it comes to command and control procedures, the Russian approach alternates between the decentralized and centralized ends of the spectrum. In the first phase of creating and maintaining deterring potential, cumulative *coercion* is not a preplanned effort driven by specific top-down orders. "Deterring potential" emerges out of the host of activities conducted by the organs of the strategic community, which function in a rather independent and not necessarily coordinated manner. General political directives and the zeitgeist drive them.[120] For example, a high level of decentralization, self-synchronization, and pre-delegation of authority to state and non-state actors characterizes the CP line of Russian IO. The Kremlin either leverages the influence potentials, which these endeavors generate, for the needs of informational coercion, or disassociates from them if this serves the needs of the moment.[121] The same tendency to delegate is observable in the DT sphere of Russian IO.[122] The level of centralization apparently increases as the situation becomes concrete. The Kremlin may rigidly regulate the whole system, in some cases even "manually," when it enters specific crises and turns coercion (deterrence or compellence) from an amorphous potential into a crystallized combat mission communicated through concrete orders to subordinates.

Cumulative coercion may be confusing. In the Russian discourse, "limited use of force" features as a separate means of deterrence, next to "intimidation" and "defense." For more than a decade, several Russian military experts argued that operational friction on the informational TVD (i.e., routine CP and DT engagement/penetration/exploitation of the enemy) blurs the demarcations between intelligence gathering, coercive influence, and actual fighting. They recognized this as a tendency worldwide, and argued for adoption of the same approach in Russia.[123] Such an approach may result in misperceptions and unintended escalation. Western scholarship differentiates between "strategy of control," i.e., war, and "strategy of influence," i.e., coercion. The former is about forcefully imposing one's will on the adversary. The latter is about diplomacy that involves threats.[124] In the informational domain, the lines between brute force (i.e., "strategy of control") and signaling a willingness to employ it (i.e., "strategy of coercion") become blurred. Informational deterrence is more contestable than its nuclear or conventional analogues. In contrast to the latter realms, where the capacity to demonstrate resolve or establish credibility through direct engagement is either impossible (the nuclear realm) or limited (the conventional realm), in the informational domain friction is more feasible; the damages are tolerable. As a result, in serial limited friction, which is the essence of informational deterrence *à la Russe*, it is not clear where "influence" ends and "control" starts. For the actor on the receiving end of the influence campaign, it is difficult to understand whether it is "coercive signaling" or a situation where the adversary is using "brute force" to "control." In practical terms, the latter means "war" and demands a different type of response, not necessarily informational in nature. Since informational signals are not purely words, but friction that has tangible consequences in the physical and behavioral domains, and since they also convey the message that more (violence) may come if the enemy does not comply with the demand, for the actor on the receiving end the situation turns into one of "intra-war coercion."[125]

COMPARATIVE PERSPECTIVE

Convergence and divergence of the Russian and U.S. approaches is a dialectical phenomenon. Both Moscow and Washington occupy certain positions on the spectrum pertaining to various aspects of coercion in the informational sphere. Their locations are relative and constantly changing, as their thinking on the subject matter is constantly evolving, often in reaction to engagement by and/or occurrences taking place on the other side. Still, since certain predominant inclinations of both actors have been shaped by the fundamental traits of the strategic cultures of both countries, they are likely to remain intact rather than metamorphose radically in the observable future. Several asymmetries between Moscow and Washington are evident on the matter of informational coercion. First, in the U.S. the field of cyber deterrence is more codified doctrinally than in Russia, although Western academics report skepticism and reservations in the U.S. expert community regarding the effectiveness of this tool of coercion. Russian experts, and apparently the strategic community as a whole, are more optimistic than their U.S. counterparts regarding the value of informational (cyber) coercion. That said, doctrinal codification and elaboration in Russia apparently lag behind the U.S. Second, apparently the Russian and Western (U.S.) approaches to informational war, and informational deterrence in particular, demonstrate a certain level of isomorphism. In contrast to its initial excessive focus on the CP aspects of IW, Russia is expanding the place of DT (cyber) components under the same rubric of informational war, On its part, Washington is seeking to balance its initial technocentric focus with greater attention to the "soft," nondigital effects of informational (cyber) war, seeking a better synthesis between projecting DT force and executing CP influence.[126] Still, the initial inclinations of both actors remain intact. The Russian approach seems better suited to harmonically synthesizing both sides of the informational coin, both in theory and to a certain extent in practice, than the U.S. approach, which seems to be more compartmentalized, in conceptual and organizational terms, and playing catch-up with its competitors, in particular Russia, in its approach to "information age statecraft."[127] Finally, convergence is evident on the matter of *cumulative coercion*. Since 2018 several experts have been popularizing within the U.S. strategic community the notion of shifting from episodic engagements to something more permanent, under the term *persistent engagement*. This "cyber persistence," like the Russian approach, blurs the line between *coercion* and *warfare*. It seeks "to remove the escalatory potential"[128] through protracted offensive-defensive friction. The latter shapes adversarial behavior persistently, as opposed to operational restraint where engagement is reserved for wartime.[129] The impact of these ideas is visible in the U.S. Cyber Command Vision (circa 2018).[130] European policymakers apparently have distanced themselves from this concept, viewing it as aggressive and inappropriate.[131] The difference seems to be that while the U.S. is trying to catch up, the Russian strategic community has been thinking and operating in this way longer than the U.S.

What accounts for such a unique Russian approach to deterrence with all its above-outlined peculiar characteristics? How is it that the Russian expert community has managed to catch up with Western theoreticians and practitioners in the learning competition on the art of deterrence? The following chapter grapples with these puzzles and outlines the cultural, ideational, and conceptual sources of Russian conduct.

CHAPTER 3

CULTURAL SOURCES OF DETERRENCE *À LA RUSSE*

WHERE DO THE DISTINCTIVE characteristics of the Russian approach to deterrence emanate from? How has the Russian expert community, despite its relatively belated arrival to the deterrence club, managed to catch up with and even outperform, in certain regards, Western theoreticians and practitioners of this strategy? What informs the style of operational design and the logic of combat planning of the Russian strategic community when it embarks today on coercive operations? This chapter explores the historical, conceptual, and cultural sources, which have conditioned the genealogy of deterrence *à la Russe*, and which remain intact today. The aim is to illustrate how these factors account for one or several characteristics of the Russian approach to deterrence.

The chapter argues that the basic instincts of Russian strategic culture, its style of war and organizational procedures, and several professional terms and principles from Soviet-Russian military and intelligence operational art have been shaping the modus operandi of deterrence *à la Russe*. Arguably, these ideational-cultural factors play an even larger role in regulating the Russian practice of this strategy than formal doctrine. They have constituted the professional norms, part and parcel of the operational code and DNA of the Russian practitioners, when they embarked on conceptualizing deterrence theory in the early 1990s. These factors are likely to continue shaping the future Russian development of this strategy. The scholarship supports this claim. When military organizations encounter new technology, or receive a demand from the political leadership against the backdrop of a high level of uncertainty and low doctrinal guidance, they tend to do what they know to do well from before. They lean on the traditional principles of operational art, professional beliefs, organizational culture, and instincts from the previous era.[1]

In the international security literature, these nonmaterial factors that regulate operational choices and professional conceptualization in national security affairs fall under the rubric of strategic culture. In the case under scrutiny, works on Russian strategic culture offer the most relevant reservoir of data to unpack the factors, which have conditioned the Russian conceptualization of deterrence. During the last decade a bourgeoning body of research has supplemented the preexisting corpus of knowledge on the Russian strategic culture, way of war, and military tradition. The literature on the subject roughly arrived in three waves. The first wave of research appeared during the late Cold War and laid the foundation for this corpus of knowledge on the ideational-cultural sources of Soviet (Russian) strategic conduct.[2] Extending through the 1990s, when explorations of Russian strategic behavior fell into relative intellectual disfavor, the second generation of literature was comparatively minor and largely advanced along similar lines. The focus was mainly on diagnosing change and continuity in the strategic tradition against the backdrop of transition to the post-Soviet era.[3] Then the third wave of research emerged, reflecting the revived interest in Russian national security policy and the sources of the Kremlin's conduct. The aggregate effects of Vladimir Putin's Munich speech in 2007, Moscow's subsequent gambits in Georgia, Ukraine, and Syria, and the Kremlin's strategic assertiveness in the Near Abroad and worldwide turned Russia into one of the main competitors of the collective West, stimulating a new wave of exploration of Russian strategic culture. The year 2014 was definitely a watershed.

This wave of scholarship, of which this book is part, has been offering cultural-ideational explanations for the Kremlin's national security choices and certain characteristics of Russian strategic-military conduct.

The authors have leaned on the preexisting corpus of knowledge from the earlier generations of literature and revisited the primary and secondary sources from the Tsarist, Soviet, and post-Soviet eras to produce new insights on various aspects of Russian strategic culture. Specifically, the current wave of literature has been examining the impact of cultural factors on contemporary Russian decision-making and strategic thought,[4] on various aspects of military art and operations,[5] on intelligence craft,[6] and on the Kremlin's policies toward the West, Asia, Middle East, and the Near Abroad.[7] In addition to the above in-depth studies, several works have offered panoramic explorations of change and continuity in Russian strategic culture.[8]

Exploration of Russian strategic culture vigorously continues worldwide, and the research on the subject is inconclusive. Still, one already benefits from a relatively solid corpus of knowledge. The aggregate body of findings from the three generations of literature is immediately handy for this book, which seeks to decipher the cultural-ideational sources of deterrence *à la Russe*. The above works have produced insights immediately relevant for this study. The latter builds on the former but also addresses the existing caveats regarding our knowledge. Specifically, the book contributes to the literature on Russian strategic culture by exploring the nexus of cultural factors and the evolution of the Russian theory of deterrence—a matter on which the existing corpus of knowledge has remained largely silent.

Particular qualities pertaining to the Russian strategic tradition, which feature in the current body of research, are more relevant than others in explaining deterrence *à la Russe*. The analysis below highlights three subcategories of factors—cultural, ideational, and historical—and then hypothesizes about their impact on the Russian style of deterrence. *Cultural factors* stand for the features of Russian strategic tradition that transcend specific historical periods, i.e., the Tsarist, Soviet, and post-Soviet. *Ideational factors* stand for traits in the military art and intelligence tradition, mainly from the Soviet era.[9] *Historical legacies* stand for specific formal practices, methods, and ideas, also inherited from the Cold War era. The chapter argues that these factors have been shaping and conditioning the contemporary Russian theory and practice of coercion. This triple typology is relative and the accuracy of such taxonomy is debatable, since factors from various categories overlap. The book, however, offers this categorization for the sake of analytical clarity and in order to make the main argument accessible.

IMPRINT OF CULTURAL FACTORS

Several traits, which are central to Russian strategic culture, and which Russian military thought and operational behavior have manifested over history, have informed and conditioned the way in which the Russian expert community has developed knowledge about deterrence. In contrast to the historical and ideational factors, which pertain to doctrinal concepts and principles of operational art, cultural factors relate to something more amorphous and deeply ingrained in the general culture—the style of thinking and norms of conduct in military affairs.

Holistic–Dialectical Cognitive Style and Approach to Strategy

One sociocultural element that shapes a state's strategic behavior and constitutes the foundation for its way of war is the national *cognitive style*, which informs how individuals prefer to perceive, organize, and process information. It applies to the collective level as well and refers to the dominant reasoning traits, which recur in the intellectual activity of a given society or professional community. Specifically, in the latter regard, the literature presumes that a certain sociocultural background and particular cognitive style produce a mentality, which guides and shapes the imagination and reasoning of military experts. International security scholars claim that national cultural context and cognitive style matter, and the empirical evidence suggests that distinct techniques for generating knowledge in military affairs do exist in different countries. A particular strategic community may differ in its approach, instincts, and inclinations from its counterparts belonging to a different cultural milieu. Given certain cultural-cognitive characteristics, some conceptual approaches become possible and others less so in a given strategic community. Due to cultural factors, military organizations may vary in their propensity to conceptualize and practice certain aspects of strategy and operations.[10]

The Russian cognitive-cultural style may have an impact on strategy conceptualization and the style of its execution. Russian experts argue that deterrence *à la Russe* is symptomatic of the holistic, or systemic, approach (*kompleksnii/sistemnii podhod*) that characterizes the Russian art of strategy in general.[11] A holistic approach, which in the literature bears a name similar to the Russian cognitive style (*holistic-dialectical*), stands for an all-embracing view of reality that grasps the big picture, sees issues in different dimensions as interconnected within one generalized frame, and describes every element of reality as being in constant interplay with other segments in frames of one meta-system. Cultural-cognitive psychologists also qualify the *holistic* thinking style as *dialectical*, meaning that it recognizes contradictions and synthesizes opposing propositions.[12] A predilection for holism is prominent throughout the Russian intellectual tradition and cognitive style in literature, religious philosophy, and the sciences.[13] It has also been projected onto the strategic style and military thought,[14] and exemplified in the design, planning, and execution of military operations.[15] *Holism* also entails viewing strategy as an uninterrupted, permanent engagement, with no divide between peacetime and wartime, which is waged in the domestic, the adversary's, and the international spheres. Within the holistic approach there is a distinction between war and peace only as regards the intensity of the effort to impose one's strategic will, but not the essence of the endeavor, which remains the same through all stages of the competition. Competition with the adversary is seen as protracted, occurring toward, during, and following kinetic phases of interaction.

Apparently, this inclination toward holism, which is emblematic of the Russian approach to strategy, may account for the *broader meaning* of deterrence (i.e., use of the term to refer to preserving and changing the status quo, and to a repertoire of intrawar coercion moves aimed at shaping the battlefield dynamic), its *wider scope* (i.e., spanning both wartime and peacetime), and larger *number of domains* (i.e., military and nonmilitary). Apparently, it also accounts for a *tendency to merge* forceful and nonforceful modes of operation in one coercion scheme and a sophisticated ability to operate across domains simultaneously, which seemingly comes more naturally to the products of the Russian mental-ideational environment than to their Western counterparts. The dialectical aspect of the holistic cognitive style apparently may account for the presence of, and attention to, the other side in strategic considerations, which in turn may explain the tailored approach to deterrence, sensitivity to subjectivity, and skillful ability to calibrate damage that deterrence *à la Russe* manifests. For the product of a dialectical cognitive milieu, reality, as well as the deterrence equation stemming from it, is a function of one and one's competitor interacting, and not of mere static balances, an insight from which emanates another strategic instinct—the inclination to constantly shape the adversary. Thus, the dialectical approach is related to reflexive control and perception management and via them to deterring by shaping, which the Russian philosophy and style of deterrence manifest.

Disconnection Between Theory and Practice

The Russian intellectual tradition, strategic legacy, and style of management often manifest a disconnection between words and deeds. Exploring the sources of this trait is beyond the scope of this research, which refers to it as a given phenomenon. This trait, the other side of the holistic coin, has manifested itself often throughout Russian history in various fields of intellectual and practical activity of the state. A fixation on generating holistic, fundamental schemes has made Russians traditionally good at theory, but extremely bad at implementing ideas. Russian nonmilitary scientists and military theoreticians can be very advanced in their conceptualizations, but the system as a whole can be pathologically bad in implementing these advanced theories. Inept realization of sophisticated concepts often recurred in Soviet military affairs. More often than not the holistic and profound visions of Soviet theoreticians failed to turn into concrete, practical deeds. The focus of Russian-Soviet military theory more often than not has been on the wishful outcome, rather than on the starting point.[16]

The gap between the theoretical and the feasible, however, has never stopped the Russians. Soviet military thinking was future-oriented and repeatedly manifested wishful thinking based upon expectations, while ignoring current realities and neglecting problems. The Soviets were traditionally good at theorizing innovative concepts, but often limited themselves to abstract considerations and remained the prisoners of their futuristic visions. Theories and even training were about future war—the war that could take place after weapon plans were to have been fulfilled. Announcing a project gave it a reality, even if it would be years before it was actually realized. Military theoreticians often debated futuristic visions without concrete and complete calculation of their feasibility. Soviet military thought often became a function of abstract ideas, where sophisticated doctrines were incompatible with the country's operational capacity to implement them.[17]

Andrew Monaghan skillfully depicts this characteristic of the Russian intellectual and managerial tradition, and applies it to military affairs by using the metaphor of *oblomovshchina*, a "talismanic belief that putting things down on paper is the same as doing them."[18] *Oblomovschina*, a term introduced in an 1859 novel and classic of Russian literature by Ivan Goncharov and then popularized by poet and literary critic Nikolai Dobroliubov, turned into an allegory for the chronic evils from which Russian society suffers: a mixture of apathy in decision-making and lethargy in execution, procrastination, and above all—a tendency toward inactive musing, sophisticated, profound, and unhurried albeit unpractical contemplation.[19] This belletristic rendition parallels the argument of cultural psychologists about the Russian inclination toward "descriptive" rather than "procedural knowledge" (i.e., viewing Russia as being and not as doing culture).[20] Several other traits of the Russian managerial tradition accompany and enhance this disconnection between words and deeds—i.e., an inability to translate advanced strategic theory into actual posture and effective combat potentials.[21]

Also, despite the holistic approach to strategy, Russian reality is rife with systemic breakdowns (*sistemnii sboi*) and unrealized visions, due to such traits of Russian professional conduct as: recklessness (*razgildiastvo*), negligence (*khalatnost'*) and carelessness (*bezolarabenrnost'*), resulting in an overall mess and chaos (*bardak*) in both planning and execution.[22] Various aspects of the Russian campaign in Ukraine, at least during its initial stage, have well manifested these traditional pathologies.[23]

The dissonance between advanced and sophisticated military theory and the state's actual ability to implement it, an ill of the Russian strategic-managerial tradition, may account for the incoherence that the Russian nuclear modernizations, posture, and doctrinal visions have been manifesting. On several occasions during the last decades, and in certain regards today, advanced Russian theoretical deterrence postulates and conceptual constructs of cross-domain coercion, sometimes even more sophisticated than their Western analogues, have not always been supported by the actual assets and industrial capabilities, linked to feasible posture and realistic operational procedures, and calibrated among the different segments of the Russian strategic community.[24] The above claim regarding detachment from the arsenal, which should supposedly support it, comes with a caveat. This cultural tendency has its pros as well. Since the frames of objective reality and feasibility considerations have not perturbed, let alone restricted, Russian military conceptual knowledge development and strategic imagination, Russians have often thought "outside the box" about the emerging character of war, and come up with innovative and creative theories of victory. Though at times unrealistic and infeasible at home, their intellectual products have been competitive and outdone in sophistication the analogues in other, wealthier and more practical countries.[25]

Morale and Psychological Factors vs. Material Factors in the Russian Culture of War

The Russian culture of war tends to emphasize morale and psychological-cognitive factors over material-technological ones. Although Russian strategy, generalship, and operations over history have appreciated the technological aspects of war, they relied heavily on the soft aspect of strategy and the resource of human mass to make up for traditional Russian technological-material inferiority. This was not a simplistic approach that merely meant outnumbering the enemy with expendable cannon fodder, but a peculiar metaphysics about overcoming the enemy qualitatively, morally. The Russian nonmaterial military edge had three expressions: a higher level of one's stratagem and theory of victory (i.e., military cunningness and operational creativity); an emphasis on moral superiority and fighting for a higher and just cause, as the main sources of soldiers' motivation and fighting spirit; and a higher level of morale and psychological fortitude of the individual serviceman, and of the whole formation, to ensure stamina, bravery, and unit cohesion. In short, according to the Russian strategic belief, battles are won by men, by the spiritual and psychological power of the servicemen, by a higher level of endurance in the face of combat hardship (i.e., outfighting by outsuffering and outlasting the enemy), and not by machines, technology, or other material factors. Traditional Russian military romanticism holds that Russian soldiers have been blessed with compensatory moral qualities that allow them to fight with inferior equipment yet prevail nonetheless. This military metaphysics has been dialectical, viewing war as a contest and clash between the moral-spiritual powers (*moral'no-duhovnye sily*) of the adversaries. Thus, in parallel with enhancing the morale and psychological fortitude of one's own troops, this philosophy prescribed attacking, undermining, and suppressing the perception, resolve, and spirit of the enemy—a topic to which Russian military art has paid significant attention over history.[26]

With the transformation of warfare following the revolutions in military affairs, notwithstanding technological modernizations following military debacles, the Russian armed forces have never become technocentric, in contrast, for example, to the U.S. military, where a technocentric theory of victory, conditioned by the American strategic culture, tends to lean on sophisticated machines. The Tsarist, Soviet, and contemporary Russian military leaders believe that technology by itself is lifeless, divorced from the moral-psychological aspects of war, despite being backed by a scientifically developed doctrine and theory of victory. In part, traditional Russian technological backwardness accounts for the aversion to technophilia, but arguably to an equal if not greater extent, the above strategic belief accounts for it. Even in the framework of the attempts to increase the technological quality of warfare, the cognitive-psychological component has been primus inter pares.[27]

These soft aspects of strategy have retained a similar status in the Russian military to this very day. The contemporary manifestation of the latter propensity in the current version of Russian military thought is the concept of *informational struggle* or *warfare* (*informatsionnaia bor'ba* or *voina*), aimed, in a nutshell, at imposing one's strategic will on the adversary by cognitive-psychological and digital-technological forms of influence. Even during the nuclear and IT (cyber) RMAs, the Russian military brass has continued to perceive psychological-cognitive components as the main center of gravity of the enemy system. In keeping with this norm of strategic culture, in the current Russian theory of victory and recent military innovations, procurement of state-of-the-art weaponry has not overshadowed the soft sides of strategy. The leading role of *informational struggle* in new-generation warfare–era operations, the centrality of this notion within Russian official doctrine, and recent conceptual[28] and organizational[29] innovations in this field are contemporary expressions of this traditional Russian norm of war.[30]

The primacy of morale and psychological-cognitive factors over material ones in Russian strategic narratives and military mythology may account for *perception* having become the center of gravity of a military campaign, for the natural comprehension of *psychological aspects* of the art of coercion, and for the sensitivity to *subjectivity*, which the Russian approach to deterring damage has manifested. Also, this cultural trait naturally predisposes toward and makes it possible to integrate various forms of influence (nuclear, conventional, and nonmilitary) in a holistic campaign aimed at shaping and manipulating the adversary's perception and decision-making processes. By extension, it accounts for the propensity as well as the capacity to practice *reflexive control*, more naturally and skillfully than in strategic communities that build their theory of victory on outperforming the enemy by superior industrial-technological-financial prowess. Generating and exploiting military surprise (*vnezapnost'*) in order to put an adversary off-balance psychologically, a dictum of the Russian military tradition, has apparently come in handy for, and may have informed, *coercive signaling* and *strategic manipulations*, when Russian experts started contemplating deterrence *à la Russe*. Finally, together with other factors, this trait apparently accounts for the wave of conceptualization of informational deterrence.

IMPRINT OF IDEATIONAL FACTORS

After the Soviet collapse, once deterrence was no longer anathema and became canonized, there were several intellectual enablers, which helped the Russian expert community overcome the crisis of knowledge, convert to the philosophy underlying deterrence theory, and develop it further. These ideational factors, i.e., factors related to the formation of ideas, were central to the intellectual-conceptual climate in which Russian experts operated. They offered a reservoir of ideas for inspiration, adoption, and adaptation to the emerging deterrence theory. These ideas, inherent to the traditional Tsarist-Russian culture of military thought, have been circulating within the strategic community but were, as a rule, not institutionalized officially. Prior to the arrival of *deterrence*, for a long while there were other tools, forceful and nonforceful, in the traditional Russian strategic inventory aimed at shaping the perception, morale, and choices of the adversary, and in this way promoting Russia's goals. *Reflexive control*, *military cunningness*, and *active measures* are concepts central to traditional Russian military thought and art of intelligence. Each of them related, in its own way, to management of adversarial behavior based on a distorted picture of reality and manipulation of perception. As such, these ideas closely corresponded with the mechanism of coercion. This section hypothesizes about the imprint these ideational factors may have left on several features of deterrence *à la Russe*.

Reflexive Control and Perception Management

The Soviet concept of *reflexive control*—a practice of perception management in strategic situations—has been handy for the development of deterrence theory, despite being inapplicable exactly as is. Reflexive control (*refleksivnoe upravlenie*) is a complex of measures that forces the adversary to act according to a false picture of reality in a predictable way, favorable to the initiator of the effort, and seemingly benign to the target. It stands for both the process of influence and the desired end-state.

Incepted within the Soviet nonmilitary scientific community dealing with the formal management problems of applied mathematics and cybernetics, this term migrated incrementally to the social sciences in general, military theory in particular, ever since informing Russian military-strategic thought across the services and organizations of the strategic community.[31] In a nutshell, *reflexive control* in strategic affairs and military interactions seeks to manipulate the adversary's picture of reality, misinform it, and interfere with the decision-making processes of individuals, organizations, governments, and societies, and to shape their strategic choices and operational behavior. Even if not mentioned by name or mentioned under a different term, *reflexive control* is the spirit and rationale, which saturates the theory and practice of Russian military-political conduct on all levels of strategic activity, from the highest to the lowest, and has been observed in recent Russian military and intelligence operations.[32]

It would be wrong, however, to equate *deterrence* with *reflexive control*.[33] Although the two concepts share similarities because they deal with perception management, *reflexive control* diverges from *deterrence* in one major way. *Reflexive control*, at least as it is presented in the Russian intelligence, psychological, and management literature, implies, as a rule, that one is shaping the behavior of the adversary clandestinely, in a way that seems benign to the victim. The object of influence is unaware that it is doing something that is actually detrimental to itself and beneficial to its adversary, because its picture of reality has been manipulated. In contrast, in coercion, one seeks to signal a threat that will overtly affect the calculus of the adversary and force the latter to make a deliberate even if undesired decision that runs against its basic interest. Deterrence for Russian experts is an art of strategic gesture (*isskusstvo strategicheskogo zhesta*), which implies, as opposed to the clandestine reflexive control, overt, even if ambiguous, strategic signaling and open communication with the adversary through force demonstration, deployment, and even limited employment. The desired effects of this art of force and will demonstration (*iskusstvo demostratsii sily I voli*) range from dissuading the adversary from a certain move to putting him in a situation of "political zugzwang."[34] This figure of speech, which Russian scholars have borrowed from chess, refers to a situation where the player is compelled to move a piece on the board to a weaker position, which results eventually in an overall strategic disadvantage. This figurative rhetoric resonates perfectly with the Western logic of coercion, but differs from reflexive control, where strategic zugzwang is attained in a clandestine way, unbeknown to the object of influence.

Military Cunningness and Deception

Military cunningness is the art of manipulating the deployment and employment of forces and information in a way that inclines the enemy to make a move that is damaging to him. The element of bluff and deception ingrained in this art serves a useful purpose in a situation of strategic signaling, where the initiator of deterrence needs to communicate credible resolve and capability behind its threat, even if the threat does not reflect the real state of affairs—which makes this craft a useful source of learning and export for coercion missions. Military cunningness (*voennaia khitrost'*) is a term in the Russian professional terminology, which stands for indirectness, operational ingenuity, and stratagems that exploit the weaknesses and avoid the strengths of the adversary. Russian military dictionaries define it as a segment of military art encompassing creative, unorthodox actions, which deceive the enemy and provoke him into making mistaken and damaging moves.[35] The English and Chinese term *stratagem*—a scheme aimed at deceiving the enemy— is the closest approximation to Russian *military cunningness*.[36] In the Tsarist, Soviet, and Russian traditions it featured as one of the central components of military art, which complements, multiplies, and sometimes substitutes for the use of force to achieve results in operations,[37] and is seen as integral to the military profession.[38]

In the Russian professional discourse, *asymmetry*, or asymmetrical approach (*asimetrichnyi podhod*), sometimes featuring also as indirect actions (*nepriamye deistviia*), is a frequent euphemism for *military cunningness* and stands, like the latter, for a stratagem pitting one's strengths against the opponent's weaknesses. The prominence of this term, not to mention of this thinking, in the current Russian discourse and approach to strategy is not unprecedented. Long before the publication of the current military doctrines, making reference to asymmetry and indirect approach became a bon ton among the military brass and political leadership discussing the correlation of forces and countermeasures to the West. The previous burst of asymmetry conceptualization in Russian military thought dates back to the 1980s, when Soviet experts sought effective countermeasures to the U.S. Strategic Defense Initiative. Andrei Kokoshin—one of its proponents then, and today one of Russia's leading defense intellectuals—has been popularizing the term *asymmetrical approach* in the professional discourse since the 1990s.[39] The implication for deterrence is obvious. Apparently, a propensity for asymmetrical thinking makes it more natural to maneuver across domains to compensate for one's weaknesses, and this may account for the cross-domain modus operandi of the Russian deterrence style.

When institutionalized as an organizational effort, military cunningness assumes the form of *maskirovka* in the realm of military affairs, and *active measures* in the realm of intelligence. The art of *maskirovka* stands for a repertoire of denial, deception, disinformation, propaganda, camouflage, and concealment, which aims to hide one's intentions and capabilities on all levels of political-military activity (i.e., strategic, operational, and tactical *maskirovka*). By manipulating the adversary's picture of reality, *maskirovka* produces favorable operational conditions for promoting one's goals. While *military cunningness* is usually a term for the personal skill of a given commander or a reference to a necessary virtue of operational art, *maskirovka* stands for the institutional endeavor of the specific military organization. As a process designed to mislead, *maskirovka* implies active and even forceful actions aimed at foiling adversarial intelligence collection efforts. The practice and logic of *maskirovka* is widespread beyond the military, having spread to every organ involved in strategic interaction, be it in politics, diplomacy, or intelligence (where it usually features under the term *konspiratsiia*). This does not mean, however, that Russian commanders have always paid the prescribed attention to this effort or executed it by the book.[40] Nonetheless, several best practices of *maskirovka* indeed have generated surprises from the tactical to the strategic levels.[41]

Active Measures and Combat Aktivnost'

Active measures (*aktivnye meropriiatiia*), often referred to using the Western term *political warfare*, is the Soviet-Russian term for the repertoire of clandestine operations (measures) aimed at influencing adversarial states, organizations, groups, and key individuals. The cumulative effect of *active measures* is to influence the course of international affairs in a favorable direction.[42] *Active measures* differ from intelligence, in the Western sense of the term, in the emphasis on action and dynamism. These measures are not about exploring and explaining reality (collection and analysis) through espionage, which is the canonical Western understanding of the intelligence craft, but about actively shaping reality by using clandestine means. It is an endeavor of offensive character (*nastupatel'ny kharakter*), aimed at either imposing one's will on the adversary or forcing it to expose his plans and act in conditions unfavorable to him.[43] The resonance with coercion is inescapable. The *active measures* notion has exactly the same rationale needed in the contemporary Russian operational art of deterrence, which mixes *forceful* and *nonforceful measures* within one coercive campaign. The emphasis on dynamic engagement of an offensive character is another similarity.

Active measures rest on nonforceful forms of psychological-cognitive influence (propaganda and disinformation) mixed with interference in foreign political life (sowing discord between the main adversary and its allies and driving wedges between adversarial governments and their populations), and may be augmented by the surgical use of force (ranging from a sole agent, to support an insurgency, and up to a limited military operation), aiming in tandem to shape the strategic perception and operational behavior of the adversary and to undermine his state from within.[44] The highest aim of this tactic has been consciously (through persuasion) or unconsciously (through manipulation) to elicit desired behavior (specific or general) from the "ignorant masses" that will be favorable to the initiator of active measures. A special KGB directorate produced a reservoir of practical and theoretical knowledge on this craft, which was accessible to other organs of the Soviet and then Russian strategic community. It not only disseminated knowledge in the formal sense (doctrine and operational procedures), but also has created the intellectual-cultural climate in which practitioners (beyond the intelligence community, in the military, for example) have been socialized and professionally cultivated.

Active measures, as a craft in the Russian art of intelligence, were incepted in parallel to, and thus probably in conjunction with, a similar principle of Russian military art—*aktivnost'*—during the same post-Revolutionary and post–Russian Civil War period, as part of the splash of intellectual activity in all social-cultural spheres of Soviet society. Although not related directly, the notion of proactively shaping the adversary's behavior that is intrinsic to the linguistic meaning of the word *sderzhivanie*, a core feature of the Russian practice of this strategy, resonates with the theory and practice of *aktivnost'*. The latter, often featuring in the professional literature as *boevaia aktivnost'* or *aktivnsot' boevykh deistvii*, is probably best translated to English as "combat dynamism." It was incepted in the early stages of Soviet military theory as a formal dictum or principle of military conduct, which in a nutshell stands for "uninterrupted influence on the adversary" (*nepreryvnoe vozdeistvie na protivnika*) in all forms of military activity, both defensive and offensive, aimed at shaping the enemy in a desired way. In a broader strategic sense, this professional dictum of Soviet and then Russian military thought implies seizure of the combat initiative and an uninterrupted effort, even if through minor, local, tactical military engagements, to shape the operational and strategic conduct of the enemy toward the forthcoming, implicitly major, battle. As a formal dictum of tactics it also informs the professional spirit, mental predisposition, and style of conduct expected from the Soviet and Russian commander, especially one designing and managing combat activities on the operational level of war. The notions of initiative and dynamism, embedded in the term *aktivnost'*, have also been central to operational creativeness (*operativenoe tvorchestvo*), one of the central qualities that is expected of the Russian military commander and corresponds, on the lower levels of combat activity, with the Western notion of mission command.[45] Combat *aktivnost'* is also one of the formal coefficients in the contemporary

Russian methodology for evaluating *beosposobnost'*—the combat potential of the order of battle.[46]

Persistent Engagement of the Adversary

A related notion is the dictum of persistent engagement of the adversary—the logic that has been central to the preexisting Russian military and intelligence traditions. Such terms as systemic influence [on the adversary] (*systematicheskoe vozdeistvie [na protivnika]*) and systematic combat activities (*sistematicheskie boevye deistivia*) epitomize this logic. According to the official dictionaries, in a nutshell, "systematic combat activities" is one of the major forms of force employment across the services and types of operations. It stands for "execution of separate operational missions by a limited number of forces and means for a long period of time, with limited aims such as: uninterrupted influence on the adversary (*nepreryvnoe vozdeistvie*), paralyzing (*skovivanie*) his activities and inflicting damage on him, creation of favorable environmental conditions (*sozdanie blagopriiatnykh uslovii obstanovki*) prior to the introduction [to the battle] of the main forces." These systematic combat activities "are usually conducted in the intermissions between operations, battles (*srazheniia*) and strikes."[47]

Systematic combat activities was and is a set of separate engagements and strikes, by operational-tactical size formations and separate combat platforms, "conducted according to a unified plot and plan for a long period of time in a designated zone, for the sake of accomplishing operational and operational-tactical missions. They are conducted both during the pauses between the operations and simultaneously, with them, within and beyond the TVD." Systematic combat activities may include intelligence and counterintelligence operations, radio-electronic struggle, and single or massive fire strikes on separate or group targets (e.g., strikes on single naval, ground, and air vessels, as well as on larger concentrations and groupings of forces, such as airfields). The eventual effect of these informational-radio-fire strikes should ensure the attainment of the higher-order operational goal.[48] This, one of the oldest principles of Russian military thought, has featured in the professional milieu since the interwar period. It is so deeply ingrained in the professional mindset that Russian senior officers utilize it as a framework of analysis not only to describe their own combat activities, but also to make sense of the adversary.[49]

The notion of persistent engagement of the adversary, which aims to ensure a positive correlation of means and forces, is also in keeping with several traditional Russian intelligence principles. While contemporary Russian military thought is still wrestling with, and often confuses between, coercion and war fighting, Soviet intelligence thinking already in the 1970s skillfully disaggregated and merged under one conceptual roof what experts today define as "coercion" and "use of brute force." The then corpus of knowledge had a clear relevance to the Russian approach to informational deterrence, and more likely than not shaped it. Arguably, several types of KGB operations, which were codified in the professional dictionaries and training manuals, offered the most relevant basis for crafting informational coercion operations today. All of them relate to repulsion of adversarial subversive activities (*podryvnye deistviia*) and best illustrate this.

The first type of operation was *prevention (preduprezhdenie) of adversarial subversion.*[50] Limited use of force was inherent in this type of operations and was designed to prevent aggression from materializing. Thus, this first type of operation strongly resonates with the logic behind the Western notion of conflict prevention by means of *deterrence*—preservation of the status quo. Although written in the 1970s, the prose even uses the term *uderzhanie*—a term from the same linguistic word family as *sderzhivanie.* Alongside the first type of operations, there were operations aimed at *compellence*—i.e., restoring the status quo ante bellum (aggression), after the enemy has already initiated subversive activities, which one seeks to halt. This second type of operations—*seizure (presechenie) of adversarial subversion*—stood for "operational activity of the state security organs, aimed at halting (*prekratit'*), by operational means, methods and measures, the subversive activities which the enemy has been conducting."[51] Thus, the then-Soviet intelligence interpretation of operational seizure was similar to the Western notion of intrawar coercion or compellence.

A related, albeit unwritten principle of operational art of Soviet intelligence, which also possibly contributed to the professional mindset of the Russian practitioners contemplating deterrence, was the notion of "systematic engagement of the adversary." Analogous to the principle of systematic combat activities, it was never formalized as a military term. However, in the practice of Soviet intelligence since the 1920s, it was one of the leitmotifs of the professional craft, honed over generations of practitioners.[52] The closest formal approximation in the Soviet intelligence vocabulary would be the notion of "prophylactics"—operational measures used in the phase prior to maturation of the plot of aggression and operational preparations for it, in terms of both intentions and capabilities. "Prophylactic measures" (*profilakticheskie meropriiatiia*) in the Soviet intelligence craft preceded "preventive" and "seizure" operations (and ultimately sought to substitute for them by eliminating any need to conduct them),[53] exactly as in Soviet military art "systematic combat activities" preceded a "major combat operation," either to substitute for it or in order to prepare optimal conditions for its opening. The KGB's differentiation between general and specific prophylactic methods (*metody chastnoi I obschei profilaktiki*) perfectly corresponded with the notion of general and specific deterrence and ways and means of attaining them.

Systematic engagement of the adversary was a handy principle for the third type of Soviet intelligence operations—*inducement to halt subversion* (*sklonenie k prekarscheniiu podryvnoi deiatel'nosti*). This term paralleled the Western notion of coercion, and unpacked the mechanism of influencing the strategic calculus of the adversary. *Inducement to halt subversive activities* was a method of operational prevention (*presechenie*)[54] of adversarial subversion, the essence of which is the influence (*vozdeistvie*) of the organs of state security by operational means and measures on the consciousness (*soznanie*) and will (*voliu*) of the adversary, which incites (*pobuzhdaiut*) him to halt subversive activities. Inducement to halt subversive activities can be based on convincing the adversary of the inevitability of the nonbeneficial consequences in case the subversive activities continue. The desire to avoid these consequences will be a motivation not to continue subversive activities.[55] The logic, letter, and spirit of this Soviet intelligence conceptualization of deterrence, especially its amalgamation of punishment and education, strongly resonate with the Soviet and universal philosophy and lexicon of deterrence in criminology and the penal process and code.[56]

These principles from Soviet operational art in military and intelligence affairs, which preceded the current wave of thinking about informational coercion, probably left the most significant marks. They were not theory detached from practice, but an applied terminology that guided the training and operational activities.[57] Given that in contemporary Russia at least half of the functions and arsenals on which informational coercion, in its CP and DT forms, rests are the responsibility of the intelligence organs of the strategic community, and given that the majority of the senior and midcareer officers had their formative educational and professional experiences during the Soviet era, these principles of the Soviet intelligence craft are more likely than not to have been projected, deliberately or in a subtle way, on the design and employment of informational deterrence and coercion operations. Thus, the terminology and theory underlying the operational art of the Soviet intelligence organs may have been even more advanced than their military analogues in offering useful insights and concepts for contemporary Russian operators contemplating the art of informational coercion. In sum, the notion of persistent engagement, epitomized by the principles of the Russian intelligence and military art, also helps to grasp how Russian theoreticians and practitioners think about deterrence. To a certain, arguably significant extent, this notion informed what this book defines as cumulative coercion—generating, maintaining, and utilizing deterrence potential by constant friction with the adversary, especially in the informational realm.

IMPRINT OF HISTORICAL LEGACIES

This section traces the contributions of the formal doctrinal concepts, which were intrinsic to the Soviet era, to the contemporary Russian conceptualization of deterrence. Specifically, it focuses on the military-technical revolution (MTR) ideas associated with Marshall Nikolai Ogarkov, on the reasonable sufficiency concept from the *Perestroika* era, and on the Soviet professional methodology for calculating the correlation of forces and means (COFM). Arguably, these three Soviet constructs from the late Cold War made conversion to deterrence easier and the Western canons of this theory more accessible when the Russian expert milieu began contemplating this strategy. During the early 1990s these legacies created a favorable intellectual climate and fertile conceptual soil for deterrence ideas and methodologies, enabling this strategy to flourish within the Russian expert community, the lion's share of which were products of Soviet military education. Although these legacies resound in current Russian military thinking, one should neither exaggerate their contribution nor underestimate it. All three have left an indirect but significant imprint on the evolution of Russian views, as they provided major building blocks for what would turn into deterrence *à la Russe*.

Ogarkov's Vision and the Legacy of the Military Technical Revolution
Marshall Nikolai Ogarkov's vision of war provided a useful frame of reference for conceptualizing conventional deterrence. Ogarkov, the Chief of the General Staff (1977–84), has been mostly associated with the concept of military-technical revolution (MTR), also known as revolution in military affairs (RMA)—two terms that Soviet military science used interchangeably to refer to a radical military innovation.[58] Ogarkov and his colleagues utilized these conceptual lenses to identify the emerging RMA brought on by the impact of information technologies (IT). In a nutshell, they saw future military organizations as reconnaissance-strike complexes (RSCs) consisting of three segments: a family of advanced intelligence collection and target acquisition capabilities, formations employing long-range, standoff precision-guided munitions, and automated command, control, and communication systems linking the first two segments together. They envisioned future war as a clash of RSCs, which, as a matter of choice, could be kept nonnuclear. The combat potentials encapsulated in advanced conventional weapons, intelligence, and communication systems made the achievement of the political ends of war feasible by nonnuclear means.[59] The U.S. defense community internalized some of Ogarkov's MTR ideas, as a generic diagnostic tool and as an argument about the implications of the IT revolution for the character of war.[60] In Russia, such novelties and defense transformations

as *RSC, self-sufficient combined-arms groupings of forces, strategic directions,* and *joint strategic commands* are an acknowledged inheritance from the Ogarkov era,[61] and Russian commentators qualify the operation in Syria as the first-ever realization of Ogarkov's vision of RSC.[62]

As compared to Ogarkov's contribution to Russian military modernization, his influence on the conceptualization of deterrence has been underexplored.[63] One should not exaggerate and read into Ogarkov's writings a conceptualization of either deterrence or intrawar coercion. That said, his impact should not be overlooked. Ogarkov's seminal works on a conventional theory of victory in the IT-RMA era provided a conceptual format for Russian thinking on escalation management and on the relationship between nuclear and nonnuclear operations. One can trace back to Ogarkov the current Russian quest to craft a balanced military consisting of conventional general-purpose forces, capable of generating nonnuclear deterrence, and forces of strategic (nuclear) deterrence,[64] although the Soviet marshal argued for a disjunction of the nuclear and conventional domains. For the reasons outlined in the previous chapter, Ogarkov was not talking about deterrence, neither about a nuclear equalizer of conventional inferiority nor about the nonmilitary forms of influence merged with conventional forces—the themes at the heart of deterrence *à la Russe.* For the post-Soviet Russian military brass, however, his argument about the conventional RSC becoming comparable, in term of the effects produced, to tactical-operational nuclear weapons, and thus capable of assuming some of their combat tasks, implied by extension why and how missions of deterrence, previously associated only with nuclear capabilities, could extend to conventional weapon systems.[65]

Michael Kofman traces the Russian calibrated approach to discrete levels of damage back to Ogarkov, and may have a point. Ogarkov was moving away from the assumption that prolonged nuclear war is possible and survivable, and promoted instead the notion of a protracted conventional phase of war. He indeed emphasized conventional, entirely nonnuclear, strategic operation on the TVD as one of the characteristics of the then-emerging military regime, and called for making the division of nuclear and conventional war into the centerpiece of planning, albeit unsuccessfully. Kofman takes the interpretation of Ogarkov a step further, suggesting that the Soviet marshal saw tactical nuclear weapons as an intermediate escalation management tool in the transition from the conventional to the nuclear phase of war.[66] Research based on primary sources is required to support or refute Kofman's proposition; however, if this premise is correct, contemporary deterrence *à la Russe* should credit Ogarkov even more.

Reasonable Sufficiency Legacy

Apparently, the Soviet *reasonable sufficiency* concept has been informing the intellectual predisposition of the Russian strategic community when it contemplates damage calibration and the cross-domain rationale. Reasonable sufficiency (*razumnaia dostatochnost'*), sometimes "reasonable defensive sufficiency," is a term that originated in Soviet military-political thought at the dusk of the Cold War, in response to a dilemma the Kremlin faced: how to maintain an adequate correlation of forces in the standoff with the U.S. and continue generating military power, but without bankrupting the Soviet economy. Articulated during Gorbachev's tenure, this guiding principle of Soviet national security management during the *Perestroika* era meant, in a nutshell, that a minimal arsenal had to be procured to defend against (and implicitly deter) any external strategic threat. Reasonable sufficiency (RS), with its nonoffensive orientation, was an antipode to unreasonable superfluity (*nerazumnaia izbytochnost'*), which had characterized, in the view of the then political leadership, the previous Soviet offensive force posture and buildup, and had stimulated an exhausting and self-defeating arms race. The concept, which was widespread in the lexicon of the Soviet military-political milieu, became a euphemism for limiting the scale of defense investments to the minimum possible that would still allow one to achieve one's security goals.[67]

The term did not collapse together with the Union. Although it was incepted in the specific late Soviet zeitgeist, it remained within the Russian professional lexicon and discourse, and its usage even progressed beyond national security affairs to other spheres of social science, for example into the vocabularies of Russian sociologists[68] and economists,[69] to name a few. In the contemporary Russian national security discourse,

Reasonable sufficiency has metamorphosed into a generic stratagem and professional figure of speech, hence possibly a hallmark of the contemporary Russian strategic mentality. Today reasonable sufficiency can be seen as unwritten conventional wisdom as regards identifying the golden range in various military-political scenarios between undershooting and overshooting, or between military underinvolvement and overinvolvement. In short, it is a management principle, which makes it possible to calibrate the theory of victory according to the varying circumstances in a given strategic-operational environment. Russia watchers in the West have already utilized reasonable sufficiency as an analytical lens to illustrate the raison d'être of Moscow's conduct in different national security scenarios, ranging from nuclear and conventional force buildup to the operational design of the Russian campaign in Syria.[70]

How does all this relate to the Russian approach to coercion? When incepted, the Soviet version of reasonable sufficiency was unrelated to deterrence; however, when the deterrence fashion arrived it became handy in three regards. First, Russian officials, experts, and defense intellectuals have been using reasonable sufficiency as a yardstick for the adequate quality and quantity of the Russian nuclear arsenal, and deterrence potential in general.[71] Second, reasonable sufficiency features in Russian discourse as a rationale for crafting a deterrence program spanning various domains, where elements from different spheres compensate for each other's weaknesses in different phases of war. That strategic deterrence (i.e., cross-domain coercion) resonates with the definition of reasonable sufficiency, as it appears in a widely referred-to military dictionary edited by Dmitry Rogozin, is inescapable.[72] Finally, although Russian experts do not claim that there is a direct connection between the deterrence and reasonable sufficiency concepts, their rationales strongly correspond. One may hypothesize that reasonable sufficiency, as a cloud of ideas circulating in the Russian expert community, has stimulated a more calibrated and tailored approach to damage infliction and its criteria, which the Russian discourse has demonstrated. The era of austerity forced Soviet military theoreticians to sophisticate their strategic thought even further and seek a resourceful approach to military operations, carefully calibrating the limited force to the political needs.

Similarly, Russian theoreticians of deterrence, operating under material limitations against the backdrop of the very slow military modernization, both nuclear and conventional, until the mid-2000s when the funding started to flow, have been shifting from the concept of unacceptable damage to the notion of deterring damage, extending beyond the nuclear realm to damage infliction across the entire spectrum of domains (i.e., strategic deterrence) and intolerable (*nedopustimii*) damage. It has been a progression from objective to subjective damage, which shapes the decision-making and psychology of the adversary.[73]

Legacy of the Correlation of Forces and Means Methodology

The imprint of the Soviet evaluation method known as *correlation of forces* on deterrence *à la Russe* is similar to that of *reasonable sufficiency*—it apparently shaped the analytical predisposition of Russian experts operationalizing deterrence plans and policy. Clint Reach, Vikram Kilambi, and Mark Cozad have produced what is probably, as of this writing, the deepest and widest Western analysis of the intellectual history and contemporary state of the Russian methodology for assessing the correlation of forces and means (COFM), and its application in the wide spectrum of military and national security issues.[74] In a nutshell, correlation of forces and means (*sootnoshenie sil I sredstv*) is a sophisticated formerly Soviet and now Russian evaluation method to estimate the superiority-inferiority relationship among adversarial groupings of forces in a given theater of operations, or in strategic competition as a whole (in which case it includes both military and nonmilitary factors).[75] Since COFM evaluation includes analysis of qualitative and quantitative factors in dynamic interaction, it strongly corresponds with what the Western military lexicon dubs "balance of power" or "military balances." In the Western ideational milieu, the closest approximation to an effort to grasp the dynamic aspects of the interaction and its first- and second-order effects would probably be the methodology of net-assessment, especially if COFM is applied beyond the purely military realm to measure a dynamic distribution of state power across various domains and dimensions, and to estimate in whose favor the overall balance of trends has been shifting, and what the prospective dynamic is.[76]

How does COFM relate to deterrence *à la Russe*? To start with, as a rigorously codified assessment methodology, which was institutional-ized and practiced across the Soviet defense community in the late Cold War era, COFM has been accessible to Russian military planners con-templating deterrence following the Soviet collapse. Even if there is no direct line connecting COFM to deterrence theory or to the notion of reflexive control, the same contemporary theoreticians of strategic deter-rence and experts on new-generation warfare from the Russian General Staff have been cooperating for decades with leading Soviet-Russian ex-perts on COFM. Coupled with the fact that the Russian military dis-course today is replete with this term, it suggests that there has been significant intellectual-conceptual cross-fertilization between the COFM, reflexive control, and strategic deterrence communities of knowledge.[77]

In addition to this general state of affairs, consider the following three specific encounters between COFM and the Russian approach to deterrence. First, COFM has apparently come in handy for diagnostics in support of deterrence planning. Presumably, an intellectual predispo-sition shaped by the COFM legacy could be particularly useful for the initial stages of deterrence design, when the initiator of this strategy di-agnoses the phobias and values of the adversary and its perception of competition, both in quantitative (e.g., military capabilities or economic prowess) and in qualitative (e.g., level of morale and cohesion of the troops or the scale of global appeal of one's ideology) terms. On these traits of thought the design and planning of deterrence operations rests. Second, as an intellectual construct, COFM apparently has come in handy for Russian military theoreticians seeking to identify deterring damage. When COFM merged with the cloud of ideas on reasonable sufficiency, it offered a methodological approach and analytical guidance to lean upon when calculating deterring damage and calibrating it ac-cording to the dynamic conditions pertaining to oneself, the adversary, and the strategic environment.

Finally, COFM has come in handy for Russian deterrence coercion experts, informing their thinking on how to manipulate the adversarial strategic calculus and influence his conduct. The notion that one can

shape the adversarial estimate of the COFM through military cunningness and deception is organic to Soviet strategic thought. The Russian
war tradition sees these two endeavors as part and parcel of military art
and treats them under the rubric of reflexive control. Professional skills
related to reflexive control employed against the adversarial estimate of
the COFM resonate with and bear a similar logic to shaping an adversary's behavior by manipulating his perception, employed in various situations of deterrence and coercive signaling. If one knows how the adversary estimates his combat potential (which is always done in comparison
to one's own), one can try to shape it by demonstrating certain capabilities and concealing weaknesses, eventually shifting the adversarial perception to an estimation of the correlation of forces as unfavorable, which
dissuades him from aggression. This manipulation of the perception of
reality, which is eventually exploited to shape the adversary's strategic
behavior, lies at the heart of classical coercion theory.

CHAPTER 4

CRITICAL EXAMINATION
AND CULMINATION POINT

THIS CHAPTER OFFERS a critical analysis of the Russian approach to coercion, which this book dubs deterrence *à la Russe*. It examines the latter through the lens of a generic coercion model from Western international security studies. This is a general frame of reference that can be applied to examine any organization practicing this strategy. How do Russian practitioners evaluate the effectiveness of their coercion strategies? Is the Russian strategic community cognizant that it may be sending confusing signals to the adversary and that in some respects, its coercion leads to counterproductive results? This chapter explores these questions and emphasizes those aspects of the Russian art of coercion that might lead to miscommunication, negative returns, and inadvertent escalation.

Discussion about the effectiveness of coercive measures suggests a mixed record. The chapter argues that Russian practitioners are in the midst of wrestling with what the Western literature has identified as one of the biggest challenges in the operational art of coercion—evaluating the effectiveness of one's coercive operation and diagnosing the point of its culmination. The chapter unpacks this argument in three steps. First, it outlines a generic type of coercion operations and discusses the main challenges associated with it. It then utilizes this blueprint as a lens to critically examine Moscow's balance in coercion operations. Finally, it hypothesizes about the capacity of the Russian strategic community to address the deficiencies associated with its coercion endeavors.

COERCION OPERATIONS: A GENERIC MODEL

Coercion aimed at shaping a competitor's behavior in protracted conflict, be it compellence or deterrence, demands a nuanced operational program. Although Western theoreticians and practitioners have aggregated significant knowledge on the subject, there is no canonical blueprint on how to run coercion operations. A synthesis of the Western academic literature, military planning manuals, and interviews with practitioners on both sides of the Atlantic makes it possible to draw the contours of conventional wisdom on the subject and the common pathologies and challenges associated with coercion operations.

A generic, ideal-type coercion operation (be it deterrence or compellence) consists of three phases—planning, execution, and evaluation. In the planning stage, in theory, any operational plan should be guided by a particular political goal and supported by a tailored intelligence diagnosis. The highest command authority, political or military, should provide operational planners with a concrete goal and desired effect, which will drive the coercive operation. Then the intelligence effort in support of the operation's planning begins. Assisted by intelligence experts, planners formulate assumptions about the adversary's intentions and capabilities, and about the correlation of forces and interests between oneself and the competitor. As part of this endeavor, they identify the adversary's perceptions and values that can be effectively exploited. The diagnosis encompasses what makes the greatest impression on the enemy and which critical possessions it is afraid to lose. To excel in this mission, an intimate understanding of the opponent" strategic culture is required as well as tailored intelligence collection and analysis in support of such a coercion endeavor.[1]

Once planners have identified what can effectively be held at risk, they seek ways and means to generate and exploit the adversary's apprehensions, in order to shape its strategic calculus. They put together an operational plan of concrete actions that exploits these values and phobias and shapes the adversary's choices in conjunction with a political objective. The planners decide how much force should be employed, if at all, where, and for how long, for the sake of coercive signaling. Common deficiencies in this phase include a poor link between the higher-order strategic goal and lower-order operational missions, and an operational design focused not on exploiting an opponent's strategic values and threat perceptions but on the use of one's favored arsenal, often the most technologically sophisticated, but not necessarily the most adequate.

The next stage is execution—the coercive signaling itself. In theory, one should communicate to the adversary which choice one expects the adversary to make and signal credible resolve and capability, by word and deed, to impose costs in case of noncompliance. History is replete with failures of a coercion initiator to signal to the opponent its capability, resolve, and strategic expectations. Theory therefore advises not taking for granted that the opponent has automatically absorbed and understood the coercive signals sent (be it deterrence or compellence). Evaluating how the adversary has internalized one's signals and ensuring that the evaluation rationalizes one's moves correctly is thus crucial to avoid coercion failures. A related challenge is to communicate red lines and/or inflict pain to prevent unacceptable behavior, but without escalating. Verifying that signals have been absorbed and perceived as intended is a vital but often missing part of deterrence programs.[2]

The final phase of any coercion operation is evaluation. Theory advises establishing a causal link between the coercion program that one has executed and the adversary's observed strategic behavior. Such an estimate of the effectiveness of one's endeavors is necessary toward the next round of interaction, especially if one is conducting a coercion operation in the frame of a protracted conflict. As elsewhere in the art of strategy, any coercion effort is unlikely to produce exactly the expected outcome. How does one establish the effectiveness of one's coercive efforts to shape an opponent's decision-making? In reality, the evaluation process is often even less structured than the earlier phases of a coercion operation. Its quality, form, and institutionalization vary across strategic communities. Despite a fascination with "deterrence theory," strategic communities on both sides of the Atlantic do not possess an established mechanism or institution charged with verifying the effectiveness of their coercive activities. Practitioners mostly assume rather than prove causality between the observed behavior and one's coercion endeavors. The common belief is that the effect has been achieved when the opponent engages in the desired behavior and the combat plan has been successfully executed. The problem of determining a cause-and-effect relationship between coercion and an adversary's behavior is built into the heart of deterrence theory, and is in effect one of the weakest points of practice.[3]

The evaluation challenge relates to one's ability to diagnose the point beyond which a coercive operation enters the realm of diminishing and negative returns. In protracted strategic competitions this is a major problem. Each round of interaction, even if it involves "forceful coercion," is not the ultimate final blow, but rather an episode on a continuum punctuated by escalatory flashes, confined in space and time. An accurate examination of the outcomes of one's coercive signaling, especially if that signaling involves certain forceful elements, makes it possible to plan the scale, shape, and form of subsequent operational steps, including a possible pause in, or calibration of, a coercion campaign in the long-lasting conflict.

Samuel Charap uses the term *calibrated coercion* to describe the logic of limited employment of coercive force in an extended game, which is different from a big war paradigm (when one applies overwhelming brute force to ultimately defeat an opponent).[4] Forceful coercion that employs limited force to influence an opponent's prospective choices demands a feedback mechanism.[5] Ideally, at each rung on the escalation ladder, the initiator of coercion should examine the impact of its actions to inform the subsequent rounds of engagement. Failure to conduct such diagnostics may result in the overapplication of force, which at best does not yield the desired outcome, and at worst turns into inadvertent escalation. In both cases, the operation defeats itself by pushing forceful coercion past the culmination point.[6]

The latter term was inspired by the logic of the Clauzewitzian "culminating point of victory (attack)." The nuances of the culmination logic differ in war and in coercion.[7] In both cases, however, it is a metaphor for use of force that attains the maximum possible outcome. This is when the strategist would be better off to consolidate combat gains and consider terminating the fighting, as beyond this point war brings diminishing and negative returns.[8] In the realm of coercion, both forceful and nonforceful, actors intuitively or systematically seek the "golden range" between "undershooting and overshooting." They aim to strike powerfully enough to maintain, restore, or establish new norms of strategic behavior, but without escalating to a major war. The culmination point of coercion therefore refers to a moment after which additional threats or use of force may become counterproductive. Instead of producing the desired behavior (e.g., holding aggression in check or restraining an opponent), forceful coercion becomes so devastating that it incites the enemy, which feels cornered and that it has nothing to lose, to escalate. Credible threats become so convincing that the adversary assumes that an attack is inevitable or imminent, and therefore decides to preempt it. Coercive signaling becomes more likely to incite the opponent rather than convince him to back down.[9] Eventually the coercion program's losses outweigh its gains, causing self-inflicted damage.[10]

The culmination point of coercion can be seen as a subcategory of what the international security literature dubs "non-intended escalation" and the "security dilemma" phenomenon. Indeed, culmination in coercion illustrates the inherent tension between credibility and escalation. Actors want their coercive signals to have maximum credibility. Enhancing credibility, however, may be a dangerous path. Instead of compelling or deterring the object of coercion it may lead to unintended overreaction on its part.[11] Also, the interconnection between the points of maximum effectiveness and points of maximum danger somewhat resonates with the security dilemma. This is when the means an actor employs to increase security decreases the security of the opponent. However, in contrast to the classical spiral model, which asserts that tension grows between adversaries that "focus on strengthening their military capabilities due to insecurity," here one is looking at a dynamic interaction. It is not about simply accumulating or enhancing capabilities in a static manner, but actually employing force for the sake of coercive signaling. Thus, the culmination of coercion refers to influence, forceful and nonforceful, which an actor proactively channels toward the opponent to shape its strategic behavior.[12] Another similarity between the culmination of coercion and the security dilemma is when an actor mistakenly takes "the opponents' strategy of deterrence for intimidation or compellence."[13]

SIGNALING CHALLENGE

How does deterrence *à la Russe* appear when examined through the lens of a generic coercion model? As in other cases worldwide, each stage in the execution has been more challenging to Moscow than the previous one. In accomplishing the first mission of any coercion operation—intelligence diagnosis to support combat design—the Russian strategic community has been rather effective. Scholars tend to agree that since confrontation with the collective West began to intensify in 2014, Moscow has rather accurately identified Western strategic phobias, values, strengths, and vulnerabilities, and then designated the relevant tools to exploit them for political purposes.[14] This capacity to design coercive operations along the lines of "tailored deterrence" has been based on relatively solid theoretical-methodological foundations. In their meticulous work, Kofman, Fink, and Edmonds discuss how the Russian strategic community, especially its military segment, for more than a decade has been developing elaborated mechanisms to tailor deterring damage to specific actors and to calibrate coercion in various scenarios.[15] The same knowledge has served Russian practitioners to inform and design signaling in cross-domain coercive campaigns.[16]

When already at the execution phase, i.e., the second stage of the generic model, how does Moscow ensure that competitors will absorb its coercive signals as intended and interpret red lines accurately? Since 2014, apparently not one of Russia's major military and nonmilitary tactical-operational signals has gone unnoticed. In each episode of coercion, across all domains, Moscow succeeded in communicating its resolve and capability; the Kremlin feels, however, that the West has misperceived the strategic intent of what Moscow has been trying to communicate.[17] Apparently, more often than not, Western strategic communities found Russian coercive signaling confusing and difficult to decipher.[18] The topic is somewhat underexplored and debated.[19] Views differ on the accuracy of the Western understanding of Russian signaling. Prior to the outbreak of the war in 2021, several non-Russian experts analyzing Moscow's coercive dialogue with Washington assumed that more often than not, the U.S. and NATO have misunderstood the Kremlin's forceful and nonforceful deterrence signaling.[20]

In contrast, prior to the war in Ukraine, several Russian experts doubted that the West had genuinely misperceived the Kremlin's strategic communication. Rather, they talked about intentional misrepresentation of Moscow's signaling, driven by motivated biases (which may mistakenly be taken for benign misconception).[21] Whatever the reality, those who believe that the distortion of Russian signals in the West has been genuine trace the misrepresentation to several factors. Some pertain to the West, while others relate to certain factors, which make Moscow's signals objectively confusing and challenging to interpret.

First, the asymmetry of perceptions and demonization of Russia may account for the misperception of Russian signals. There is a huge discrepancy between Moscow's reputation in the West and the Kremlin's self-perception. The majority of Western strategists see Moscow as an assertive, aggressive, offense-oriented revisionist. The Kremlin, however, believes that it is signaling from the position of a defensive, status quo power. The West qualifies Russian actions not as countercoercion (i.e., a reactive strategy aimed at preserving strategic stability) but as harbingers of reckless aggression driven by geopolitical revisionism.[22] These Western assumptions have preceded Russian coercive signaling, which only reinforced them.[23] As Andrew Monaghan demonstrated, preexisting Western views, myths, and misconceptions account at least partially for the misunderstanding of Moscow's coercive signaling in the years leading to the war.[24] The West has filtered almost every coercive signal by Moscow through the above optics. Such a dynamic is not unique to the discussed standoff. Mutual demonization that distorts strategic communications and leads to escalation and security dilemmas is a common pathology in coercive signaling.[25] This distortion does not contradict the fact that in certain episodes Moscow's cross-domain coercion has shaped Western strategic behavior in accordance with the Kremlin's preferences (on which more below).

Second, insufficient attention by Russian strategists to the communication of signals may be another reason for the Western confusion. Apparently, Russian strategists have tended to take almost for granted the Western capacity to accurately decipher the Kremlin's coercive signaling, although the general context in which these signals have been sent has often been unclear to the West.[26] According to Kristin Ven Bruusgaard, it is unclear on what basis Russian strategists assume that their intrawar coercion signaling will be accessible to the adversary.[27] Such assumptions, bordering almost on wishful thinking, may derive from the relatively insufficient attention that Russian strategic studies have paid to this subject.[28] At least in the open sources, there has been no discussion on how to ensure that the enemy neither overestimates nor underestimates Russian intentions and capabilities during forceful and nonforceful coercion. Such exploration is necessary: this is not an abstract academic issue but a practical question, central to any military organization employing coercive signaling.

Finally, the Russian modus operandi, especially in the informational segment of "strategic deterrence," may be confusing. The challenge of deciphering a competitor's intent during nonnuclear coercive signaling is not unique to Russia.[29] In the case of "strategic deterrence," especially in the informational realm, this problem becomes more complicated. Even prior to the war in Ukraine, Moscow's coercive signaling included employment of force, limited in time and scope. The evidence suggests that different segments within the Russian strategic community utilize this employment for three ends. The first is "learning"—to generate knowledge about the adversary, oneself, and the environment in order to inform force buildup, organizational structures, and concept of operations (ConOps) in the midst of an ongoing military innovation. The second is "shaping"—to influence the intentions and capabilities of the adversary in order to dissuade him from taking particular actions in peacetime and crisis, especially from undertaking the transition to wartime, but if this fails, to prepare favorable operational conditions for oneself and unfavorable conditions for the enemy in the initial period of war. The third end is "competing" internally—to generate a reputation in the eyes of the senior authority that will ensure a favorable position in the bureaucratic competition for resources and influence. By accumulating direct combat experience, which can justify resources and expansion of areas of responsibility, military organizations can enhance their prestige and weight.

This state of affairs exacerbates the diagnostic challenge and increases the likelihood of misperception and miscommunication. Only the second end—"shaping"—corresponds with the rationale of coercive signaling. The other two—"learning" and "competing"—do not. The actor on the receiving end is not necessarily capable of differentiating among the three. More likely than not, an actor will be inclined to qualify each episode as an act of coercive signaling, and to merge them all, rather than assign them to distinct categories. It is unclear whether the organs within the Russian strategic community are cognizant that they may be sending confusing signals to the adversary.

EVALUATION CHALLENGE

How do Russian practitioners evaluate the effectiveness of their coercion strategies since 2014 and up to the 2020–21 crisis leading to the war? Generalizations on the subject are problematic; Russian strategists apparently have mixed feelings.[30] Prior to the war, on the positive side, some Russian experts attributed Russia's return to the top of the U.S.'s list of national security challenges, after almost three decades of absence, to its coercive efforts since 2014. For many in the Russian strategic community, this reconciled the cognitive dissonance between their self-perception as a big power rising from its geopolitical knees, and the U.S. perception of Russia as a declining and irrelevant geopolitical actor. This return, even as a troublemaker, to the U.S.'s national security priorities allowed many in Russia to recover from a chronic post-Soviet complex of inferiority.[31] Russian coercive activities somewhat adjusted the calculus of the collective West and contributed to Moscow's strategic reputation. Demonstrations of capabilities, and the resolve to deploy and employ them across several functional and geographical domains, have enhanced the credibility of Moscow's coercive threats and contributed to the ongoing military modernization—an indirect but beneficial effect of coercion.[32] In the eyes of the collective West, the cost of conflict with Russia—or even an attempt to coerce it—is much higher today than it was prior to 2014.[33] The Kremlin's efforts to rewrite the rules of international security in Europe and globally—the main logic behind the escalation of the Ukrainian crisis since 2021—have been building on the pre-produced coercive potential.

In parallel, deterrence *à la Russe* at times has generated negative returns even prior to the war. As Kristin Ven Bruusgaard put it, "Russian deterrent behavior has produced an opposite type of response of what it seeks."[34] Andrew Monaghan echoes Ven Bruusgaard, arguing that the Kremlin faces encirclement, which its coercion efforts have been aimed at preventing.[35] How one's adversary interprets one's behavior is a notion intrinsic to an ideal-type coercion operation. However, both scholars argue that this insight occasionally has not extended to deterrence *à la Russe*.[36] Moscow has employed coercive signaling since 2008, and especially after 2014, as "counterdeterrence" against Western pressure. However, that has only solidified and intensified the latter instead of neutralizing it. Following programmatic speeches by the Russian military brass, political announcements, and demonstrations of nuclear and conventional capabilities in exercises, crises, and combat, Western strategic communities have revived and refined deterrence theory, largely neglected until then, invested significant intellectual and organizational energy in national and collective deterrence strategies, and applied coercive pressure on Russia on an unprecedented scale.

In sum, at times the Kremlin has been irresponsive to the reactions of the adversary and crossed the culmination point of coercion. The Ukrainian case illustrates this even prior to the outbreak of the war. The Kremlin aimed to distance Kyiv from the political-military institutions of the collective West, to scare NATO away from the Russian zone of privileged interests, and to preserve a favorable balance of forces in "the Western strategic direction." Moscow's coercive signaling achieved the opposite results. Not only did it push Kyiv closer to Brussels and Washington; it also prompted NATO to beef up its presence along the Russian borders, exercise regularly on a scale unseen since the Cold War, and invest in countermeasuring Russia all across its strategic periphery. On top of that, military staffs and think tanks on both sides of the Atlantic have uninterruptedly been honing theories of victory for the next war with Russia. To the Kremlin's discontent, Washington has adjusted its major pivot to Asia and begun to reallocate to Europe significant strategic attention and energy to contain and coerce Moscow, in Ukraine, all over its zone of privileged interests, and beyond.[37]

Informational coercion is another illustration. Moscow sees its digital-technological and cognitive-psychological informational operations, both forceful and nonforceful, on both sides of the Atlantic as counter-coercion during a "threatening period"—a Russian euphemism for intensive political confrontation on the verge of a major military crisis. According to Monaghan and Keir Giles, for the collective West, operating from a different ideational foundation, Russian activities come across as irrational escalation of a "hybrid war in a grey zone."[38] To understand the argument about the mixed results, one should consider the short- and long-term consequences of Russian coercive operations in the informational sphere. For example, in the case of the Bronze Soldier, a frequent countdown episode for a talk on Russian informational operations, the long-term drawbacks trumped the short-run achievements. If one confines the spectrum of analysis to this specific episode, the Russian coercion operation could be qualified as a failure—Moscow failed both to deter Tallinn from moving the statue, or compel it to bring the Bronze Soldier back. Moreover, Russia was demonized internationally, presaging the anti-Moscow sentiment that would further brew in 2008 and climax in 2014.

Another counterproductive outcome (further stimulated by the 2008 Russian informational operations in Georgia, and then in Ukraine) was the expedited creation of the Tallinn NATO cyber-excellence center and eventually the Riga Strategic Communications Center. In the long term, however, the 2007 episode and subsequent ones contributed to the general credibility of Russian informational coercion, demonstrating its capability and resolve. In the following rounds of strategic interaction with the collective West, the preproduced strategic potential enabled effective coercive signaling. What Moscow is capable of became ingrained in public consciousness. This is exactly the deterring potential that several subsequent operations sought to maintain, especially as new and more agile tools have been entering Russia's arsenal. This is not to argue that this was the initial long-term plan, which it probably was not; however, in the subsequent stages this episode contributed to the cumulative coercion. All the subsequent episodes can be seen as coercive engagements pursuing a specific coercive goal, and also a more general aim—recharging the batteries of coercion for the next rounds of strategic interaction, which Russia sees as an indefinitely protracted confrontation.

It is impossible to establish categorically whether and to what extent the alleged 2016 and 2020 (presidential), 2017 (state), and 2018 (midterm) U.S. election interference operations maneuvered U.S. voting patterns in any way. American analysts have hypothesized about the Russian intent, but not proved any causal link to the results.[39] Furthermore, new rounds of sanctions were imposed on Russia in response. That said, interfering in the elections nonetheless inflated the Kremlin's strategic reputation and provided it with reputational capital to spend in future coercive campaigns against the U.S. or any other actor. Similarly, no clear immediate advantages can be discerned in the context of the alleged hacking of French president Emmanuel Macron's campaign or Brexit. Nonetheless, both added to the cumulative effect. Given that Western strategic communities and commentators pay such disproportionate attention to subversive Russian cognitive-psychological influence—including in publications of the leading think tanks and congressional investigation commissions, not to mention the routine hype in the media—turning almost everything into Russian informational war, Moscow does not even need to signal its capabilities and resolve to make its coercive threats credible.[40] Russian informational operations have sparked the establishment of new structures in NATO, such as the Strategic Communications Centers, the dedication of a significant chunk of U.S. CYBER-COM resources to Russia, and assertive informational countermeasures under the rubric of "persistent engagement."[41] Today Moscow sees the Western "mental war" against it as an immediate and constantly mounting danger.[42]

Finally, Russian coercive signaling has further reinforced the Kremlin's preexisting reputation as a strategic adventurist waiting to exploit a land grab opportunity.[43] This image made many in Moscow unhappy; it has prompted Western punitive and preventive measures, and led to economic isolation. Although prewar sanctions have produced several positive effects for Moscow, besides not having a dramatic impact,[44] some damages have been significant, especially in such central fields for the Kremlin as AI and digitalization.[45] In sum, statements by the Russian political-military leadership and defense intellectuals suggest that they estimate the overall strategic situation and the attitude of the collective West as having worsened. It is unlikely that the grand designers and senior operators of Russian coercion techniques expected, let alone wished for, such an outcome.

WHAT ARE THE CHANCES FOR IMPROVEMENT?

Improving the analytics for evaluating coercion and diagnosing its culmination looms largest among the challenges that face practitioners of forceful deterrence or compellence worldwide. How does one recognize the culmination point? Is such evaluation feasible? Failures and successes over history have made scholars skeptical about the ability to determine culmination in advance, or in the midst of fighting.[46] This point may not be identifiable using the scientific method, being more a virtue of art and professional intuition than something that can be calculated through formal models.[47] This, however, has not deterred practitioners from refining procedures to diagnose culmination and taking it into account during coercive operations. Evidence from the U.S. and Israeli armed forces—two militaries that have been practicing the operational art of coercion, especially forceful, more than any other actor worldwide—suggests that improvement in this regard is a function of two factors: the accumulation of firsthand, especially negative, experience, and the ability of an establishment to conduct a self-critical examination to learn from its blunders, and adjust accordingly. During the last decade, on the assumption that conceptualizing the problem may enhance performance, practitioners in both countries have been refining their capacity to coerce without provoking escalation.[48]

What is the capacity of the Russian strategic community to deal with one of the biggest challenges in the operational art of coercion? How established and systematic is the evaluation of coercion effectiveness in the Russian strategic community? The evidence is mixed. Since the mid-2000s, several Russian practitioners have been exploring the theoretical-methodological aspects of coercion evaluation. In parallel with the rise of *strategic deterrence*, as theory and policy, a number of experts within the establishment have been developing formal models to measure the effectiveness of nonnuclear coercion. The tone of these publications, the most prominent of which is a 2010 book by V. M. Burenok and Iu. A. Pechatnov, has been exploratory rather than definitive. In a way it was food for thought, which the defense establishment experts offered to practitioners of "strategic deterrence." These works elaborated on Russian and foreign experience, presented evaluation as an integral part of an ideal-type deterrence operation, highlighted the main challenges, and offered ways to address them. Implicitly, they also offered blueprints for institutionalizing coercion evaluation procedures in the Russian establishment.[49] These steps toward a coherent theory for estimating coercion effectiveness emerged in conjunction with efforts to refine effectiveness evaluation in fields such as force employment in various types of strategic operations, in informational-radio-fire strikes, and the evaluation of damage inflicted on Russian forces.[50]

No data available to the author indicates whether, how, or to what extent the Russian military has adopted formal models of deterrence evaluation. If Russian practitioners lack institutionalized procedures to evaluate the effectiveness of their coercion operations, this may explain why the Kremlin's deterrence and compellence endeavors have at times crossed the culmination point. The abovementioned corpus of knowledge is insufficient, albeit relevant, for the type of coercion operations that the Russian military has been running. Ideally, there should be a model that captures the adversary's changing resolve and capability in the midst of ongoing coercive friction (i.e., intrawar coercion). What Charap dubs "calibrated coercion"[51] demands an estimate of the adversary in an action-reaction dynamic, not an evaluation of a static correlation of forces and means. The closest approximation from the world of kinetic operations, to use the Western lexicon, would be "battle damage assessment" techniques or "operational net-assessment," applied during each episode of coercive engagement to inform combat planning for the subsequent stages of a protracted campaign.[52] No professional Russian articles that deal specifically with estimating the first- and second-order strategic effects of coercive signaling, immediately after its application but still in the midst of ongoing friction, are available to the author as of this writing.

Works by Burenok and Pechatnov have applied the methodology of operational analysis (*issledoovanie operatzii*) to reflexive control theory (*refleksivnoe upravelnie*) in order to estimate one's efforts in deterrence operations. Despite the relevance, their main focus has been on the cost-effectiveness of reflexive control (i.e., coercion), rather than on forecasting the risk of a competitor's overreaction following the application of "forceful strategic deterrence" (*silovoe sratergicehskcoe sderzhivanie*).[53] In contrast, a diagnostic model is needed to prevent a competitor's overreaction during domination on "the intermediate steps of the escalation ladder"—a topic that Russian military theory and practice, in the words of Pechatnov himself, has underexplored.[54] Inadvertent escalation, another topic related to diagnosing and preventing any crossing of the culmination point, has drawn only limited Russian professional attention, as compared to the first and second phases of the generic type of coercive operation that Russian theory has explored in depth. Apparently, the absence of the topic from the professional discourse may reflect the lack of formal acknowledgment of such an endeavor as a separate procedure in the Russian military. Despite signs indicating the emergence of theory on the evaluation of deterrence operations, as of this writing it is unclear whether the Russian strategic community, and the General Staff specifically, has a coherent methodology, staff-work procedures, or an organ charged with evaluating coercion operations and diagnosing their culmination point.

Despite the challenges, the Russian military is more likely than not to improve in the matter of diagnosing the culmination point. Dedicated exploration of the subject should come as no surprise, given the elevated status of "strategic deterrence" in Russian policy, theory, and operations. A basic awareness of the problem, albeit not under this rubric, has apparently been emerging within the establishment.[55] This is a natural stage in the evolution of a community of practice, which adopts a coercive strategy, codifies it as formal doctrine, and practices it regularly.

Moreover, Russian practitioners can build on friends abroad. There is a corpus of open-source Western professional publications, both military manuals and specified periodicals, that deal with these questions and systematize the knowledge. They are easily accessible to Russian practitioners, who are exploring more and more thoroughly the Western deterrence literature and importing conceptual constructs.

Russian practitioners may be at least as good as their Western counterparts in developing an applied diagnostics for this universal professional challenge. As in other fields of deterrence theory and practice, the Russian expert community is several decades younger than its Western counterpart as regards dealing with the question of forceful coercion. If Russian practitioners begin to deal with this issue systematically, they can benefit from several preexisting corpora of professional knowledge from the Soviet-Russian military and intelligence sciences. These might not only offer useful building blocks, but make it possible to outperform their foreign colleagues. On the military side, Russian practitioners dealing with effectiveness evaluation of "strategic deterrence" already employ methods from operations research and reflexive control. In most of the works, the former is used to estimate the effectiveness of the latter. Both are established disciplines in the Soviet-Russian pantheon of sciences, civilian and military. *Operational research* offers an apparatus of methods, which the Soviet and Russian armed forces have been routinely practicing in measuring combat effectiveness and battle damage assessment.[56] Russian deterrence experts' use of a reflexive control framework is also natural, as this concept serves as the theory of victory and organizing principle of coercive operations.[57] From here it is but a short way to a designated effort to diagnose the culmination point; this today is mainly a matter of professional awareness and choice.

If Russian experts move in this direction two techniques are available to them. From the pool of military methods, Russian practitioners can lean on *qualimetry*—the use of formal models to quantify the qualitative characteristics of weapons, forces, and doctrines.[58] Since the challenge here is to measure variations in nonquantifiable factors, such as a competitor's resolve and intentions, this method may come in handy. Additional conceptual assistance may come from the Soviet-Russian theory and practice of intelligence. The most relevant concept here is *operational game* (*operativnaia igra*)—a professional term of the KGB and its successors for manipulating an adversary in a protracted intelligence operation.[59] The logic and techniques and supporting concepts (i.e., prevention, preemption, and dissuasion from subversion) of operational games, which Russian intelligence practices to this day, have much in common with the current Russian theory of forceful coercion.[60] As regards operational games, no formal technique was established for diagnosing the culmination point. However, starting from the 1970s, KGB theoreticians acknowledged this problem. Learning from their failures and successes, they systematically explored methods to prevent this undesired outcome. Usually, this was done under the rubric of struggle against cliché in thinking and operations (*shablonost' v mishlenii i operatsiiakh*)—a professional ill that leads to crossing the culmination point, according to KGB officers.[61]

In sum, Russian experts dealing with coercion operations are likely sooner rather than later to come up with an applied theory that minimizes the risk of crossing the culmination point. Beyond the realm of "strategic deterrence," in the sphere of major military operations, the Russian strategic community, the armed forces in particular, already possess such aptitude. The operation in Syria demonstrated the Russian military's capacity not to cross the culmination point of the campaign.[62] It remains to be seen the aptitude of the Russian strategic community not to cross the culminating point of war and culminating point of coercion in the current conflict in Ukraine. The next chapter will discuss this question in a more detailed manner. Here it suffices to add that the assessment problem is not only a challenge of a proper method and procedures in coercion operation, but is also rooted in pathologies of civil-military relations. As already mentioned above, and as Lawrence Freedman demonstrates in his work on the politics of strategic-military leadership, this is not necessarily uniquely Russian problem or the result of Russian cultural approach to coercion (both deterrence and compellence) but a universal challenge pertaining to the supreme command dialectics.[63]

CHAPTER 5

WAR IN UKRAINE AND AVENUES
OF FUTURE RESEARCH

WHAT'S NEXT FOR DETERRENCE *à la Russe*? How is the Russian theory and practice of coercion likely to evolve after the war in Ukraine? What are the promising avenues of future research? This chapter offers initial thoughts on these questions. This book was submitted to the press prior to the war in Ukraine—a military clash of a size and scale unseen in Europe since World War II. As of this writing, the war continues to unfold and appears to be turning into a protracted conflict. The contours of the big picture are still emerging. Until the initial fog of war dissipates, probably after the first cessation of massive fighting, conclusions are premature.

Western scholars are just beginning to explore various aspects of Russian strategy and operations in depth. The topic of coercion will loom large among these endeavors. In parallel, the Russian expert community has begun its systematic examination of the war. As in the West, exploration in the field of "strategic deterrence" is likely to become one of the avenues of Russian postwar learning. There is already sufficient evidence from Ukraine to pose initial questions about Moscow's wartime behavior and to frame the postwar research agenda in the realm of deterrence *à la Russe*. This chapter first couples preliminary insights from the war with the book's findings and then outlines several avenues of prospective research.

WAR IN UKRAINE

The Russian invasion of Ukraine thus far has been a forceful phase of a prolonged coercive campaign. The decision to invade had several drivers—regional, global, and ideological. Beyond the issue of Ukraine, fundamental security aspirations and geopolitical frustrations, which had been aggregating for decades, drove the Kremlin to war. In a nutshell, the Kremlin initiated the crisis and eventually invaded Ukraine to rearrange the post–Cold War world order, terminate the unipolar moment in world history, and demonstrate the limits of U.S. power. The Kremlin initiated the crisis in autumn 2021. Its ultimatum submitted in December demanded Ukrainian neutrality, a pledge not to join NATO, security guarantees from the U.S., and a reversal of the current NATO posture. Since then, Moscow has been steadily ascending the escalation ladder. The Kremlin aimed to deter Ukraine from further approach with the alliance, to keep it within its sphere of geopolitical influence and compel the U.S. to accept at least some of its demands. Moscow apparently did not expect all of its requests to be met. Some of those, like a demand to return to the pre-enlargement posture, were obviously unrealistic. Still, the Kremlin anticipated minimal concessions, at least with regard to the status of Ukraine. Apparently, in the Kremlin's view, war was not inevitable. Acceptance of some of the demands, such as finding a proper definition on neutrality of Ukraine, and engagement, even a nominal one, in discussing the adjustments of the European security architecture, might have prevented the employment of force. More empirical evidence is needed to support or refute this proposition. Moscow apparently saw the NATO responses and even rounds of shuttle diplomacy as adamant refusal to accept even the basic parts of the Russian ultimatum.

An interview with Andrei Sushentsov, one of the leading Russian experts close to the establishment and a dean of the Russian Foreign Ministry's elite university of international relations, is indicative of the then Kremlin's logic. Sushentsov spoke in early February, when the Kremlin apparently realized the vanity of its nonforceful compellence. He described the standoff as the first step of a higher-stakes phase in Russia's protracted conflict with the West. According to him, Russian coercive engagement since late 2021 aimed "to force the West to agree to new security architecture for Eastern Europe." The aim of keeping the threat of war ever-present, argued Sushentsov, was to compel the West to consider concessions it had avoided until then.[1] The uncertainty of the prewar situation was meant to communicate the seriousness of ignoring Russian concerns.[2] To signal the credibility of its intentions, Moscow incrementally amassed forces near the border. After three months of muscle flexing, when the nonforceful rungs of coercion did not deliver, Moscow moved on to forceful means of influence (*silovye metody vozdeistvia*).

Does the Russian invasion constitute a failure of coercion? Yes and no. If judged by the classical theoretical metrics, this resort to force underscores the futility of coercive influence. On the other hand, if judged by the Russian canon, invasion is merely a transition to the forceful stage of coercive pressure. As the first chapters of this book have explained, deterrence *à la Russe* is not so much about rhetorical threats as it is about concrete engagement aimed at imposing one's strategic will on the competitor. Proactive endeavor and preemptive action underlie the meaning of the Russian term *sderzhivanie*. The Kremlin expected its nonforceful coercion to produce results. When it did not deliver, Moscow turned to forceful influence. Russian conduct since autumn 2021 may therefore be seen as a single holistic coercion campaign, nonforceful and then forceful.

Putin, in his opening speech of the "special military operation," framed the invasion as the preemption of a larger war. Such framing of coercion somewhat corresponds with the concept of *mabam*—campaign between the wars—which lies at the heart of Israeli deterrence theory. It refers to surgical strikes and special operations conducted against an opponent's valuable military assets and critical infrastructure, and in order to forcefully prevent the acquisition of advanced capabilities. The use of limited force should dissuade the adversary from initiating large-scale aggression that otherwise would demand massive retaliation.[3] When the initial invasion aimed at quick victory fell to pieces, the Russian military began adapting. Several rounds of combat adjustments boiled down to more firepower, brute force, and urban combat. Fragmentation and destruction of the Ukrainian military, coupled with annihilation of the defense-industrial infrastructure, followed by strategic operation against critical infrastructure since October 2022, became the Russian theory of victory.

The war has been unfolding in a nuclear atmosphere from the outset. The omnipresence of the nuclear dimension has been in keeping with the logic of cross-domain coercion that this book has outlined. In the weeks leading up to the invasion, the Kremlin introduced the nuclear element to produce a cordon sanitaire around the emerging theater of operations. In other words, nuclear manipulations produced around the battlefield a sphere of the possible within which conventional operations could achieve results. The aim was to contain the military activity in the realm of a "local conflict" and prevent it from turning into a "regional war." The image of unacceptable consequences produced by this cross-domain coercion was aimed at paralyzing Western assertiveness and responsiveness.

The nuclear signaling aimed to prevent any NATO intervention and to keep to a minimum the stream of armaments. Rhetorical signals included various references by Putin and senior officials to the risk of escalation to nuclear war. In addition to the constantly mounting forces, the nonverbal signaling included the readiness exercise (which was not pre-planned) in all three legs of the Russian nuclear triad. During the first week of war, to enhance this cordon sanitaire, Putin introduced a special combat regime in the forces of strategic deterrence (i.e., strategic and nonstrategic nuclear weapons and nonnuclear dual-use long-range weapons).

As the previous chapters have explained, Russian theory views the employment of "pre-nuclear" or *conventional* deterrence capabilities as a prelude to nuclear coercion. According to Russian doctrinal views, the merger of pre-nuclear and nuclear tools into one system of coercion expands Russian options on the escalation ladder. Threatening to launch and actually conducting long-range conventional precision-guided strikes, selective or massive, with discriminating damage to the military and civilian infrastructure, should signal the last warning before limited low-yield nuclear use. From the outset, Moscow has been regularly employing advanced munitions and platforms that are dual use—i.e., capable of carrying both conventional and nuclear warheads. In many episodes, the employment of these capabilities has served tactical-operational needs to a lesser extent but constituted strategic signaling. The massive strategic operation against the critical infrastructure began only in October 2022, but nuclear signals escorted it from the outset.

How effective was Moscow's initial intrawar coercion? Moscow succeeded in deterring NATO from intervening directly. This was somewhat easy, obvious, and effortless, due to the mix of the Western self-deterrence and Russian, especially nuclear, deterrence threats. It was much more challenging to deter the massive transfers of arms, supplies, and intelligence to Ukraine. The challenge became even bigger for Moscow, when deterrence of the West and compellence of Ukraine became almost equally prominent in Moscow's intrawar coercion. Starting from summer to autumn 2022, the Kremlin started to aim its coercion to compel Ukraine to cease fire and enter into negotiations on Russian conditions. By the end of 2022, coercion as war termination mechanism has not delivered. As of this writing, Moscow failed to compel Ukraine to surrender even by using dual use systems, nuclear and other nonconventional threats, and strategic operation against critical infrastructure. Allegations of perceived chemical, biological, and radiological threats turned into a central motif of informational coercion, aimed at enhancing coercive credibility and preparing the ground for further escalation, whether conventional or nuclear. Similarly, the messianic rhetoric accompanying the verbal and nonverbal signaling aimed to communicate an eagerness to escalate and gave an existential aura to the war. In the first eigtheen months of war, Moscow's implicit nuclear signaling as a war-termination mechanism and/or as a compellence tool did not work.

From the outset, experts saw the risk of Russian nuclear escalation as low, but nonetheless real and the highest in decades. Several prominent acting and former U.S. officials considered a scenario of nuclear escalation to be unlikely but more probable than ever before. Considering contingency plans, they argued that NATO had plenty of conventional resources to respond, and that nuclear retaliation was only a last resort.[4] The predominant recommendation of the Western experts was to qualify the Russian signals as a coercive bluff and disregard them. Experts assumed that the more attention was paid to these signals the more it played into the hands of the Kremlin.[5]

The likelihood of the Kremlin's employment of a limited nuclear option is increasing if Moscow qualifies NATO's growing involvement as threatening to its existence and territorial integrity. At a certain point, transfers of advanced intelligence, command and control, and standoff fire capabilities may enable the Ukrainian forces to employ sophisticated reconnaissance-strike complexes. This could lead to instances of local superiority over the Russian forces. If the effect of such tactical superiorities translates into operational-level achievements, Moscow may find itself in a daunting strategic situation in Ukraine. Russian doctrine would qualify such a scenario as a transition from local conflict to regional war. Other potential triggers include unbearable costs of the conflict, Ukrainian strikes into Russian territory or an unstoppable offensive into Donbas or Crimea, and a desire to terminate the war by having Ukraine surrender unconditionally.

The more daunting the Kremlin considers the situation in the front to be—that its nonnuclear escalations arsenal has been exhausted, and its nuclear rhetoric is futile—the higher the probability to escalate nonconventionally. As of this writing, we have not yet reached this phase. By the end of winter 2023, the Kremlin apparently estimated it has enough military and nonmilitary means of escalation (energy and food leverages, chemical weapons, cyber, strategic operations against critical infrastructure, besides the ongoing fighting fueled by mobilization). The nuclear rhetoric that accompanies the current conventional fighting—a Russian cross-domain coercion cocktail—is likely to continue. As of this writing, the Kremlin apparently estimates that its coercive rhetoric is still delivering. However, the repeated nuclear intimidations unsupported by actions may be approaching the culmination point, after which negative returns devalue coercion credibility. If the Kremlin senses any inflation in threats, it will consider switching to nuclear muscle flexing.

This phase is likely to precede limited nuclear use. Arguably, rather than opt for a surprise attack, Moscow will progress through the muscle-flexing phase gradually, making visible "strategic gestures"—a Russian euphemism for coercive signaling aimed at deterring and compelling. The "gestures"—various demonstrative activities with strategic and non-strategic nuclear arsenals—should communicate credible capabilities and resolve to climb the escalation ladder. The aim will be the same as that of the nuclear rhetoric today—to coerce the U.S. to compel Kyiv to negotiate and accept a cease-fire, and to deter NATO from further support of Ukraine. It could also be a war-termination mechanism.

Activities may include elevation of alert levels as close as possible to full readiness. In the strategic triad, this may include increased numbers of ground, naval, and air patrols away from the bases. In the nonstrategic nuclear weapons (NSNW), it may include transport of nuclear containers from central storage closer to the means of delivery. The transport teams may stay next to the delivery platforms, just a few steps away from turning over the armed weapons to the operators from the "conventional" forces. These "gestures" will be decisive enough to communicate credibility, but slow enough to allow the West to take notice of them, digest the information, and adjust accordingly. The Kremlin is unlikely to skip up the escalation stairs, but will advance through this phase incrementally to generate maximum effectiveness. This phase can last for weeks.

Indications of this phase will be twofold. First will be unusual, dangerous, and escalatory shifts in the deployment posture of strategic and nonstrategic platforms. Another indicator will be a deviation in the rhetoric: no longer hints and figures of speech from politicians or propagandists, but concrete announcements by the military brass about elevation of the alert level in the nuclear C_2 and forces, and an outline of expectations from the adversaries. This modus operandi will resemble Moscow's coercion on the eve of the war, when in parallel with the ultimatum to Ukraine the Kremlin also engaged in conventional muscle flexing.

Moscow cannot sustain this phase for too long. (This is another similarity to its prewar coercion by concentration of forces.) The Kremlin will wait and see whether the signal has achieved any effect before climbing the next rung of the ladder. A nuclear test followed by limited use is the watershed. The latter, even if conducted on the battlefield, will still be driven by the coercion logic of escalation for the sake of de-escalation, not by pursuit of a functional operational effect. The eventuality of limited nuclear use cannot be ruled out. However, the Kremlin will do everything possible, including prolonging the nuclear muscle-flexing phase to the maximum, to deter and compel without actual use. As of this writing, Moscow assumes that the balance of interests is in its favor and that the West will not retaliate with nuclear weapons. Implicitly, all the rest the Kremlin can tolerate. It therefore expects the credible prospect of further escalation, which its nuclear muscle flexing will spark, to push the West to back off.

Why did the Kremlin's pre-invasion coercion fail? Did the West miss Moscow's signals? Did it qualify them as a bluff? Or, rather, did the West get Moscow's communication right but decide not to back off? As of this writing, there is insufficient data to provide a categorical answer to this question. The ambiguity of the red lines has been a feature of Moscow's approach to coercion. Prior to the war, competing schools of thought existed on this matter. Some Russia watchers have argued that Moscow's red lines intentionally are blurred to enhance coercive power. According to this view, the aim of this stratagem is to let the enemy exaggerate the actual Russian capabilities and intentions.[6] An alternative view argues that Moscow's red lines are truly nonexistent, and that the Russian experts themselves are debating them.[7] Although these questions have drawn major attention during the last decade, when the war broke out they were still unresolved. The war further underscored this conundrum.

Who crossed the culmination point of coercion in this war? Views differ. One could argue that Moscow's coercion strategy yielded negative returns. It refocused the U.S. from China to Russia. It expanded (i.e., via requests from Finland and Sweden to join) and consolidated NATO, with the alliance demonstrating its most enhanced decision-making and decision-execution capacity ever. In Ukraine, the Kremlin's coercion further reinforced the national identity and cemented the Western orientation. Ukraine has turned into a testing range of

Western weaponry against Russia; some of the advanced and longer-range weapons that Kyiv has acquired are exactly the capabilities that the Kremlin wanted to prevent them from having. Russia has become a pariah state; the implications of the sanctions are likely to be multidimensional and long-lasting, and have already produced the biggest ever social-economic risks to the regime. The invasion has discredited, perhaps even endangered, the national ideology and civil religion. Finally, already in war, the Kremlin crossed the culmination point when it did not terminate the "special military operation" once the initial plan went awry. After the first week, this war turned into an inadvertent escalation yielding negative returns.

According to an alternative view, it was the West that crossed the culmination point. Among the first to promote this view were John Mearsheimer and Dimitri Simes. Their takes on the genealogy of the war are indicative.[8] According to this view, the Western policies toward Moscow since the late 1990s, instead of producing the desired behavior (e.g., holding aggression in check or restraining an opponent), provoked escalation. It was the Western indifference to Russia's repeated calls over the years, climaxing in the ultimatum of late 2021, that led to this war. That attitude incited the Kremlin to preempt rather than back down. Prior to the war the Kremlin already saw the regime in Kyiv as a Western geopolitical proxy. Within this broad framework, it is not unconceivable that Putin indeed considered Western military aggression against Russia to be inevitable or imminent, and therefore decided to preempt. Washington was cognizant of that view. It estimated the risk of invasion as high and apparently tried to deter Moscow from taking this step. It revealed intelligence about the Russian preparations to delegitimize the move, and possibly to dissuade the Kremlin from making it. The prewar threat of sanctions (which in the end turned out to be more forceful that either Western capitals or Moscow apparently expected) turned out to be too vague to deter the Kremlin. According to this view, Washington indeed may have aimed to prevent the war, but it was the lack of response to the ultimatum that provoked the invasion. Moscow, according to this interpretation, felt that the West again simply ignores Russian interests altogether, and apparently took Washington's strategy of deterrence for intimidation and compellence, and as a harbinger of the forthcoming escalation.

AVENUES OF FUTURE RESEARCH

Even prior to the Russian invasion, this book had identified several known unknowns pertaining to deterrence *à la Russe*. The preliminary insights from the war in Ukraine further underscore some of these lacunae of knowledge and have added novel research questions. The following five topics loom largest as promising avenues of exploration. For some of this future research the same cultural analysis that this book employs seems to be an appropriate methodological fit. An alternative approach would be to conduct focused comparative case studies employing hypothesis testing that draws on theoretical insights about political and organizational behavior.

Prevention in Russian Strategic Thought

How does "prevention," a strategic concept that is gaining attention among the Russian experts, relate to deterrence *à la Russe*?

In his opening speech of the war, Putin framed the operation as a preventive strike. His historical frame of reference was straightforward—Moscow would not repeat the Kremlin's mistake on the eve of Hitler's Operation Barbarossa in 1941. It would preempt in order to save the colossal costs of tomorrow's war. Such framing occurs against the backdrop of a bigger conceptual trend in the Russian expert community. During the last several years there has been a splash of professional interest among Russian military experts in the role of prevention (*uprezhdenie* or *preventivnye deistviia*) in the art of strategy. The concept originated in the current Russian military discourse at the intersection of three bodies of literature: works on "strategic deterrence," works on "asymmetrical measures," and works on "strategic operations" (i.e., the highest form of combat activity of the Russian military).[9] This splash of interest in Russian expert circles is a novel trend, but prevention itself is an old postulate.[10]

The advocacy of prevention relates to the Russian perception of the "time factor" in modern war. The agility and speed of long-range hypersonic systems pose new threats—the U.S. "global missile defense" and "prompt global strike." Experts argue that a massive strike by tens of thousands of missiles on the objects of the Russian civilian-military critical infrastructure, on the nuclear arsenal, and on the national command-and-control centers would result in a "military knockdown or knockout." According to this estimate, the adversarial offensive and defensive (interception) capabilities nullify the Russian retaliation capacity—launch on warning and second strike. Thus, the only way to repulse the aggression properly is to preempt. The aim of preventive measures is to disrupt adversarial intentions. "Disruption of forthcoming aggression" (*sryv agressii*) becomes more important than success in the initial stage of war (which might be too late).[11]

At present, several Russian military experts present the nonnuclear preventive strike as the only viable option for Russian decision-makers to contain war. They see "prevention" as a separate category within the nomenclature of "asymmetrical military-technological measures aimed at deterring the adversary from initiating military conflict." The definition applies to large-scale regional or local war, or to the transition of a simmering conflict into massive combat activities. In 2022 the Russian high command explicitly ordered that a theory of prevention by "asymmetrical military-technological means" be developed for the full range of conflicts. The end result would be a coherent deterrence concept that drives procurement, doctrine, and missions from the strategic to the operational-tactical echelons.[12]

Novel nonnuclear strategic weapon systems feature as the main tool of prevention.[13] Proponents of this view call for the inclusion of "preventive strike" in the system of strategic operations. The novelty should supplement the "strategic operation for destruction of critically important objects."[14] In the experts' estimate, as of 2021, the Russian armed forces possessed sufficient capabilities to execute such an asymmetrical response on the strategic level to deter large-scale war. However, the operational-tactical echelons lacked sufficient capabilities to prevent lower-intensity conflicts (i.e., regional wars and local conflicts with non-state adversaries).[15] Evidence suggests that the MoD and the GS have charged uniformed theoreticians with developing doctrinal concepts and organizational modifications related to "preventive strategic strike."

However, as of this writing, there is certain mishmash in the Russian references. Three questions loom large. First, it is unclear how the notion of "prevention" relates to the Russian concepts of "strategic deterrence" (i.e., cross-domain coercion) and "escalation dominance" (i.e., intrawar coercion). Second, on the doctrinal level, how will the concept of prevention, if codified officially, refer to other types of Russian strategic operations? Will there be a certain hierarchy among them?[16] Relatedly, it is important to establish the relationship between the concept of prevention and the Strategy of Active Defense and Strategy of Limited Actions, if these are at all relevant concepts after the war. Finally, there is a question regarding the role of intelligence support for the decision to opt for a preemptive strike. Putin's decision to embark on a preemptive war in Ukraine underscores this question. According to the Russian sources, "absolutely credible evidence about the inevitability of aggression" is a precondition for preventive strike.[17] Such warning is universally expected from intelligence organs. Russian sources hint at certain novelties, which should emerge in the intelligence affairs related to prevention. The exact nature of these innovations is unclear and invites a separate exploration.[18]

Emerging Technologies and Chemical Weapons

How does the Russian expert community see the impact of emerging technologies, in particular AI and the new generation of chemical weapons, on the conceptualization of coercion?

During the last decade the Russian expert community, like their colleagues worldwide, has been exploring the impact of emerging technologies on the art of coercion. Several competing schools of thought have produced a corpus of knowledge on this matter.[19] There is sufficient data to explore the following questions. Do Russian experts see emerging technologies as an enabler of or an obstacle to coercion in the nuclear, conventional, subconventional, and informational realms? How, in the Russian view, does human-machine dialectics project on the postulates of coercion? Can machines substitute for men to conceptualize the rationale of an adversary and design an operational plot for deterrence and compellence campaigns? Or are machines limited to supporting the mechanical aspects of combat planning and execution of a human-made operational plot? How does AI relate to strategic intuition? Can it produce counterintuitive plots beyond human imagination? What are the objective and human-imposed limits of AI in coercion operations? Which decisions should and which should not be delegated to machines based on strategic, ideological, and normative considerations? Which schools of thought exist on each subject matter in the Russian military? There has been a massive exodus of Russian IT experts during the war. Will this brain drain affect the Russian attitude to the above questions? Will it shape a preference for certain tools of coercion over others?

The process through which emerging technologies are changing the character of war is known as a revolution in military affairs (RMA). RMA is not about technology per se, but about the capacity to envision its doctrinal and organizational implications. Funds for technological R&D and procurement do not guarantee that a military organization can anticipate an RMA or exploit it properly. The Soviet military outperformed its more technologically advanced and wealthier competitors in the U.S. in grasping the shifts in the character of war at the dawn of the IT era, during the 1980s. Today, again, Russia is among the world leaders in exploring the implications of AI for security affairs, including the strategy of coercion. Comparing and contrasting the Russian discourse on the above topics with parallel discussions in the West is a promising line of inquiry. Where do these discussions diverge and converge? Where do Russian experts agree and disagree with their Western counterparts exploring similar questions? Are there any topics that feature in the Russian debate that the Western exploration has overlooked?

The new generation of chemical weapons is another related line of inquiry. During the last decade chemical weapons have drawn increasing attention in Russian strategic thought. Russian experts have been learning lessons about the coercive and battlefield potential of this capability. Apparently, research and development of a new generation of chemical weapons, in particular nonlethal munitions, has been conducted at a certain scale. Russian discourse mentions this capability in several regards. First, it features as a tool of informational coercion, when staged false flag operations are used to justify subsequent escalatory steps, conventional or nonconventional.[20] In addition, it has emerged as another intermediate stage within the complex of pre-nuclear deterrence. Nonlethal chemical weapons that do not violate legal prohibitions represent an innovative capability that features as a battlefield tool and tool of intrawar coercion.[21] On the escalation ladder, nonlethal chemical weapons may precede coercion by conventional fire systems. As such, they are akin to cyber and radio-electronic means of engagement in the transitional stage from nonforceful to forceful coercion.

What role is Russian military theory likely to attribute to these emerging capabilities? Which lessons will Russian experts take from the war in Ukraine about the coercive potential of these weapons? Are chemical weapons seen as an instrument of strategic signaling, a coercion tool, or part of the battlefield arsenal? What is the perceived effectiveness of each application according to Russian sources? How do ideas on chemical weapons correspond with the cross-domain coaction (i.e., strategic deterrence) theory? How do Russian experts see this capability in relation to nuclear and nonnuclear tools of coercion? As of this writing, these questions have been underexplored in the West.

Evolution of Informational Coercion

What is the Russian mechanism to deter mental and cultural aggression?

The Russian corpus of knowledge on informational coercion is significant, albeit still minor as compared to its nuclear and conventional analogues. Although the Russian expert community has been developing this knowledge almost in parallel with the other two, an official policy of informational deterrence is nonexistent as of this writing. It should come as no surprise if the topic gains higher prominence as part of the updates of state policy in the field of informational security.[22]

In the latter realm, Russian practitioners frame the confrontation with the collective West as a "civilizational contest."[23] They attribute to their adversaries a quest "to change the Russian cultural code," reprogram the national DNA, and "transform Russian strategic culture."[24] The argument runs as follows: the aim of foreign influence is to discredit the value system of the ruling elite and inject alien ideology and fake norms. The end goal is to control the mentality of the population and establish bogus national interests in the collective consciousness.[25] Subversive change of the value system forces the victim to voluntarily make ideological concessions, which in turn leads to geopolitical, military, and economic acquiescence. The adversary destroys the victim's state-social management system,[26] and demoralizes and neutralizes the military without resort to kinetic violence.[27]

In recent years, three themes—"mental wars," "spiritual security," and "strategic culture"—have been central to the Russian discourse on informational coercion. These concepts are interrelated. Since the 2000s the term *spiritual security* has appeared in the Russian national security white papers as an object of defense and deterrence.[28] The concept of "mental war" is a recent official variation on the theme of informational-psychological security.[29] In parallel, the argument that Russia's adversaries aim to reshape Russian strategic culture has been gathering momentum.

How do Russian experts conceptualize the coercion mechanism in mental war? How do they plan to deter adversarial efforts to transform Russia's traditional values and strategic culture? Which countermeasures, passive and active, do they contemplate employing? Are noninformational, i.e., forceful means of deterrence conceivable for this task? Do they take asymmetrical threats into consideration and how do they imagine a symmetrical response—reshaping the strategic culture of the adversaries? How might the Kremlin use religion for purposes of coercion and countercoercion? The Russian Orthodox Church has been the Kremlin's comrade-in-arms in several national security enterprises prior to[30] and during the war.[31] The church collaborates with the state to ensure the loyalty, patriotism and morale-spiritual fortitude of the citizens. How do the Russian experts view the targeting of adversarial spiritual security? Do they envision the leveraging of religion to morally and spiritually decompose the decadent West? These are promising avenues of future inquiry.

Religion and Coercion

How does religion relate to strategic deterrence? In this war, the Kremlin fostered its image as a faith-driven actor to enhance coercive potential.

How effective has this strategy been? How likely is the Kremlin to exploit this approach in future?

Since the Soviet collapse the nuclear arsenal in Russia has been steadily acquiring a divine aura. Moscow started the war at the peak of a three-decade-old nexus between the Orthodox Church and the nuclear forces—a singularity known as Russian nuclear orthodoxy. It is based on a public belief, with which Putin himself concurs, that in order to preserve its traditional (i.e., Orthodox) national character, Russia needs to ensure its being a strong nuclear power; and vice versa, to guarantee its nuclear status, it has to preserve traditional values as the main source of internal spiritual-moral well-being. Some aspects of this phenomenon have been only a ritualistic façade; not everyone has subscribed to the notion. However, it does illustrate the zeitgeist—a mixture of politicized religious philosophy and militarism.[32]

Prior to the war this combination had already gained prominence in Russian politics. The political myths of Holy Rus', the Third Rome, and Russia's civilizational role have become applied notions.[33] Putin's philosophical views have become integrated into his geopolitical vision and policy choices. At times, his rhetoric has been replete with religious-metaphysical ideas and apocalyptic figures of speech[34] in relation to nuclear weapons and beyond.[35] The Kremlin merged strategic and religious justifications behind the gambits in Crimea[36] and the Middle East[37] and has provided the messianic branding for the war in Ukraine.

Several factors account for this peak of messianic fervor. In prewar Russia, the hard-nosed pragmatism of the authoritarian regime,[38] conservatism,[39] nostalgia for imperial greatness,[40] and a religious sense of historical mission[41] drove the Kremlin's policies. Religious motives have not ultimately informed Russian statecraft. However, the public representation of Russia as a *katechon*, a shield against the apocalyptic forces of evil, has become omnipresent and predated the war in Ukraine.[42] Such an approach resonates with the Russian Orthodox Church, which has its own imperial and military propensities.[43] Finally, the traditional Russian glorification of "death on military duty"—an act of martyrdom on behalf of fellow compatriots, brothers in arms, and Holy Russia—has seen a revival. In Russian military discourse, this combat duty to "lay down one's life for one's friends" has the connotation of a religious commandment. Presenting the killed in action as martyrs has been a trend since the Syrian operation.[44] It is a leitmotif of the agitprop in Ukraine.[45]

Prior to the war scholars had registered the Kremlin's use of religion to promote its national security goals.[46] Arguing that the Russian leadership is unlikely to test its martyrdom,[47] some have categorized the religious rhetoric as reflexive control.[48] Others concur that the image of a faith-driven decision-maker can contribute to bargaining.[49] In war, apparently, the Kremlin has started to exploit its reputation as a faith-driven actor to enhance the credibility of its coercive signaling. Putin has framed this war in almost transcendental terms, and has promoted his messianic image in the eyes of competitors.

The logic behind this choice is as follows: the image of being a staunch religious believer provides an actor with a reputation, which secular actors lack. Religious actors come across as being undeterrable, an image that enhances the credibility of their threats in coercive bargaining and makes their competitors question the relevance of classical deterrence.[50] The faith-driven strategic actor, along the lines of the "madman theory," opts for extreme preferences—i.e., perceives the costs of war as being unusually low, attributes unusually high value to the issue at stake, for which apparently there is no reason to fight, has an unusually high tolerance of risk,[51] and demonstrates a readiness to bet against the odds.

Do the Kremlin and its propagandists intentionally blend nuclear posturing with eschatological rhetoric to enhance coercive signaling? On the assumption that the Kremlin deliberately exploited the image of a faith-driven actor to foster coercion, how effective was it during the war in Ukraine? What lessons have Russian strategists learned from this episode? Are the Western analytical models adequate for diagnosing prospective Russian conduct? What lessons for general deterrence theory does this episode offer? The inclination to merge messianic rhetoric and escalatory signaling may extend beyond the war in Ukraine and beyond Putin's tenure in the Kremlin. Without overstating the probability of this eventuality, it is safe to assume that the Kremlin will maintain ambiguity on this issue, increasing Western confusion.[52] Thus, exploration of the above questions may be a separate avenue of research both for Russia watchers and for scholars of coercion theory.

Brutality, Coercion, and the Russian Way of War

Does the Russian military intentionally utilize brutality for coercion purposes? If so, what are the driving forces behind this strategy, its rationale and mechanism?

Brutality in war refers to individual atrocities conducted by soldiers on the ground, intentional targeting of civilian objects, and acts of collective punishment including starvation, instigating a refugee and humanitarian crisis and scaring away the population by conventional and nonconventional strikes or the threat of them. Have the massive civilian casualties and collateral damage been unavoidable consequences of war, or an intentional operational design of the Russian command in this war? Drawing initial lessons from the battlefields of Ukraine, several Western experts have assumed that the Russian military has been compensating with atrocities for poor battlefield performance. Others have assumed that Russia weaponizes brutality as a tool of coercion. On this view, atrocity is a deliberate choice aimed at terrorizing the enemy forces and population and coercing them into submission. In a nutshell, this means that the Russian theory of victory combines fighting and coercive terrorization.

If the brutality attributed to the Russian forces operating in Ukraine was indeed a massive phenomenon and not an exceptional episode, what can explain it? Does it manifest a deeply rooted, distinct style of war? Does it express the general, nonmilitary Russian culture? Or is it in line with other examples of military brutality worldwide that derives from situational factors, such as the degradation of humanity in war, coupled with frustration at the lack of achievements? Was brutality in Ukraine a bottom-up phenomenon, a top-down directive, or a combination of both? How long-lasting and deep-rooted is this phenomenon?

One should differentiate between two interrelated albeit distinct issues. One question concerns the social-cultural sources of Russian brutality on the level of the individual soldier, who is a product of Russian society in a given historical epoch. This question relates to the culture of brutality in the armed forces and beyond, in all aspects of Russian life during the last several generations. If one's dignity is trampled on in the garrison and if one has been brutalized in all spheres of everyday life since childhood, one is likely to do the same in war. The other question concerns the extent to which the military command and political leadership deliberately exploit this somewhat organically engrained brutality for the purposes of coercion.

In the Soviet and Russian military, even if brutality on a massive scale has occurred and then been exploited for the purposes of intimidation, there was no written doctrine or order sanctioning this type of activity.[53] It is unclear, as of this writing, which of the atrocities in Ukraine were ordered by the political leadership and high command, and which occurred due to the tacit permission, or even encouragement, of the officers on the ground. Apparently, in most of the cases, the initial impulse came from rank-and-file soldiers on the ground, and commanders on various levels seem to have preferred not to intervene and thereby encouraged the spread of the phenomenon.

The deep mechanics of this phenomenon in Russia, its patterns and connection to organizational and strategic cultures and to civil-military relations, have been underexplored. This invites a long list of research questions. Did the Russian political leadership and military command intentionally unleash atrocities to coerce Ukraine into unconditionally surrendering? If the utilization of brutality was a deliberate choice, how did the high command envision the coercive mechanism of this tactic? Does the Russian military possess a stratagem, written or unwritten, of intentionally targeting civilians for the sake of coercion? Under what circumstances do the Russian rank and file, and the military organization as a whole, become more prone to committing atrocities? Which factors incline the political leadership and military command to utilize this propensity for coercion? What makes this propensity increase or decrease? What should we expect in future military campaigns? If there is a deliberate intent to use brutality to coerce, is there a division of organizational labor in this regard? What is the role of Rossgvardia, the internal military troops, an extension of the NKVD military units, which conducted most of the coercive and punitive operations?

If the utilization of brutality is indeed an established coercive strata-gem, then how do Russian servicemen and the Russian public come to terms with this development? Have additional formative experiences left an imprint? What was the impact of the brutalization observed and pos-sibly absorbed from foreign militaries by the Russian armed forces? A certain number of Russian commanders have been exposed to such coer-cive performance in recent conflicts by local militaries in the Middle East and Africa, in Syria in particular. There have been claims that Rus-sian forces deliberately used such coercive tactics in tandem with the Syrian military. Coercive manipulation of the civilian population has been evident in the functioning of the Russian reconciliation centers in Syria. Has there been an intentional or subconscious emulation of the foreign culture of war, which proved to be effective? What lessons have the Russians learned from Syria? To what extent have these lessons been applied during the war in Ukraine, if at all? All of the above can be a separate avenue of prospective research.

Foreign Sources of Learning

As the Russian expert community continues to develop knowledge on coercion theory and practice, does it have any foreign sources of intel-lectual inspiration? Is the Russian pivot to Asia going to project on the Russian conceptualization of coercion? Is any intellectual stimulus from China likely to supplement the traditional Russian tendency to learn from the West?

Prior to the war, and even more so after it started, Russia has been pivoting to Asia.[54] This strategic reorientation may bring with it an intel-lectual predisposition. As regards the conceptual inspirations in the matter of coercion, Russian experts have been absorbing intellectual stimuli from both East and West. They have acknowledged variance in the approaches across different strategic cultures and sought to culti-vate the Russian style while critically examining foreign evidence.[55] Tra-ditionally, in the realm of informational coercion, as in many other do-mains, the main source of inspiration has been the West. The U.S. cyber innovations have been the principal frame of reference for Rus-sian knowledge development, modernization of capabilities, and conceptual-organizational transformations. However, somewhat in contrast to the nuclear and conventional realms, in the informational sphere growing attention is also being paid to the Chinese experience during the last decade. Russian experts are closely following Chinese conceptual innovations in the field of informational, network-centric, and cyber warfare(s). Russian sources are learning from the Chinese approach to informational and cyber deterrence and are familiar with the U.S. views on the Chinese approach.[56]

An interest in the Chinese approach and its appeal to Russian experts is somewhat unsurprising. Chinese discourse, in particular in the informational sphere, parallels the Russian approach in at least three regards: both imply a certain level of constant operational friction; both see perception as the center of gravity; and both merge under one rubric the notions of deterrence and compellence. According to Russian sinologists, the Chinese term for deterrence, *veishe*, implies deterrence—forcing the enemy to break off aggressive actions against China (*zastavit' otkazatsia ot vrazhdebnykh deistvii*)—and compellence—forcing the enemy to commit actions in the interest of China. As such, both *veishe* and deterrence *à la Russe* are closer to the Western notion of coercion.[57] Consequently, it may be useful to establish whether and to what extent the Chinese approach informs the Russian. Do these similarities represent Russian conceptual emulations of the Chinese case? Or does this convergence between the approaches derive from factors unrelated to learning and is owing to certain similarities in strategic culture, military thought, and style of warfare?

Deterrence Scholarship and Cross-Cultural Research

Do Western and non-Western practitioners tend to blur the line between coercion and war fighting? If so, what are the sources and consequences of this phenomenon? Exploring this question is a promising line of work for the current wave of deterrence scholarship in Western academic circles.

The "fourth wave" of deterrence literature, especially the notion of a "tailored approach," has informed the argument of this book. Further, the latter's findings correspond with certain claims of the so-called "fifth wave" of scholarship.[58] Whichever wave of research this book belongs to, it offers to the current research program on deterrence the following hypothesis. Arguably, the Russian case demonstrates a blurring of the line between coercion and war fighting. Available evidence suggests that this apparently is not unique to deterrence *à la Russe*. Rather, the current character of war predisposes both Western and non-Western communities of practice to adopt a similar approach to "deterrence."

Various actors demonstrate this propensity in different domains, some in the informational realm and others in conventional deterrence. Preliminary observations suggest that this trend has been evident among those communities of practice that operate under one or more of the following conditions: 1) actors who have formulated applied deterrence theory to inform their operational planning; 2) actors who have conducted this conceptualization against the backdrop of protracted conflicts punctuated by outbreaks of kinetic clashes, usually limited in time and scope; 3) actors who have developed coercion schemes for the nonnuclear realms but against the backdrop of their nuclear arsenals. In all these cases, preexisting strategic traditions have been shaping the approach of a given actor to the conceptualization of coercion.

Limited use of force (i.e., permanent low-level operational friction) became an integral element of informational and noninformational coercion during the last decade worldwide. This regular, albeit limited, use of force makes it difficult to differentiate where coercion ends and where war fighting starts. This line was once somewhat conceptually clear. Now practitioners worldwide tend to obscure it. For example, the U.S. approach in the cyber realm (i.e., "persistent engagement") demonstrates this inclination. The current Israeli approach to conventional deterrence, also known as "campaign between the wars" (*mabam*), and the Iranian doctrine of "forward defense" for deterrence (*bazdarandagi*) illustrate the same trend.[59] The Chinese conceptualization of deterrence implies a certain level of constant operational friction to realize its coercive goals.[60] Western strategic studies distinguish between deterrence and use of brute force. Evidence from all the above cases challenges this classic academic taxonomy.

Is there still a benefit to making this theoretical distinction? If so, what are the criteria for making it? Comparative cross-cultural research on this matter has the potential to advance deterrence theory. Future works can either refute or refine the above proposition. Such exploration will also advance knowledge on variations and congruence in the conceptualization of coercion under the impact of cultural factors and on mutual influence among strategic communities worldwide. Are there any additional peculiarities in other national approaches to coercion strategy, within and outside the Western world? Do practitioners in strategic communities worldwide learn from each other? How does the knowledge diffuse? Who serves for whom as the source of inspiration and who emulates whom? These questions are, as of this writing, underexplored. Research on this matter lies at the intersection of the current waves of literature on strategic culture and deterrence theory.

CONCLUSION

THIS BOOK HAS DESCRIBED the genealogy of the Russian approach to deterrence, highlighting the cultural, ideational, and historical factors that have shaped the Kremlin's prewar and intrawar coercive conduct. The intellectual history of Russian deterrence, which this book has offered, also provides ways to contemplate the prospective evolution of this strategy in Russia following the war in Ukraine.

The book explored the phenomenon at the intersection of three bodies of work—theory of strategic culture, deterrence theory, and Russian affairs. As of this writing, these fields of applied scholarship are witnessing a major renaissance and preoccupy theoreticians and practitioners on both sides of the Atlantic. This book has contributed to all three literatures.

By analyzing a case outside Western strategic thought, which traditionally has dominated deterrence theory, the book demonstrated how strategic concepts evolve differently in various ideational contexts. Utilizing cultural explanations to demonstrate the logic that underpins the Russian approach, it has articulated a model of the cultural imprint on strategic thought.

The findings of this study suggest the adoption of an idiosyncratic approach to exploring coercion. The concept of "tailored deterrence"—adjusting a deterrence program to the nature of a specific actor—is already common wisdom. This study has showed that the understanding of the deterrence strategies of different actors should be tailored as well. Emerging in a specific cultural context, deterrence conceptualization is not universal and varies across strategic communities.

What accounts for the difference between the Russian conceptualizations of coercion and the Western version of this strategy? This was the main research question of *The Russian Way of Deterrence*. The book has argued that the singularities of the Russian approach emanate from Russian strategic culture, national mentality, and military and intelligence traditions. It demonstrated how the latter have been conditioning the former. The sections below summarize the main findings of the book and outline avenues of prospective research on the art of coercion in Russia and elsewhere.

GENEALOGY OF DETERRENCE À LA RUSSE

The intellectual history of the Russian approach to coercion has been relatively short but eventful. When deterrence theory ceased to be anathema following the Soviet collapse, what had heretofore been rejected was not only canonized, but also turned into the Holy Grail for the Russian strategic community. With the zeal of new converts, Russian experts, operating from a position of daunting qualitative and quantitative military inferiority during the first decades of the post-Soviet era, stormed the corpus of knowledge on deterrence, which has accumulated in the West since the 1950s. They studied it, critically adopted some of it, and have developed, through almost thirty years of exploration and debate, their own version of deterrence. Following several stages of evolution, the Russian art of deterrence has become a complex of nonnuclear, informational, and nuclear types of influence encapsulated in a unified cross-domain program.

At least prior to the war, the Russian political leadership, senior military brass, and doctrinal publications most often had been using the term *strategic deterrence* in reference to coercion efforts. This concept seeks to integrate all available capabilities—nuclear, nonnuclear, and informational (cyber)—into one coercive influence effort. To convey the logic of this approach, one may use the non-Russian term *cross-domain coercion*. It denotes the Russian notion of a host of efforts to deter and compel adversaries by orchestrating soft and hard instruments of power (nuclear, nonnuclear, and nonmilitary) across various domains, regionally and globally, through all phases of interaction.

Prior to the Russian invasion of Ukraine, Russian deterrence discourse was relatively more synchronized, coherent, codified, and aligned with the force buildup programs, doctrine, and posture than ever before. Nonetheless, substantial internal and external incongruences still exist. When discussing deterrence, Russian experts and their Western colleagues often mean different things when using the same terms and use different terms to refer to the same things. In part, this pluralism reflects the fact that *strategic deterrence* is an umbrella term under which a variety of definitions coexist. In part, it reflects the uncertainty about the extent to which the political leadership has embraced the military theory. And in part, it reflects the fact that the theory of deterrence is continuing to evolve in Russia. Also, it reflects traditional disconnect in Russia between advanced theory in military affairs and actual practice of strategy and operations.[1]

As a scholarly theory and as a national security practice, deterrence *à la Russe* is about five decades younger than the Western version. It has been entering Russian military science and the professional lexicon incrementally. In the course of catching up, the Russian expert community has been adopting certain terms from the Western lexicon and has given them a Russian cultural reading. The end result is a unique terminology, meanings, and approach to deterrence that differ from the Western conceptualization.

As indicated by the etymological origins of the term *sderzhivanie* (deterrence), the Russian approach implies proactively shaping the strategic behavior of the adversary. The interpretation of this concept in the Russian strategic lexicon is much broader in terms of rationale and scope of application than the meaning that Western experts have in mind. In a nutshell, deterrence *à la Russe* stands for the use of threats, sometimes accompanied by limited use of force, to maintain the status quo ("to deter" in Western parlance), to change it ("to compel" in Western parlance), to shape the strategic environment within which the interaction occurs, to prevent escalation, and to de-escalate. The term is used to describe signaling and activities both toward and during military conflict, and it spans all phases of war. As such, the Russian interpretation of deterrence is closer to the Western conceptualization of "coercion," in its prewar and intrawar forms. In 2021 a certain novelty emerged in the Russian systematization. Probably for the first time, a leading military periodical, *Military Thought*, clearly differentiated between coercion, deterrence, and compellence.[2]

In the nuclear and conventional realms, Russian experts have tended to downplay the Western *punishment versus denial* typology. Rather, they have focused on the *forceful versus nonforceful* taxonomy, which in their view is more useful for the purposes of the operational art of deterrence. Deterrence *à la Russe* has been honing its proficiency in being flexible across domains of influence and in calibrating damage to the adversarial strategic psychology, at least to the same extent as in the West, where academic experts and practitioners appreciate these qualities, which lie at the heart of tailored deterrence in planning and execution.

Informational coercion is a less elaborated construct than the conceptualization of nuclear and conventional deterrence in Russia. Russian experts have recognized the impossibility of replicating classical principles of deterrence in the informational realm verbatim. In terms of maturity, the current state of *informational coercion* (deterrence)—i.e., the evolution of strategic theory, and official doctrinal codification—parallels that of the Russian conceptualization in the nuclear and conventional realms when it was of comparable age, in the early post-Soviet era. The evolution of strategic theory, especially within the military community, and remarkably during the last decade, is indicative of an effort to crystallize and operationalize a coercion mechanism in the informational sphere.

The conceptualization of informational coercion and the organizational structures, operational procedures, and procurement policies in this sphere are likely to become more coherent. The pace of articulation and codification may be even higher given the importance that the Kremlin attributes to digital sovereignty and informational security, following the war in Ukraine and the new rounds of sanctions. It should come as no surprise if in the observable future Moscow attains the same level of coherence in national doctrine, ConOps, organizational structures, and force-buildup programs in the realm of informational deterrence, comparable to the nuclear and conventional analogues.

In some aspects, the philosophy of informational deterrence parallels its nuclear and nonnuclear analogues, whereas in others it differs from them. Russian thinking on informational deterrence is similar to the conceptualization of the nuclear and conventional forms of this strategy in being holistic, broad, and cross-domain. Informational deterrence stands for the threat, or limited employment, of digital-technological and cognitive-psychological forms of influence against the adversary to attain the political goals. Russian thinking implies the employment of *informational deterrence* in pure and in cross-domain forms. The latter means threatening an informational strike not only to prevent informational aggression but also to shape the opponent's behavior in other fields, including kinetic operations.

Since the mid-2000s, when the concept of *strategic deterrence* began gathering momentum, the discourse has tended to conflate the employment of *informational struggle* as a tool of *war* and as a tool of *coercion*. Similarly, Russian authors tend to conflate cyber and radio-electronic means of informational influence, and to assume that the offense-defense distinction is somewhat irrelevant in the informational realm. More often than not, Russian authors have blurred the distinction between informational operations in peacetime, crisis, and war.

The main dissimilarity lies in the serial use of limited force, psychological and technological, which is central to informational deterrence. This book has introduced the term *cumulative coercion* to better convey the Russian modus operandi in the informational sphere. *Cumulative coercion* stands for constant low-intensity engagement of the adversary that is designed to produce generic "deterring potential," which one can leverage according to specific operational needs. Damage in the informational realm is more tolerable than in the conventional and nuclear spheres. This feature enables this unlimited use of limited force. As a result, coercion and fighting in the informational sphere often become indistinguishable from each other. "Learning," "shaping," and "controlling" are often intertwined within Russian informational operations.

Another dissimilarity relates to the typology. Prior to the war in Ukraine, deterrence by *denial*, deterrence by *punishment*, and deterrence by *international regulations* were the three forms of coercive influence that loomed largest within the Russian discourse on informational deterrence. In the nuclear and conventional realms the Russian expert community has tended to downplay the *punishment versus denial* typology, and to focus instead on the *forceful versus nonforceful* taxonomy. In contrast, the Russian discourse on informational deterrence has utilized the *punishment versus denial* taxonomy to a much greater extent.

One explanation may be a difference in how knowledge has emerged in the informational as opposed to the nuclear and conventional realms. In the latter, knowledge did not evolve in parallel but first originated in the West and then, following a delay of several decades, Russian experts dived into the topic. In the case of informational coercion, on the other hand, in a way it has been a competition of learning; both actors have sought to outperform each other conceptually. Years of mutual learning, shaping, and emulation may explain the conceptual isomorphism between the Russian and Western approaches in the realm of *informational coercion*.

THE IMPACT OF STRATEGIC CULTURE

What accounts for the unique Russian approach to coercion with all its peculiar characteristics? How has the Russian expert community managed to catch up with Western theoreticians and practitioners? This book has argued that several historical, conceptual, and cultural factors have conditioned the genealogy of deterrence *à la Russe*. Arguably, these factors are likely to continue shaping the future Russian conceptualization of this strategy after the war in Ukraine as well.

Cultural Factors

Several traits central to Russian strategic culture, which Russian military thought and operational behavior have manifested over history, informed and conditioned the way in which the Russian expert community developed knowledge about deterrence and operationalized it. An inclination toward holistic-dialectical thinking, which is emblematic of the Russian approach to strategy, may account for the *broader meaning* of deterrence (i.e., use of the term to refer to both preserving and changing the status quo, and to a repertoire of intrawar coercion moves aimed at shaping the battlefield dynamic), its *wider scope* (i.e., spanning both wartime and peacetime), and larger *number of domains* (i.e., military and nonmilitary).

Apparently, it also accounts for a *tendency to merge* forceful and non-forceful modes of operation in one coercion scheme and a sophisticated ability to operate across domains simultaneously, which seemingly comes more naturally to the products of the Russian ideational environment. The dialectical aspect may account for the attention to the other side in strategic considerations, which may explain the tailored approach, sensitivity to subjectivity, and ability to calibrate damage. For the product of a dialectical cognitive milieu, reality is a function of the interaction between one and one's competitor rather than mere static balances. This trait relates to the inclination to constantly shape the adversary, which the Russian style of deterrence manifests.

The dissonance between sophisticated theory and the state's ability to implement it, a traditional Russian strategic-managerial pathology, may account for the incoherence that the Russian nuclear modernizations, posture, and doctrinal visions have manifested. On several occasions during the last decades, and in some regards today, Russian conceptual constructs of cross-domain coercion, sometimes even more sophisticated than their Western analogues, have not always been supported by the actual assets and industrial capabilities, nor linked to feasible posture and realistic operational procedures, nor calibrated among the different segments of the Russian strategic community. This cultural tendency, however, has had its pros, too. Since the frames of objective reality have not restricted the Russian conceptual imagination, Russians have often thought "outside the box" about the emerging character of war, and come up with innovative theories of victory. Though at times infeasible at home, their intellectual products have been competitive and outdone in creativity and sophistication their analogues in other, wealthier countries.

The primacy of morale and psychological-cognitive factors over material ones in Russian strategic narratives may account for *perception* having become the center of gravity of a military campaign, for the natural comprehension of the *psychological aspects* of the art of coercion, and for the sensitivity to *subjectivity*, which the Russian approach has manifested. Also, this cultural trait naturally predisposes toward integrating various forms of influence (nuclear, conventional, and nonmilitary) in a holistic campaign aimed at shaping the adversary's decision-making processes. By extension, it accounts for the propensity as well as capacity to practice *reflexive control*, maybe even more naturally and skillfully than in strategic communities that build their theory of victory on outperforming the enemy by superior industrial-technological-financial prowess. The exploitation of surprise in order to put an adversary off-balance psychologically, a dictum of the Russian military tradition, may have informed deterrence *à la Russe*. Together with other ideational factors, this trait apparently accounts for the wave of conceptualization of informational deterrence during the last decade.

Ideational Sources
Deterrence *à la Russe* is neither *reflexive control* nor *military cunningness* nor *active measures*. However, these constructs have been central to Russian military thought and tradition of warfare. They were more than just generic theories of victory or principles of military-intelligence operations. These concepts informed and shaped the professional spirit, mental predisposition, and style of conduct widespread among Russian national security practitioners when they embarked on crafting coercion strategy. Since the Soviet collapse these ideational factors, all of which deal with various ways and means of shaping the adversary's behavior without or with limed use of force, enabled the development of Russian coercion theory (i.e., mechanisms of deterrence and compellence).

Each ideational source offered something. The concept of *reflexive control*—a practice of managing adversarial decision-making and behavior in strategic situations through manipulation of the picture of reality—offered a general philosophy handy for the development of deterrence theory. That said, the two concepts do differ. While *reflexive control* is about shaping the behavior of the adversary clandestinely, in a way that appears benign to the victim, *deterrence* for Russian experts is an art of strategic gesture, which implies, as opposed to *reflexive control*, overt, albeit ambiguous, strategic signaling and open communication with the adversary through force demonstration, deployment, and even limited employment.

Military cunningness is the art of manipulating the deployment and employment of forces and information in a way that inclines the enemy to make a move that is damaging. The practice of *maskirovka*, an institutionalized expression of this art, stands for a repertoire of denial, deception, disinformation, propaganda, camouflage, and concealment. It aims to hide one's intentions and capabilities on all levels of political-military activity, to manipulate the adversary's picture of reality, and to produce favorable operational conditions for promoting one's goals. This stratagem, in which the element of bluff and deception is ingrained, offers handy skills for the situation of signaling, when the initiator of deterrence needs to communicate credible resolve and capability behind one's threat, even if the threat is a bluff.

Finally, *active measures*, a term taken from the Soviet-Russian intelligence craft, refers to the repertoire of influence operations directed at adversarial states, organizations, groups, and key individuals, and aimed at consciously (through persuasion and limited force) or unconsciously (through manipulation) eliciting desirable behavior. These measures, although waged by intelligence organs, are not about exploring and explaining reality, which is the canonical Western understanding of the intelligence craft, but about actively shaping the strategic environment. The tradition of active measures has apparently informed the Russian operational art of deterrence. Both share the same coercion rationale. Also the dynamic and offensive character of *active measures* corresponds with the linguistic meaning of *sderzhivanie* and a core feature of the Russian practice of this strategy—proactively shaping the adversary by a mix of forceful and nonforceful measures.

A related source of influence was *aktivnost'*—a principle of combat dynamism in Russian military art, which stands for uninterrupted engagement of the adversary. Like *active measures*, *aktivnost'* aims to seize the initiative as early as possible in order to shape the enemy toward a major encounter (during the threatening period, in the initial stage of war, or prior to a big battle). On the strategic level, it aims to influence the correlation of forces in one's favor. Relatedly, the military concept of "systematic combat activities," which implies uninterrupted operational influence on the adversary in the intermissions between major battles, and several types of KGB operations, under the rubric of "inducement to halt subversive activities," apparently offered the most relevant basis for crafting informational coercion.

Historical Legacies

Three historical legacies—the *military-technological revolution* ideas associated with Marshall Nikolai Ogarkov, the *reasonable sufficiency* concept from the *Perestroika* era, and the Soviet professional methodology for calculating the *correlation of forces and means*—have provided major building blocks for deterrence *à la Russe*. Ogarkov was not writing on deterrence per se. However, his works on the conventional theory of victory provided a useful frame of reference for Russian experts to conceptualize conventional deterrence and to contemplate the relationship between nuclear and nonnuclear operations. One can trace back to Ogarkov the Russian quest to craft a balanced military of conventional general-purpose forces, capable of generating nonnuclear deterrence, and forces of strategic (nuclear) deterrence. For the Russian military brass, his argument about the conventional reconnaissance-strike complex becoming comparable, in terms of the effects produced, to tactical-operational nuclear weapons, and thus capable of assuming some of their combat tasks, implied by extension why and how missions of deterrence, previously associated only with nuclear capabilities, could extend to conventional weapon systems.

The legacy of the *reasonable sufficiency* concept has been informing the intellectual predisposition of the Russian strategic community when it contemplates damage calibration and the cross-domain rationale. In post–Cold War Russia, reasonable sufficiency, a euphemism for limiting the scale of one's investments to the minimum possible that will still make it possible to achieve one's security goals, turned into a generic stratagem, which seeks to calibrate the theory of victory according to the varying strategic-operational circumstances. Russian experts use reasonable sufficiency as a yardstick for the quality and quantity of the nuclear arsenal and the deterrence potential. It features in the discourse as a rationale for crafting a deterrence program spanning various domains. The Russian discussion on calibration, subjectivity, and the psychological aspects of damage is a good illustration of a tailored approach to deterrence, which rests on the philosophy of reasonable sufficiency.

Finally, the Soviet evaluation method known as *correlation of forces and means* has shaped the analytical predisposition of the Russian experts operationalizing deterrence. The imprint of *correlation of forces and means* on Russian military planners following the Soviet collapse has been threefold: First, this method apparently has come in handy for Russian experts for diagnosing the phobias and values of the adversary. Second, it has apparently come in handy for military theoreticians seeking to identify deterring damage. Finally, it has apparently informed the thinking of Russian coercion experts on how to manipulate the adversarial perception of reality and shape the adversarial strategic calculus.

CRITICAL EXAMINATION

As for other practitioners worldwide, each stage in the execution of coercion operations has been more challenging to Moscow than the previous one. Communicating coercive signals has been more challenging than operational design and planning and initial intelligence diagnosis of the competitor. Apparently, the Russian strategic community has been rather effective in its intelligence analysis of competitors in support of combat planning for coercive operations. (The nature of the Russian intelligence blunder on the eve of the invasion to Ukraine remains to be explored.) However, ensuring that competitors absorb its coercive signals as intended and interpret redlines accurately has proven to be a more challenging task for Moscow.

Prior to the war, the distortion of Russian signals in the West apparently resulted from several factors. Some pertain to the West; others relate to the Russian style of coercion, which makes Moscow's signals objectively challenging to interpret. First, preexisting Western misconceptions may account, at least partially, for the misunderstanding of Moscow's signaling. Second, the insufficient attention of Russian strategists themselves to communication may be another reason. Apparently, there has been a tendency among Russian strategists to take almost for granted the Western capacity to decipher the Kremlin's coercive signaling. Finally, the modus operandi of deterrence *à la Russe* may confuse actors on the receiving end of coercive signaling. For audiences trying to decipher the rationale of the Kremlin's signaling, the task is more daunting due to Moscow's style of coercion. The Russian strategic community utilizes forceful engagement for three ends: "to learn"—to generate knowledge about the adversary, oneself, and the strategic-operational environment; "to shape"—to influence the intentions and capabilities of the adversary; and "to compete" internally—to ensure a favorable position in the internal bureaucratic competition over resources and influence. Only the logic of "shaping" corresponds with the rationale of coercive signaling. This state of affairs adds to the diagnostic challenge.

Russian practitioners are apparently in the midst of wrestling with one of the biggest challenges in the operational art of deterrence for any actor—evaluating it and diagnosing its culmination point. Russian experts consider an effectiveness estimate to be an integral phase of any deterrence operation. They possess a certain theoretical-methodological apparatus in support of combat-planning procedures in this regard. The applied knowledge on the subject has been evolving in the Russian strategic community for more than a decade, but it still suffers from certain conceptual shortcomings. The extent to which effectiveness evaluation has become an institutionalized procedure in Russian deterrence operations is unclear. Russian practitioners apparently have been diagnosing the culmination point of coercion intuitively rather than systematically. Cases of negative returns may be attributed to certain deficits in the existing knowledge and its poor utilization, and also to the nature of the civil-military relations. This situation is not uncommon for other actors practicing forceful coercion worldwide.

Russia's evaluation of the effectiveness of its own coercion strategies since 2014 and up to the beginning of the war in 2022 seems to be mixed. On the pro side, Russian experts would attribute to coercive friction

Russia's return to the top of the U.S. list of national security challenges and a position of certain parity with Washington in the international arena. Russian coercive activities have somewhat adjusted the calculus of the collective West and contributed to Moscow's strategic reputation and coercion potential. At least prior to the war in Ukraine, the cumulative effect of the latter, in Moscow's estimate, enabled it to promote its aspirations and challenge the geopolitical status quo.[3]

In parallel, deterrence *à la Russe* has apparently generated diminishing and negative returns. The Ukrainian case and evidence from the informational theater of operations prior to the war demonstrate that the Kremlin is experiencing encirclement and pressure, which its coercion efforts were aimed at preventing in the first place. Also, Russian coercive signaling further reinforced the Kremlin's preexisting reputation among some in the West as a strategic adventurist waiting to exploit a land grab opportunity, resulting in NATO's enhancement and the beefing up of defense and deterrence initiatives vis-à-vis Russia. One could argue that on several occasions, if not overall, the Kremlin has crossed the culmination point of coercion. This was true already prior to the invasion. Russian prewar and intrawar coercion further exacerbated this tendency.

Among other factors, first and foremost the politics of supreme command and the nature of the civil-military relations, the source of the failure relates to the methodology of evaluating one's own coercive endeavors. Since the mid-2000s, several Russian practitioners have been exploring the theoretical-methodological aspects of coercion evaluation. A number of experts have been developing formal models to measure the effectiveness of coercion. Despite being relevant, this corpus of knowledge is insufficient for the type of coercion operations that the Russian military has been running. Ideally, a technique is needed that captures an adversary's changing resolve and capability in the midst of ongoing coercive friction (i.e., intrawar coercion). This topic was underexplored by Russian military theory and practice when the war started. As of this writing, it is unclear whether the Russian strategic community, the military in particular, has a coherent methodology, staff-work procedures, or organ charged with such a mission as deterrence operations in general, diagnosing the culmination point of coercion in particular.

The professional challenge related to the culmination point of coercion is universal. The Russian armed forces may be at least as good as other militaries in developing an applied diagnostic capacity for this tipping point. A basic awareness of the problem, albeit not under this rubric, has apparently been emerging within the Russian establishment. This is a natural stage in the evolution of a community, which adopts coercive strategy. On this issue the establishment benefits from several preexisting corpora of knowledge from the Soviet-Russian military and intelligence sciences. These may offer useful building blocks to inform its current endeavor. On the military side, Russian practitioners dealing with the evaluation of coercion effectiveness already employ methods from two fields: operations research and reflexive control. In most of the works the former is used to estimate the effectiveness of the latter. Both are established disciplines in the Soviet-Russian pantheon of sciences, civilian and military.

If Russian experts move in this direction two additional techniques are available to them. From the pool of military procedures, Russian practitioners can lean on *qualimetry*—the use of formal models to quantify the qualitative characteristics of weapons, forces, and doctrines. Since the challenge here is to measure variations in nonquantifiable factors, such as a competitor's resolve and intentions, this method may come in handy for diagnosing the tipping point of strategic considerations. Additional assistance may come from the Soviet-Russian intelligence discipline. The most relevant concept here is *operational game*: a professional term for manipulating an adversary in a protracted intelligence operation. KGB theoreticians and practitioners acknowledged the problem of crossing the culmination poinxt, and systematically explored methods to prevent this outcome. The Russian operation in Syria demonstrated the capacity of the military not to cross the culmination point of the campaign. Time will show whether Moscow is capable of replicating this in Ukraine. As of this writing this does not seem to be the case.

Moreover, one may find it notable that Russian experts and scholars do not engage with the possibility that their coercive efforts may fail or backfire. Critical discussions examining the effectiveness of one's coercive strategy are rather widespread in the U.S. and in Israel, two states that have been investing significant intellectual and organizational energy into the theory and practice of coercion. It is to be seen if such self-examination will gather momentum in Russia during the war or after. Examination of this kind seeks to distill actionable generic insights for the procedures of coercive operations. However, essentially, it is a discussion about the nature of civil-military relations. It is unclear whether there will be a proper political-cultural climate in Russian that enables experts from the strategic community to engage in such examination, at least during the war and in its immediate aftermath. The postwar Soviet expert and scholarly communities went through similar challenge, when examining intelligence failure of 1941, which was essentially the blunder in the relationship between the political leadership and supreme command. It remains to be seen if the Russian scholars of deterrence, which follow their Western colleagues, will emulate this essential element for the development of strategic theory.

AVENUES OF FUTURE RESEARCH

What's next for deterrence *à la Russe*? How are the Russian theory and practice of coercion likely to evolve after the war? What are the promising avenues of future research? As of this writing, the war in Ukraine is unfolding, and any conclusion would be premature until the first cessation of massive fighting. Still, there is already sufficient evidence from the war to pose initial questions and to frame the prospective research agenda on the matter of coercion.

Prior to the Russian invasion, this book identified several known unknowns pertaining to deterrence *à la Russe*. The preliminary evidence from Ukraine further underscores some of these lacunae of knowledge and adds novel queries. The following seven topics loom largest as promising avenues of exploration in the realm of coercion.

First, there is a question regarding the role of preventive and preemptive military operations in Russian strategic thought. How does "prevention," a strategic concept that since recently has been drawing more attention among Russian experts, relate to deterrence *à la Russe*? What is the relationship between this concept and "strategic deterrence"? How does this emerging notion relate to other types of Russian "strategic operations" and escalation management?

Second, as elsewhere worldwide, there are questions pertaining to emerging technologies. How does the Russian expert community see the impact of AI, machine learning, and big data analytics, and of the new generation of chemical weapons, on the conceptualization of coercion? Do Russian experts see these technologies as enablers of or as obstacles to coercion in the nuclear, conventional, subconventional, and informational realms? What role does Russian military theory attribute to chemical weapons in coercive operations?

Third, there are questions pertaining to the evolution of informational coercion—a topic that is likely to gain greater prominence in the near future. How do Russian experts conceptualize the coercion mechanism in mental war? How do they plan to deter adversarial efforts to transform Russian values and strategic culture? What intentions, capabilities, and modi operandi do they attribute to the adversary? Which countermeasures, passive and active, do they contemplate employing? Are noninformational, i.e., forceful, means of deterrence conceivable for this task?

Fourth, due to the unprecedented prominence of the Orthodox Church and the social functions of faith in Russian national security, there is a question regarding the relationship between religion and coercion. How does religion relate to strategic deterrence in Russia? In its war in Ukraine the Kremlin has fostered its image as a faith-driven actor to enhance coercive potential. How effective has this strategy been? How likely is the Kremlin to exploit this approach in the future and what are the likely innovations in the field?

Fifth, the war in Ukraine has put on the research agenda the subject of brutality in the Russian way of war and its relationship to coercion. Does the Russian military intentionally utilize brutality for coercion purposes? If so, what are the driving forces behind this strategy, its rationale and coercive mechanism?

Sixth, there is a question regarding the sources of Russian learning and knowledge development. The Russian expert community will continue developing knowledge on coercion theory and practice. What are likely to be its foreign sources of inspiration? Is the Russian pivot to Asia going to project on the Russian conceptualization of coercion? Is any intellectual stimulus from China likely to supplement the traditional Russian tendency to learn from the West and use it as a frame of reference in strategic and military affairs?

Finally, there are theoretical questions pertaining to international security scholarship. The new waves of deterrence and strategic culture literature are gathering momentum. The findings of this book suggest that a promising line of work for both disciplines would be comparative cross-cultural research. Specifically, exploration could focus on variations in the conceptualization of coercion under the impact of cultural factors, on mutual influence among strategic communities, and on the diffusion of conceptual knowledge on coercion within and outside the Western world. In addition, there is a question regarding the distinction between deterrence and brute force. As several Western and non-Western practitioners tend to blur the line between coercion and war fighting, the question arises as to any practical benefit of this theoretical distinction.

All of the above questions lie at the intersection of three subfields of international security scholarship—theory of strategic culture, deterrence theory, and Russian affairs. This book has offered to the community of Russia watchers, and to scholars and practitioners of international security at large, initial leads toward exploring all of the above.

NOTES

INTRODUCTION

1. For the author's earlier efforts to explore the impact of cultural factors on strategic behavior in Russia and elsewhere, see Dmitry (Dima) Adamsky, *The Culture of Military Innovation: The Impact of Cultural Factors on Revolution in Military Affairs in Russia, the US and Israel* (Stanford, CA: Stanford University Press, 2010); "Cross-Domain Coercion: The Current Russian Art of Strategy," Paris, IFRI, 2015; "From Israel with Deterrence: Strategic Culture, Intra-war Coercion and Brute Force," *Security Studies* 26, no. 1 (2017); "From Moscow with Coercion: Russian Deterrence Theory and Strategic Culture," *Journal of Strategic Studies* 41, no. 1 (2018); "Russian Campaign in Syria: Change and Continuity in Strategic Culture," *Journal of Strategic Studies* 43, no. 1 (2020).

CHAPTER 1

1. These sections are based on Dmitry (Dima) Adamsky, "Strategic Culture," in John Baylis, James Wirtz, and Jeannie Johnson, eds., *Strategy in the Contemporary World* (Oxford: Oxford University Press, 2022); Lantis, 2014; Libel, 2020.

2. Lantis, 2017.

3. The characteristics of physical and political geography—climate, territory, natural resources, landscape, and lines of ground and naval communication—usually feature as key elements, which over centuries have given rise to certain instincts and behavioral inclinations. Variations in the political geography of a state over history (proximity to stronger enemies, contestation of borders, their natural defensibility or lack thereof) may explain a state's siege mentality or lack thereof, and its preferences and capacity for certain forms of warfare over others (for example, an inclination toward ground warfare over naval warfare). Economic and technological prowess or backwardness may account for a tendency toward either symmetrical or asymmetrical warfare, and maybe even for the adoption of certain forms of government and economy rather than others. Nonmaterial factors include a state's social texture, general managerial tradition, style of government, and the attitude toward authority. Religion, as a source of values and traditions, the national cognitive style, and transnational norms are additional sources of influence. The imprint left on national memory by major formative experiences, and the lessons learned from them, are another source. Lantis, 2017; Farrell and Terriff, 2001; Acharya, 2004; Emily Goldman and Leslie Eliason, *The Diffusion of Military Technology and Ideas* (Stanford, CA: Stanford University Press, 2003).

4. Ibid.

5. Latnis and Charlton, 2011; Karasek, 2016; Bloomfield, 2012.

6. For example, the military organizations of Germany and Japan after World War II, and of the Warsaw Pact countries following the Soviet collapse, deliberately parted ways with their earlier professional ethos and decided to fundamentally reinvent their styles of warfare, norms, and professional practices Bloomfield, 2012; Colin S. Gray, *Out of the Wilderness: Prime Time for Strategic Culture* (Fort Belvoir, VA: Defense Threat Reduction Agency, 2006); Tomas Karasek, "Tracking Shifts in Strategic Culture," *Obrana A Stratgie* 1 (2016); Alan Bloomfield, "Time to Move On: Re-conceptualizing the Strategic Culture Debate," *Comparative Security Policy* 33, no. 3 (2012): 437–61; Anja Dalgaard-Nielsen, "The Test of Strategic Culture: Germany, Pacifism and Preemptive Strikes," *Security Dialogue* 36, no. 3 (2005); Tamir Libel, "Explaining the Security Paradigm Shift: Strategic Culture, Epistemic Communities, and Israel's Changing National Security Policy," *Defense Studies* 16, no. 2 (2016): 137–56.

7. Ibid.

8. Bloomfield, 2012; Lantis, 2004, 2017; Libel, 2020.

9. Jack Snyder, *The Soviet Strategic Culture: Implications for Nuclear Operations* (Santa Monica, CA: RAND, 1977), 8. By introducing his paradigm, Snyder codified wisdom that had been circulating in communities of practice for centuries. From antiquity to the modern era, classics of strategy from East and West, Thucydides, Sun Tzu, and Carl von Clausewitz, to name just a few, have claimed that culture influences military styles, battlefield conduct, and preferred theories of victory across nations (Lantis, 2017; Howard, 1991).

10. Gray, 1981; Booth, 1981; Evangelista, 1988; Lantis, 2005.

11. Colin Gray, "Strategic Culture as Context: The First Generation of Theory Strikes Back," *Review of International Studies* 25, no. 1 (January 1999).

12. Klien, 1991; Wilson, 1992; Kupchan, 199. The second generation of scholarship corresponded with the rise of constructivism in IR, which boosted the strategic culture research program. Wendt, 1995; Katzenstein, Keohane, and Krasner, 1998; Hopf, 1998; Lergo, 1995; Hudson, 1999.

13. Katzenstein, 1998; Farrell, 2002; Thomas Berger, *Cultures of Antimilitarism: National Security in Germany and Japan* (Baltimore: Johns Hopkins University Press, 1998).

14. Rosen, 1995, 1996; Avant, 1994; Banchoff, 1999; Friedberg, 2000.

15. Farrell, 1996; Zisk, 1993; Eden, 2004, Johnston, 1995; Kier, 1997, Mahnken, 2002).

16. Goldman and Eliason, 2002; Mahnken, 2004.

17. Howard, 2013, Schulz, 2012, book 2021; Long, 2009; Brun and Valenci. Edward Last, *Strategic Culture and Violent Non-State Actors: A Comparative Study of Salafi-Jihadist Groups* (London: Routledge, 2021); Assaf Moghadam, "Motives for Martyrdom: Al Qaeda, Salafi Jihad, and the Spread of Suicide Attacks," *International Security* 33.3 (Winter 2008/2009).

18. Michael Eisenstadt, *The Strategic Culture of the Islamic Republic of Iran* (Washington, DC: Washington Institute, 2015); Ayse Irem Aycan Ozer, "Iranian Strategic Culture," *Middle Eastern Studies* 8, no. 2 (2016): 44–67.

19. Jacqueline Newmyer Deal, "China's Approach to Strategy and Long-Term Competition," in Thomas Mahnken, *Competitive Strategies for the 21st Century* (Stanford, CA: Stanford University Press, 2012); Thomas G. Mahnken, *Secrecy and Stratagem: Understanding Chinese Strategic Culture* (Washington, DC: Lowy Institute for International Policy, 2011).

20. Fritz Ermarth, "Russia's Strategic Culture," in *Strategic Culture and WMD*; Dima Adamsky, *The Culture of Military Innovations* (Stanford, CA: Stanford University Press, 2010).

21. James Stratfrod, "Strategic Culture and the North Korean Nuclear Crisis," *Security Challenges* 1, no. 1 (2005): 123–33; Van Jackson, *On the Brink: Trump, Kim, and the Threat of Nuclear War* (Cambridge: Cambridge University Press, 2018).

22. Michael Wills, Ashley J. Tellis, and Alison Szalwinski, *Understanding Strategic Cultures in Asia-Pacific* (National Bureau of Asian Research, 2016).

23. Darryl Howlett and John Glenn, "Nordic Strategic Culture," *Cooperation and Conflict* 40, no. 1 (2005): 121–40.

24. Thomas Mahnken, *Technology and the American Way of War* (New York: Columbia University Press, 2008); Eitan Shamir, *Transforming Command: The Pursuit of Mission Command in the US, British, and Israeli Armies* (Stanford, CA: Stanford University Press, 2011); Michael Raska, *Security Strategy and Military Change in the 21st Century* (London: Routledge, 2015); Theo Farrell, Terry Terriff, and Frans Osinga, *A Transformation Gap: American Innovations and European Military Change* (Stanford, CA: Stanford University Press, 2010).

25. Jeannie Jonson, Kerry Kartchner, and Jeffrey Larsen, *Strategic Culture and Weapons of Mass Destruction* (London: Palgrave Macmillan, 2009).

26. Becker, 2017; Zyla, 2017; Echevaria, 2017, Lantis, 2009; Libel 2020.

27. Discursive institutionalism (an explanation of how institutions affect behavior and how the interaction of various organizations accounts for national security choices) and employing computational social science methods to formulate and test midrange theories lie at the heart of this endeavor. Becker and Melesky, 2017; Tamir Libel, "Rethinking Strategic Culture: A Computational (Social Science) Discursive-Institutionalist Approach," *Journal of Strategic Studies* 43, no. 5 (2020): 686–709.

28. Christopher Meyer, "The Purpose and Pitfalls of Constructivists Forecasting: Insights from Strategic Culture Research for the EU's Evolution as Military Power," *International Studies Quarterly* 55, no. 3 (2011): 669–90; Jeffrey Lantis, "Strategic Cultures and Security Policies in the Asia-Pacific," *Contemporary Security Policy* 35, no. 2 (2014): 166–86; Tamir Libel, *European Military Culture and Security Governance: Soldiers, Scholars and National Defence Universities* (London: Routledge, 2016); Heiko Biehl, Bastian Giegerich, and Alexandra Jonas, *Strategic Cultures in Europe* (Berlin: Springer, 2013); Jordan Becker and Edmund Malesky, "The Continent of the Grand Large? Strategic Culture and Operational Burden Sharing in NATO," *International Studies Quarterly* 61, no. 1 (2017): 163–80.

29. Bloomfield, 2012; Hill, 2015; David Haglund, "What Can Strategic Culture Contribute to Our Understanding of Security Policies in the Asia Pacific Region?"

Contemporary Security Policy 35, no. 2 (June 2014): 310–28; Ronald Krebs and Jennifer Lobasz, "Fixing the Meaning of 9/11," *Security Studies* 16, no. 3 (August, 2007): 409–51; Jeannie Johnson, *The Marines, Counterinsurgency, and Strategic Culture: Lessons Learned and Lost in America's Wars* (Washington, DC: Georgetown University Press, 2018); Peter Mansoor and Williamson Murray, eds., *The Culture of Military Organizations* (Cambridge: Cambridge University Press, 2019); Rebecca Zimmerman, Kimberly Jackson, Natasha Lander, Colin Roberts, Dan Madden, and Rebeca Orrie, *Movement and Maneuver: Culture and the Competition for Influence Among the U.S. Military Services* (Washington, DC: RAND, 2019).

30. Ahmed Hashim, *Iranian Ways of War* (Oxford: Oxford University Press, 2021); Olga Oliker, *Between Rhetoric and Reality: Explaining the Russian Federation's Nuclear Force Posture* (PhD diss., Massachusetts Institute of Technology, 2018); Sally White (Oxford University Press, forthcoming).

31. Yaacov Falkov, *Change and Continuity in the Russian Intelligence Culture* (forthcoming, 2021); Itai Shapira, "Israeli National Intelligence Culture and the Response to Covid-19," *War on the Rocks*, November 12, 2020; Bob de Graaff, *Intelligence Communities and Cultures in Asia and the Middle East* (New York: Lynne Reinner, 2020); James Wirtz, *Understanding Intelligence Failure* (London: Routledge, 2016); Bar-Joseph and McDermott (2017).

32. Beatrice Heuser and Eitan Shamir, eds., *Insurgencies and Counterinsurgencies: National Styles and Strategic Cultures* (Cambridge: Cambridge University Press, 2016); Austin Long, *The Soul of Militaries: Counterinsurgency Doctrine and Military Culture in the US and UK* (Ithaca, NY: Cornell University Press, 2016).

33. Jeannie L. Johnson, Kerry M. Kartchner, and Marilyn J. Maines, *Crossing Nuclear Thresholds: Leveraging Sociocultural Insights into Nuclear Decision-making* (London: Palgrave Macmillan, 2018); *Strategic Culture and WMD: Culturally Based Insights into Comparative National Security Policymaking* (London: Palgrave Macmillan, 2009); Paul Bracken, *The Second Nuclear Age* (New York: St. Martin's Griffin, 2013).

34. Frans Osinga and Tim Swejis, *Deterrence in the 21st Century* (The Hague: Springer and Asser Press, 2021).

35. Joshua Libben, "Am I My Brother's Peacekeeper? Strategic Cultures and Change among Major Troop Contributors to UN," *Canadian Foreign Policy Journal* 23, no. 3 (2017): 324–39.

36. A. M. Williams, "Strategic Culture and Cyber Warfare: A Methodology for Comparative Analysis," *Journal of Informational Warfare* 19, no. 1 (2020): 113–27; Wirtz, "Cyber War and Strategic Culture"; Gregory Rattray, *Strategic Culture and Cyberwarfare Strategies* (SIPA, 2018).

37. For example, see Lawrence Freedman, *Deterrence* (Cambridge: Policy Press, 2004); T. V. Paul, Patrick Morgan, and James Wirtz, *Complex Deterrence* (Chicago: University of Chicago Press, 2009).

38. For example, see Robert Jervis, "Deterrence Theory Revised," *World Politics* 31, no. 2 (1979): 289–324; Knopf (2010); Lupovici (2010); Osinga and Swejis (2021); Sean Monaghan.

39. Jeffrey W. Knopf, "The Fourth Wave in Deterrence Research," *Contemporary Security Policy* 31, no. 1 (April 2010): 1–33; Amir Lupovici, "The Emerging Fourth Wave of Deterrence Theory—Toward a New Research Agenda," *International Studies Quarterly* 54, no. 3 (September 2010): 705–32; Sean Monaghan, "Deterring Hybrid Threats: Towards a Fifth Wave of Deterrence Theory and Practice," *Hybrid CoE Papers* 12, no. 3 (May 2022).

40. For example, see Erik Gartzke and Jon Lindsay, *Cross-Domain Deterrence: Strategy in an Era of Complexity* (Oxford: Oxford University Press, 2019); King Mallory, *New Challenges in Cross-Domain Deterrence* (Santa Monica, CA: RAND, 2018); Tim Sweijs and Samuel Zilinick, "The Essence of Cross-Domain Deterrence," *Annual Review of Military Studies*, 2020.

41. For example, see Sean Monaghan (2022); Frans Osinga and Tim Sweijs, *Deterrence in the 21st Century: Insights from Theory and Practice* (The Hague: Springer and Asser Press, 2021), especially introduction and conclusion; Michael Ruhle, *In Defense of Deterrence* (National Institute of Public Policy, April, 2020); Tim Prior, "Resilience: The Fifth Wave in the Evolution of Deterrence," *Strategic Trends* (Zurich, 2018).

42. Sean Monaghan, 2022.

43. Mark Galeotti, The *Weaponization of Everything: A Field Guide to the New Way of War* (New Haven, CT: Yale University Press, 2022).

44. Sean Monaghan; Patrick Morgan, "The State of Deterrence in International Politics Today," *Contemporary Security Policy* 33, no. 1 (2012). Also see Amir Lupovici, "Toward a Securitization Theory of Deterrence," *International Studies Quarterly* 63, no. 1 (2019): 177–86.

45. Sean Monaghan, 2022.

46. Sean P. Larkin, "The Limits of Tailored Deterrence," *Joint Force Quarterly*, no. 63 (4th Quarter 2011): 47–57; Patrick K. Morgan, "Evaluating Tailored Deterrence," in *NATO and 21st Century Deterrence*, Forum Paper No. 8, ed. Karl Heinz Kamp and David S. Yost (Rome: NATO Defense College, 2009); Alexander L. George, "The Need for Influence Theory and Actor-Specific Behavioral Models of Adversaries," in *Know Thy Enemy: Profiles of Adversary Leaders and Their Strategic Cultures*, ed. Barry R. Schneider and Jerrold M. Post (Maxwell, AL: USAF Counterproliferation Center, 2003), 271–310.

47. Colin Gray, "Out of the Wilderness: Prime Time for Strategic Culture," *Comparative Strategy* 26, no. 1 (2007): 1–20; Jeffrey Lantis, "Strategic Culture and Tailored Deterrence," *Contemporary Security Policy* 30, no. 3 (December 2009): 467–85; Keith Payne, "Understanding Deterrence," *Comparative Strategy* 30, no. 5 (November 2011): 391–92; Elaine Bunn, "Can Deterrence be Tailored?" *Strategic Forum*, no. 255 (January 2007).

48. Jeffrey Lantis, "Strategic Culture and Tailored Deterrence: Bridging the Gap Between Theory and Practice," *Contemporary Security Policy* 30, no. 3 (2009): 467–85.

49. For example, see Rosen, "Competitive Strategies."

50. Snyder, 1977; Shu Guang Zhang, *Deterrence and Strategic Culture: Chinese-American Confrontations, 1949–1958* (Ithaca, NY: Cornell University Press, 1993).

51. Christopher Twomey, *The Military Lens* (Ithaca, NY: Cornell University Press, 2010); Dean Cheng, "An Overview of Chinese Thinking about Deterrence," and Nori Katagiri, "Japanese Concepts of Deterence," in Osinga and Swejis.

52. Hassan Ahmadian and Payam Mohseni, "Iran's Syria Strategy: The Evolution of Deterrence," in Osinga and Swejis; Ephraim Kam, "Iran's Deterrence Concept," *INSS Strategic Assessment* 24, no. 3 (July 2021); Guy Freedman, "Iranian Approach to Deterrence: Theory and Practice," *Comparative Strategy* 36, no. 5 (2017): 400–12; Afshon Ostovar, "The Grand Strategy of Militant Clients: Iran's Way of War," *Security Studies* 28, no. 1 (2018): 159–88; Michael Eisenstadt, *The Strategic Culture of the Islamic Republic of Iran* (Washington, DC: Washington Institute, 2015).

53. Boaz Atzili and Wendy Pearlman, *Triadic Coercion* (Columbia UP, 2018).

CHAPTER 2

1. As of this writing, the following works have been among the most prominent knowledge generators: Kristin Ven Bruusgaard, "Russian Nuclear Strategy and Conventional Inferiority," *Journal of Strategic Studies* 44, no. 1 (2021): 3–35; Katarzyna Zysk, "Escalation and nuclear weapons in Russia's military strategy," *The RUSI Journal*, no. 2 (2018); Michael Kofman and Anna Loukianova Fink, "Escalation Management and Nuclear Employment in Russian Military Strategy," *WOTR*, June 23, 2020; Dave Johnson, *Russia's Conventional Precision Strike Capabilities, Regional Crisis, and Nuclear Threshold* (Livermore, CA: CGSR, 2018); Clint Reach, Vikram Kilmbi, and Mark Cozad, *Russian Assessments and Applications of the Correlation of Forces and Means* (Washington, DC: RAND, 2020); Andrew Monaghan, *Dealing with the Russians* (Manchester: Manchester University Press, 2019); Keir Giles, *Moscow Rules* (London: Chatham House, 2019); Samuel Charap, "Strategic Sderzhivanie: Understanding the Contemporary Russian Approach to Deterrence," *Marshall Center Security Insight*, no. 062, September 2020; Lukas Milevski, "Russia's Escalation Management and a Baltic Nuclear Weapons Free Zone," *ORBIS* 66, no. 1 (2022): 95–110.

2. Hines et al., *Soviet Intentions*, 1–2, 22–24, 26, 50; Arbatov and Dvorkin, *Revising Nuclear Deterrence*, 17–19; Keith B. Payne, *The Fallacies of Cold War Deterrence and a New Direction* (Lexington: University Press of Kentucky, 2001), 26–27; Sinovets, *Dvulikii Ianus ili teoriia iadernogo sderzhivaniiav XXI veke*, 39, 49–50; L. N. Nezhinskii and I. A. Chelyshev, "O doktrinal'nykh osnovakh sovetskoi vneshnei politiki'," *Otechetsvennaia Istoriia*, no. 1 (1995): 5–12.

3. Hines et al., *Soviet Intentions*, 15–17, 21.

4. Kokoshin, *Strategicheskoe Upravlenie*, 68; Sinovets, *Dvulikii Ianus*, 33–4. See Hines et al., *Soviet Intentions*, 37–38.

5. Alexei Fenenko, "Between MAD and Flexible Response," *Russia in Global Affairs*, June 22, 2011.

6. Blank, "Beyond the Reset," 351; Hines et al., *Soviet Intentions*, 39.

7. Sinovets, *Dvulikii Ianus*, 12, 40–43; Arbatov and Dvorkin, *Revising Nuclear Deterrence*, 17–19.

8. Beatrice Heuser, "Victory in a Nuclear War? Comparison of NATO and WTO War Aims," *Contemporary European History* 7, no. 3 (1998): 311–27.

9. Adamsky 2010; Grinevsky, Akhromeev, Varennikov.

10. Kokoshin, *Strategicheskoe Upravlenie*, 317–18; Shevtsov et al., *Takticheskoe iadernoe oruzhie v Evrope*, 11–12.

11. S. V. Kreidin, "Global'noe I regional'noe sderzhivanie," *VM*, no. 4 (1999); S. V. Kreidin, "O problemakh global'nogo I regional'nogo sderzhivaniia," *VM*, no. 5 (1998); Ivasik et al., "Iadernoe oruzhie'"; Trenin, *Russia's Nuclear Policy in the 21st Century Environment*, 17–19.

12. John G. Hines, Ellis M. Mishulovich, and John F. Shull, *Soviet Intentions, 1965–1985* (Germantown, MD.: BMD Federal, 1995), 16; Sergei Karaganov, "Preodolet' sderzhivanie'," *Rossiiskaia gazeta*, April 6, 2011; Amir Lupovici, "The Emerging Fourth Wave of Deterrence Theory—Toward a New Research Agenda," *International Studies Quarterly* 54, no. 1 (2010): 717; Henry Trofimenko, *Changing Attitudes towards Deterrence* (Los Angeles: University of California Press 1980), 10–12.

13. Aleksei Arbatov, "Zdravyi smysl I razoryzhenie'," *Rossiia v global'noi politike*, no. 4 (2010), 180; Sinovets, *Dvulikii Ianus*, 73; Trenin, *Russia's Nuclear Policy*, 13.

14. For the first attempt, see V. L. Grin'ko and S. I. Kohan, "Kontseptsiia sderzhivaniia: strategicheskai stabil'nsot' v sovremmenukh usloviiakh'," *VM*, no. 4 (1993).

15. M. A. Gareev, "Itogi deiatel'nsoti AVN za 2008 I zadachi akademii na 2009 god'," *VestnikAVN* 26, no. 1 (2009).

16. Arbatov and Dvorkin, *Revising Nuclear Deterrence*, 4; Muntianu and Tagirov, "O iadernykh silakh zamolvite slovo'."

17. M. A. Gareev, "Strategicheskoe sderzhivanie," *Strategicheskaia Stabil'nost'* 46, no. 1 (2009): 2–13; V. Ia. Shatokhin, "Iadernaia Sostavliiaiuschaia," *Strategicheskaia Stabil'nsot'* 46, no. 1 (2009): 35–40; S. A. Modestov, "Strategickeskoe sderzhivanie na teatre," *Strategicheskaia Stabil'nost'* 46, no. 1 (2009); Protasov and Kreidin, "Sistemy upravleniia'"; B. A. Koniakhin and V. I. Kovalev, "Mekhanism realizatsii strategiches-kogo," *Strategicheskaia Stabil'nost'* 46, no. 1 (2009) 27–31; Korobushin, "Nadezhnoe strategicheskoe iadernoe"; Muntianu and Tagirov, "Nekotorye problemnye voprosy"; R. G. Tagirov, Iu. A. Pecahtnov, and V. M. Burenok, "K voprosu ob opredelenii urovnei'," *VestnikAVN*, no. 1 (2009).

18. Zagorski, *Russia's Tactical Nuclear Weapons*, 25.

19. Sirotinin, "Sderzhivanie agressii'," 6; Zagorski, *Russia's Tactical Nuclear Weapons*, 26; Rukshin, "Iadernoe sderzhivanie"; Protasov et al., "Systemy upravelniia"; Iu. G. Shushkanov and V. N. Gorbunov, "O nekotorykh aspektakh teorii I praktiki priminenia vooruzhennykh sil," *VM*, no. 1 (January 2010): 24.

20. Dmitry (Dima) Adamsky, "Russian Nuclear Incoherence," *Journal of Strategic Studies* 37, no. 1 (2014): 91–134.

21. V. V. Matvichiuk and A. L. Khriapin, "Sistema strategicheskogo sderzhivaniia'," *VM*, no. 1 (2010); "Metodicheskii podkhod k otsenki," *SS* 46, no. 1 (2009): 51–55; S. A.

Bogdanov and V. N. Gorbunov, "O kharaktere vooruzhennoi bor'by'," *VM*, no. 3 (2009); V. P. Grishin and S. V. Udaltsov, "Iadernoe sderzhivanie," *Vestnik AVN*, no. 1 (2008); V. V. Korobushin, "Nadezhnoe strategicheskoe iadernoe sderzhivanie," *Strategicheskaia Stabil'nost' (SS)* 46, no. 1 (2009): 14–18; A. A. Protasov and S. V. Kreidin, "Sistemy upravle-niai voiskami'," *SS* 46, no. 1 (2009): 23–26; V. V. Korobushin, V. I. Kovalev, and G. N. Vinokurov, "Predel sokrascheniia SIaS," *Vestnik AVN* 28, no. 3 (2009); A. V. Muntianu and R. G. Tagirov, "Nekotorye problemnye voprosy," *SS* 53, no. 4 (2010): 69; "O nekotorukh aspektakh vliianiia globalizatsii," *SS* 54, no. 1 (2011): 25–28.

22. Adamsky, 2015, 2017, 2018, 2019.

23. Michael Kofman, "Drivers of Russian Grand Strategy," *FRIVARLD Briefing* no. 6, 2019; "Assessing Russian Fait Accompli Strategy," *Russian Analytical Digest*, November 2020; Andrew Monaghan, "Understanding Russia's Measures of War," *Russian Analytical Digest*, November 2020; *Blitzkrieg and the Russian War of War* (Manchester University Press, forthcoming). On the blitzkrieg analogy applied to the current character of war, also see Rolf Hobson, "Blitzkrieg, the RMA, and Defense Intellectuals," in Dmitry (Dima) Adamsky and Kjell Inge Bjerga, eds., *Contemporary Military Innovation: Between Anticipation and Adaptation* (London: Routledge, 2012).

24. V. Gerasimov, "Vektory razvitiia voennoi strategii," *KZ*, March 4, 2019; Aleksandr Pinchiuk, "Zdes' nauchiat pobezhdat'," *KZ*, September 4, 2019.

25. For example, see Maxim Suchkov and Seam Teck, *Buduschie Voiny* (Moscow: Valdaiskii Kluv, 2019), 10–24.

26. Editorial, "Sovetnik Shoigu zaiavil o mental'oi voine SShA protiv Rossii," *Kommersant*, March 25, 2021.

27. A. G. Saveliev, *K Novoi Redaktsii Voennoi Doktriny* (Moscow: URSS, 2009), 182.

28. V. M. Burenok and O. B. Achasov, "Neiadernoe sderzhivanie'," *VM*, no. 12 (2007); V. V. Sukhorutchenko, A. B. Zelvin, and V. A. Sobolevskii, "Napravlenie issledovanii boevykh," *VM*, no. 8 (2009); R. G. Tagirov, Iu. A. Pecahtnov, and V. M. Burenok, ":K voprosu ob opredelenii urovne," *Vestnik AVN*, no. 1 (2009).

29. Viktor Litovkin, "Andrei Kokoshin," *NVO*, May 20, 2011; "Bomba spravliaet iubilei," *NVO*, November 26, 2010; Igor' Varfolomeev, "Iadernaia deviatka," *KZ*, May 25, 2011; Viktor Ruchkin, "Balans interesov," *KZ*, December 28, 2010.

30. A. A. Kokoshin, *Obespechenie strategicheskoi stabilnosti* (Moscow: URSS, 2009), 183–86; *Iadernye konflikty v XXI veke* (Media Press, 2003), 87–91; Efimov, *Politiko-Voennye Aspekty*, 152–55.

31. *VD*, paragraphs no. 22, no. 27, March 2010.

32. *VD*, 2014.

33. "Strategicheskoe sderzhivanie," "Demonstratsionnye deistviia," in *VES*.

34. Sterlin, Protasov, and Kreidin; Ponomarev, Poddubnyi, and Polegaev. Kristine Ven Bruusgaard was among the first within the Western scholarly community to highlight the prominence of the term and concept *strategic deterrence* in Russian theory and practice. Kristine Ven Bruusgaard, "Russian Strategic Deterrence," *Survival* 58, no. 4 (2016): 7–26.

35. Adamsky, IFRI, 2015; Suchkov, 2021.

36. Sterlin, Protasov and Kreidin; Ponomarev, Poddubnyi and Polegaev; Iu. A. Pechatnov, "Retrospektivnyi analiz evoliutzii kontsepsii sderzhivaniia," *Vooruzhenie I ekonomika* 1, no. 9 (2010): 11–15; "Teoriia sderzhivaniia: genesis," *Vooruzhenie I Ekonomika* 35, no. 2 (2016).

37. American policymakers also almost never (if ever) describe what they do or seek to do as compellance or coercion. Those Russian scholars are also loath to do it. I am thankful to an anonymous reviewer for this point.

38. Pechatnov.

39. Sterlin, Protasov, and Kreidin; Ponomarev, Poddubnyi, and Polegaev.

40. In a way, this resonates with George's original definition of coercive diplomacy, which tried to make the case for the analytical distinction between coercive diplomacy for offensive purposes (blackmail) as opposed to defensive purposes (coercive diplomacy). The author would like to thank Tim Sweijs for sharing this observation.

41. Fenenko; Pechatnov.

42. This claim should be conditioned to a certain extent. The line between deterrence and compellence is at times not that clear on Western parlance, too. The notion of "reestablishing deterrence" after an adversary has already acted against one's will may come across as "compellence." Let alone academics, military planners might have even a bigger challenge with differentiating the terms properly.

43. For elaboration, see T. V. Paul, James Wirtz, and Jeffrey Knopf, eds., *Complex Deterrence* (Chicago: University of Chicago Press, 2009); Adamsky, *SS*, 2017.

44. For elaboration, see Adamsky (2015); Maxim A. Suchkov, "Whose Hybrid Warfare? How the Hybrid Warfare Concept Shapes Russian Discourse, Military and Political Practice?" *Small Wars and Insurgencies*, February 2021.

45. The two types also differ qualitatively: *denial* implies the up-front introduction of "control" to take away the benefits, while *punishment* implies cost imposition, which may be chronologically remote, geographically different, and more painful, meaning that the magnitude of retaliation may be disproportional to and in excess of the initial aggression. For an overview and critical discussion of the classical IR literature on the two types of deterrence, see Paul, Morgan, and Wirtz, eds., *Complex Deterrence*. Also see Thomas Schelling, *Arms and Influence* (New Haven, CT: Yale University Press, 1966); Glen Snyder, *Deterrence and Defense: Toward a Theory of National Security* (Princeton, NJ: Princeton University Press, 1961).

46. This argument demands some contextualization. Western scholarship acknowledges that states tend to merge both strategies of deterrence, just as they merge offense and defense in their military posture, each to compensate for the other's weaknesses. *Denial* and *punishment* have often been applied in combination, like offense and defense in military operations. However, in one's theory of victory at any given moment there is a certain proportion between the two, with an inclination toward the primacy of one strategy over the other. Western conventional wisdom accepts that a preference for a specific type of deterrence might vary over strategic cultures and within a given strategic community over time, due to transformation of the threat perception, military capability, cultural changes, or all of the above. Adamsky, "From Israel with Deterrence."

47. *Sderzhivanie nedopushieniem/razubezhdeniem/ubezdheniem chto ataka bezpolezna/ otritsaniem (uspekha)/putem vospreshenia dostupa.*

48. Interviews with Russian strategic studies scholars and experts, 2019–21. In part, this attitude reflects the relative brevity and peculiarity of *denial*'s intellectual history in the West, and in part the Russian conviction regarding the irrelevance of this dichotomy and the uselessness of overconceptualization. An alternative explanation might be that denial does not get a lot of attention because Russian sources may assume that they can not fail Western attack or battlefield victory but only punish by retaliation.

49. For example, see Michael Kofman and Anna Loukianova Fink, "Escalation Management and Nuclear Employment in Russian Military Strategy," *WOTR*, June 23, 2020; Kokoshin (2019). Offensive versus defensive deterrence (*nastupatel'noe* vs. *oboroniteln'noe sderzhivanie*) is a related, Russian variation on the theme, although it is unclear, as of this writing, to what extent this terminology and conceptualization have penetrated the lexicon of Russian practitioners. This classification somewhat resembles the Western *punishment* and *denial* taxonomy, although the differences are greater than the similarities. This notion leans on the conceptualization of *air power* (*vozdushania mosch*) and *anti–air power* (*protivovozdushnaja mosch*) as two capabilities respectively supporting each type of deterrence. The resemblance derives from the division between offensive and defensive forms of activity aimed at shaping the adversary's behavior, which in the West is the kernel of the *punishment* versus *denial* classification. See A. V. Fenenko and V. A. Veselov, "Protivovozdushnaia Mosch' v Mirovoi Politike," *Mezhdunarodnie Processi* 17, no. 2 (2019): 47–69.

50. Author's interviews with NATO practitioners involved in the writing of manuals and doctrine and operational planning of deterrence campaigns 2009–18.

51. Michael Kofman, Anya Fink, and Jeffrey Edmonds, *Russian Strategy for Escalation Management: Evolution of Key Concepts* (Washington, DC, 2020); Anya Fink and Michael Kofman, *Russian Strategy for Escalation Management: Key Debates and Players in Military Thought* (Washington, DC, 2020).

52. Ibid. Also see Kofman and Fink; Fink, 2021.

53. Pechatnov; Bartosh.

54. Pechetnov and Bogdanov. Fink, 2021; Reach, 2021; Kofman et al.; Dave Johnson, *Russia's Conventional Precision Strike Capabilities, Regional Crisis, and Nuclear Threshold* (Livermore, CA: CGSR, 2018).

55. Erik Gartzke and Jon Lindsay, *Cross-Domain Deterrence: Strategy in an Era of Complexity* (Oxford: Oxford University Press, 2019).

56. For an alternative approach to nuclear capability in frames of the overall coercion scheme, see Matthew Kroenig, *The Logic of American Nuclear Strategy: Why Strategic Superiority Matters* (Oxford: Oxford University Press, 2020).

57. Evan B. Montgomery, "Posturing for Great Power Competition: Identifying Coercion Problems in U.S. Nuclear Policy," *Journal of Strategic Studies*, February 21, 2021.

58. Safetdinov (2014); *Doktrina Informatsionnoi; Kontseptual'nue Vzgliady; Strategiia Natsionalnoi; Kontseptsiia Obshchestvennoi; Voennaia Doktrina*; Strel'tsov (2012); Antonovich (2012); V. I. Kuznetsov, Y. Y. Donskov, and O. G. Nikitin, "K voprosu o meste kiberprostranstva," *VM*, no. 3 (2014): 13–17; S. G. Chekinov and S. A. Bogdanov, "Vliianie nepriamykh deistvii," *VM*, no. 6 (2011): 3–13.

59. Timothy Tomas and Keir Giles have been among the first and the most prolific scholars in the West to highlight the uniqueness of the Russian approach and its initial contrast with the Western approach. For the early and recent examples of their works see Timothy L. Thomas, "Russia Views on Information Based Warfare," *Airpower Journal*, Special Edition (July 1996); "Information Weapons: Russia's Nonnuclear Strategic Weapons of Choice," *Cyber Defense Review* 5, no. 2 (Summer 2020): 125–44; Keir Giles and William Hagestad, "Divided by a Common Language: Cyber Definitions in Chinese, Russian and English," 5th International Conference on Cyber Conflict (CYCON), 2013; Keir Giles and Valeriy Akimenko, "Russia's Cyber and Information Warfare," *Asia Policy* 15, no. 2 (2020): 67–75.

60. Due to this unique understanding of informational security, when the Kremlin talks about *digital sovereignty*, it equally relates to both the "code" and the "content." It would be wrong to see it as purely technological. Even if friction and damage are DT, the end, which Russian strategists have in mind, is of a higher order than the cyber effect. This is true whether Russia is on the receiving or initiating end of the informational influence. The latter is just a means for CP influence and effects. Thus, in terms of tools employed, DT (cyber in Western parlance) or CP (dis/misinformation or pysops in Western parlance) or both merged within one operation, all of the above fall into the category of IW or IC.

61. For elaboration, see Adamsky, 2015.

62. For one of the first and clearest examples of this division in the setting closest to coercion, see "Sklonenie k prekrascheniu podryvnoi deiatel'nosti," *Kontrrazvedovatel'nye Slovar'* (Moscow: Vysshaia Krasnoznamennaia Shkola KGB pri Sovmine SSSR im. F.E. Dzerzhinskogo, 1972).

63. In the U.S. case, different military organs have been responsible for electronic warfare, cyber, strategic communications, and psyops operations. After almost a decade of interaction in the informational sphere, as of this writing, this asymmetry between the U.S. and Russia has been fading somewhat. For elaboration, see Sarah P. White, *Subcultural Influence on Military Innovation: The Development of U.S. Military Cyber Doctrine* (PhD diss., Harvard University, 2019).

64. A. A. Kokoshin, Iu. N. Baluevskii, and V. Ia. Potapov, "Vliianie noveishikh teknologii I sredstv vooruzhennoi bor'by na voennoe iskusstvo," *Mezdhunarodye Otnosheniia I Mirovaia Politika*, no. 4 (2015).

65. For elaboration, see Adamsky, 2015.

66. For elaboration, see Adamsky, 2015.

67. In Russia, as in the West, there is no definitional canon. Thus, Russian discourse on the subject at times turns into scholastic casuistic, so that one may lose sight of the

forest for the trees of competing definitions, which refer to the tools, objects, and subjects of informational coercion.

68. A countermeasure against malign informational influence can be informational and noninformational. To deter negative CP influence, which it sees as a strategic threat equal to WMD, Russia might employ not only CP but also DT and even noninformational, kinetic countermeasures. Thus, it is essentially asymmetrical since "deeds" are more effective than "words" in deterring "words."

69. It is also about acquiring the upper hand on the higher rungs of the escalation ladder. Russian experts trace the intellectual sources of the term *counterdeterrence* to James Schlesinger, who brought this notion with him from RAND to the Pentagon and turned it, on the Russian view, into the foundation of his "escalation dominance" concept (*eskalatsionnoe dominirovanie*). V. A. Veselov, "Iaderneyi Faktor v Mirovoi Politike," *Mezhdunarodnye Otnosheniia I Mirovaia Politika*, no. 1 (2010): 68–89; "Programma Kursa Strategicheskaia Stabil'nost'," *Mezhdunarodnye Otnosheniia I Mirovaia Politika*, no. 4 (2010): 135–51. When deterrence is formally taught in the leading Russian universities, the curriculum on international strategic stability usually presents nuclear deterrence and counterdeterrence as an interrelated dyad. Similarly, it treats *proliferation* and *counterproliferation* as a dialectical phenomenon of international security. Veselov, 2010.

70. A. Bartosh, "Strategiia I Kontrstrategiia gibridnoi voiny," *VM*, no. 10 (2018): 5–21. Since Moscow perceives itself as the target of an uninterrupted multidimensional coercion campaign by the collective West, ranging from economic sanctions, mental-cultural subversion, to military pressure (in the form of beefing up NATO force concentrations on Russian borders, exercises, and cyber probing), it qualifies its countermeasures as counterdeterrence. The latter features as forceful and nonforceful measures of an offensive and defensive nature. For example, see Sergei Kazennov and Vladimir Kumachev, "Khochesh Mira—Gotovsia k Chemu?" *NVO*, May 29, 2015. The claim that one of the main tasks of STRATCOM, of which CYBERCOM is a part, is to discredit the Russian political-military leadership in the eyes of its own population and to instill among the latter panic and defeatist sentiment, by tools ranging from public diplomacy and psyops to use of force, is indicative of the threat perception underlying the notion of counterdeterrence. Smirnov, 2018.

71. The term stood for the public exposure to domestic and foreign audiences of the groundlessness and hypocrisy of the anti-Soviet critique, dissuading both audiences from adopting the adversarial ideology. "Ideinoe razoruzhenie protivnika," *Kontrrazvedovatenlyi slovar'*. As such, ideological disarmament was a kind of counteroffensive agitprop.

72. This stream of Russian discourse usually appears under the rubric of *conventional deterrence*. In an article on strategic (nuclear and conventional) deterrence, authoritative Russian authors (active-duty senior officers at the Center of Military-Strategic Research of the GS) argue that there is "an increase in missions [of the Russian military] aimed at decreasing stability [*ustoichivost'*] and proficiency [*operativnost'*] of the enemy C4ISR systems, by employment of directed energy weapons, in particular the Combat Laser Complex *Peresvet*," as part of the Russian strategic deterrence system. According to the

article, the *Kinzhal* hypersonic missile could be used for the same purpose. A. V. Evsiukov and A. L. Khriapin, "Rol' novykh system strategicheskih vooruzhenii v obespechenii strategicheskogo sderzhivaniia," *VM*, no. 12 (December 2020): 26–30. Also see Katarzyna Zysk, "Defence Innovation and the 4th industrial revolution in Russia," *Journal of Strategic Studies*, 8 December 2020.

73. "Doktrina informatsionnoi bezopasnosti RF" (Utv. Prezidentom RF 09.09.2000), kremlin.ru.

74. The closest approximation would be what the doctrine defines as "means aimed at preventing, repulsing and neutralizing threats to the informational security of RF." Shakirov, 2020.

75. *Voennaia Doktrina RF*, 2010, kremlin.ru.

76. Kontespetual'nye vzgliady na deiatel'nost' vooruzhennykh sil RF v Informatsionnom Prostranstve," MoD RF, 2011.

77. In the document informational deterrence stood for the "creation of conditions, for lowering the risk of use of informational and communicational technologies for military-political goals, [and] for realization of activities contradicting international law, aimed against the sovereignty, political independence, territorial integrity of the states and threatening international peace, security, global and regional stability." *Voeannaia Doktrina RF*, 2014, kremlin.ru.

78. *Doktrina Informatsionnoi Bezopasnosti RF*, December 5, 2016, scrf.gov.ru.

79. Manoilo, 2003.

80. I. N. Dylevskii, V. O. Zapivakhin, S. A. Komov, and A. A. Krivchenko, "O dialektike sderzhivaniia," *VM*, no. 7 (July 2016): 6–8; S. A. Komov, S. V. Korotkov, and I. N. Dydelvskii, "Ob evolutsii sovremennoi amerikanksoi doktriny," *VM*, no. 6 (2008): 54–61.

81. A. A. Kokoshin, "Strategicheskoe iadernoe I neiadernoe sderzhivanie: prioreitety sovremennoi epokhi," *Vestnik Rossiiskoi Akademii Nauk* 84, no. 3 (2014): 195–205; O. I. Shakirov, "Kto pridet s kibermechem: podkhody Rossii I SShA k sderzhivaniiu v kiberprostranstve," *Mezhdunarodnaia Analitika* 11, no. 4 (2020): 147–69.

82. For example, see E. V. Zabegalin, "K Voprosy of opredelenii termina informatsionno-tekhnicheskoe vozdeistvie," *Sistemy Upravleniia, Sviazi I Bezopasnotsti*, no. 2 (2018): 121–50.

83. Russian experts see the latter, aimed at manipulating foreign public opinion and destabilizing the political systems of adversaries, as central to current world politics, and works under the rubrics of "counterdeterrence" and "anti–soft power" illustrate the efforts to frame this subject. For example, see Roman Rainkhard, "Novye Formy I Metody Diplomatii," *Mezhdunarodnaia Analitika* 11, no. 4 (2020): 11–19; Aleksei Fenenko, "Anti-miagkaia sila v politicheskoi teorii," *Mezhdunarodnye Processy* 18, no. 1 (2020): 40–71.

84. For example, consider avenues of future research on the "dialectics of deterrence" in the cyber realm, which GS experts designated in 2016. The experts call for the evaluation of unacceptable damage that deters the opponent and target selection criteria; the joint employment of cyber and conventional capabilities to optimize coercion; and the

formulation of an "adequate understanding" among the adversary's decision makers of the resolve to use cyber capabilities and their effectiveness. Dylevskii et al., 2016, 7–8. A certain distribution of labor and the emergence of two major epistemic communities on the subject are evident. Authors affiliated with organs, think tanks, and periodicals related to diplomacy and foreign policy tend to discuss international regulations and the CP aspects of informational security, while the military and force-employing segments of the strategic community pay about equal attention to both the CP and DT aspects of ID. As of this writing, it seems that while military periodicals cover both aspects of ID, the nonmilitary ones tend to overlook the DT aspect of this craft, and if they do take note of it then it is to refer to adversarial influence. At times, these two communities of knowledge don't intersect at all, as authors from each tend not to refer to the works and ideas of the other.

85. In other words, since "informational struggle" is employed to attain "strategic deterrence," it has often turned into a euphemism for "informational deterrence."

86. These, however, were permanently present in the overall deterrence scheme.

87. For example, see: Pavel Sharikov, "V Boi Idut Kibervoiska," *NVO* 13. no. 4 (2013); "Informatsionnoe Sderzhivanie," *RSMD* 5, no. 9 (2013).

88. "Psychological intimidation," according to them, can credibly deter and even completely dissuade from aggression, thus preventing the forceful stage of the conflict altogether. Manoilo, 2004; "Kontseptsii politicheskogo regulirovaniia informatsionno-pshychologicheskoi voiny," *Mir I Politika*, May, 12, 2012.

89. A. Manoilo, "Upravlenie psikhologicheskoi voinoi," *Politika I Obschestvo*, no. 2 (2004); S. Modestov, "Strategicheskoe sderzhivanie," *Vestnik AVN* 26, no. 1 (2009); M. Gareev, "Strategicheskoe sderzhivanie," *SS*, no. 1 (2009).

90. Informational struggle became the leitmotif of NGW, the latter being essentially a strategy of coercive influence and not of massive brute force, on the view that sophisticated means of informational influence may achieve strategic goals and downgrade the determination to resist. Cheginov and Bogdanov, 2010; Adamsky, 2015.

91. For example, see V. K. Novikov and S. V. Golubchikov, "Formy Radioelektronnoi bro'by v sovremennykh usloviiakh," *Vestnik AVN*, no. 2 (2019): 139–43; Iu. E. Donskov and A. L. Moraresku, "K Voprosu o Formakh Primenenia Chastie I Podrazdezelenii REB," *VM*, no. 7 (2018): 101–8; V. F. Lazukin, N. I. Korolev, and V. N. Pavlov, "Bazovye element taktiki voisk REB," *VM*, no. 11 (2017): 15–20; D. V. Kholunenko, V. A. Anokhin, A. S. Korobeinikov, and A. A. Lakhin, "Radioelektonnyi I Radio-Ognevoi Udary—Osnovnye Formy Primenenia Chastei REB," *VM*, no. 11 (2019): 21–27; I. Korolev, V. Pavlov, and V. Petrov, "REB v Voinakh Buduschego," *Armeiskii Sbornik*, no. 8 (2016): 39–48; V. A. Volgin, "Razvitie Form Radioelektronnogo I Ogenvogo Porazheniia Protivnikoa," *VM*, no. 4 (2010): 31–34; N. A. Kolesova and I. G. Nasenkova, eds., *Radioelektronnaia Bor'ba* (CAST, 2015): 232–33; I. Iu. Lastochkin, "Rol' I Mesto Radioelektronoi Bor'by," *VM*, no. 12 (2015): 14–19; "Perspektivy razvitiia voisk REB VS RF," *VM*, no. 12 (2020): 86–87; Viktor Khudoleev, "Strazhniki efira na pravilnom puti," *KZ*, April 15, 2020. Professional Russian military literature beyond periodicals is in sync with this trend.

92. For example, see Cheginov and Bogdanov, 2013. An example of the pure form would be to threaten to employ digital and nondigital means of interfering in internal political processes, threatening the legitimacy of elections, and employing a set of active measures to drive a wedge between the state and its allies and/or the government and its citizens. Cyberattacks or pure informational influence campaigns may involve blackmailing by threatening to conduct a hack-and-leak operation (revealing certain information to impose reputational damage and to discredit the political leadership, regime type, parties, way of life), and spreading divisive messages in old and new media to instigate internal social-ethnic tensions (*infovbros/kompromat/razglashenie inf*).

93. For example, see Iu. I. Starodubtsev, P. V. Zakalkin, S. A. Ivanov, "Tekhnosfernaia voina kak osnovnoi sposob razresheniia konfliktov v usloviiakh globalizatsii," *VM*, no. 10 (October 2020): 16–21; Martti Kari and Katri Pynnoniemi, "Theory of strategic culture: An analytical framework for Russian cyber threat perception," *Journal of Strategic Studies*, September 11, 2019. The trend is particularly clear in publications arguing that various forms of radio-electronic (RE) operations—suppression (offense), defense, and reconnaissance—have become undistinguishable from each other. These forms of RE combat activities lean on the same systems and the same units wage them. For example, see Kolodiazhnyi, Kuleshov, and Sekhovtsev; Boiko; Kolesova and Nasenkova; V. A. Balybin, "Zavoevanie prevoskhodstva nad protivnikom v upravlenii primenitel'no k operatsii (boiu)," *VM*, no. 3 (March 2016): 3–8; S. A. Gricenko, L. B. Rezancev, O. N. Skliarova, and I. Iu. Cherednekov, "Dezoragnaizacii Upravelniia Nezakonnimi Voennimi Formirovaniiami v Khode Kontrterroresticheskoi Operatsii," *Voennaia Mysl'*, no. 5 (2016): 22–27; V. I. Vladimirovski and V. I. Stuchinskii, "Obosnovanie primenenija avionosnsikh nositelei sredstv radioleletronnoi bor'bi v operativnoi glubine dlia zavoevania informatsionnogo prevoshodstva," *VM*, no. 5 (2016): 15–21.

94. Kofman, Fink, Johnson, and Reach observe a similar harmonic approach to offense and defense in a range of Russian SOs, and Monaghan registers the same in the emerging military concepts like AD, TD, and SLA. Michael Kofman, Anna Loukianova Fink, and Jeffrey Edmonds, *Russian Strategy for Escalation Management: Evolution of Key Concepts* (Washington, DC, 2020); Anya Fink and Michael Kofman, *Russian Strategy for Escalation Management: Key Debates and Players in Military Thought* (Washington, DC, 2020); Michael Kofman and Anna Loukianova Fink, "Escalation Management and Nuclear Employment in Russian Military Strategy," *WOTR*, June 23, 2020; Dave Johnson, *Russia's Conventional Precision Strike Capabilities, Regional Crisis, and Nuclear Threshold* (Livermore, CA: CGSR, 2018); Clint Reach, Vikram Kilmbi, and Mark Cozad, *Russian Assessments and Applications of the Correlation of Forces and Means* (Washington, DC: RAND, 2020); Monaghan, *Blitzkrieg* and *RAD*.

95. This assumption further underscores the Russian disinclination to draw a clear demarcation between "punishment" and "denial" (not to the same extent that the logic behind these terms features in the West). Rather, the forceful versus nonforceful and CP and DT taxonomies will be more widespread.

96. Kofman and Fink, *WOTR*, 2020.

97. 1) Does the cyber realm constitute a separate domain of warfare and is therefore a new RMA, or is it merely an evolution of war in the preexisting domains? 2) Does cyber innovation favor the offensive or defensive mode of warfare? 3) Do cyber capabilities enhance or undermine strategic stability? 4) Does the cyber tool of influence empower strong or weak actors of the international system? 5) Is cyber deterrence possible and what is its stronger form? For example, see Sebekin, 2020; Shakirov, 2020; Kokoshin, 2019, 2020 (book and articles); E. Rogovskii, "Amerikanskaia srategiia infromatsionnogo preobladaniia," *Oko Planety*, Decemebr 12, 2009; Pavel Sharikov, "Informatsionnoe sderzhivanie: Transformattsiia paradigm strategicheskoi stabil'nosti," *RSMD*, September 5, 2014; A. V. Manoilo, *Gosudarstvennaia Informatsionnaia Poltika v Osobykh Usloviiakh* (Moscow: MIFI, 2003). Although Russian experts closely follow U.S. innovations in the field of cyber warfare, and often frame their discussion on cyber deterrence in similar terms, apparently they sometimes arrive at somewhat different conclusions, often citing from the U.S. evidence.

98. Shakirov, 2020.

99. For example, see Shakirov, 2020; Leonid Kovachich, Kinolai Markotkin, and Elena Chernenko, *Gonka Tekhnologii: perspektivy II v Rossii I Kitae* (Moscow: Carnegie Moscow Center, 2020).

100. Shakirov, 2020; Tumar and Levchiuk; E. G. Lazarevich, S. K. Kolganov, and A. N. Semashko, "Tekhnologicheskaia osnova obespecheniia voennoi bezopasnosti gosudarstva," *Nauka I Voennaia Bezopasnost'*, no. 2 (2007); Konstantin Geraschenko, "Chasovye Runeta," *VPK*, no. 19 (May 21, 2019); Vera Zelendinova, "Tsifrovoi suverinetet Rossii- missiia vypolnima," *NG*, August 2020. For instance, Krutskikh, a representative of the Russian President for International Informational Security and one of leading Russian practitioner-theoreticians in the field, has been a frequent national-level channel for verbalizing this coercive signaling. A prominent example would be his paraphrase of the famous Russian proverb that "one who comes to us with a cyber sword will also die from a cyber sword." "A. Krutskikh: O Kiberugrozah I sposobakh protivodeistviia im," *Mezhdunarodnaia Zhyzn'*, April 23, 2019.

101. Apparently during recent years authors affiliated in one way or another with the REB troops have dominated the discussion and been more prolific and vocal as compared to other segments of the Russian strategic community. For example, see Lastochkin, 2015, 2020; A. S. Korobeinikov and S. I. Pasichnik, "Osobennosti metodicheskogo obespecheniia otzenki effektivnsoti REB pro modelirovanii kompleksnogo porazheniia informatsionno-upravliaiuschih system protivnika," *VM*, no. 11 (2015): 58–64.

102. For example, see Shakirov, 2020; S. A. Sebekin, "Nebkhodimost' sovershenstvovaniia doktriny sdrzhivaniia v usloviakh rosta kiberugroz," *Problemy Natsional'noi Strategii* 48, no. 3 (2018): 122–36; *Genezis i Razvitie Strategii Sderzhivaniia Kiberugroz v SShA, KNR, I Rossii* (PhD diss., IGU, 2020).

103. Zagorskii and Romashkina, 73.

104. Elena Chernenko, "Vmesto vstrechi izmenit nelzia: Kak sorvalis Rossiisko-Amerikanskie peregovori po kiberbezopasnosti," *Kommersant*, March 3, 2018.

105. Shakirov, 2020; Anastasiia Tolstukhina, "V Garmish-Partenkirkhene sobralis veduschie eksperty mira po informatsionnoi bezopasnosti," *Mezhdunarodnaia Zhyzn'*, April 27, 2018.

106. Shakirov, 2020; Sebenin, 2020; Anatolii Smirnov, "Noveishie Kiberstrategii SShA—Preambula Voiny?" *Mezhdunarodnye Protsessy* 16, no. 4 (2018): 181–92.

107. Daniel Rakov and Yochai Guisky, "Why Joe Biden Should Start a Cybersecurity Dialogue with Russia," *National Interest*, February 18, 2021; Andrew Monaghan, *Dealing with the Russians* (Manchester: Manchester University Press, 2019).

108. Keir Giles, "Russian Information War: Construct and Purpose," in Timothy Clack and Robert Johnson, eds., *The World Information War* (London: Routledge, 2021). Some even qualify recent Russian cyber engagements as coercion efforts to stimulate the U.S. administration to embark on a dialogue with Moscow on streamlining rules of conduct in the cyber realm. Rakov and Guisky, 2021; Suchkov, 2021.

109. Joseph Nye, "Deterrence and Dissuasion in Cyberspace," *International Security* 41, no. 3 (Winter 2016–17): 44–71; Soesanto and Smeets.

110. Some Russian experts even assume that the U.S. shares the basic assumption that international regulations are an effective tool of conflict prevention and deterrence. For example, see Zagorskii and Romashkina, 59.

111. Interviews with Russian international security experts, 2020–21.

112. On one occasion Krutskikh argued that there is a danger of applying the theory and practice of nuclear deterrence to the cyber realm, suggesting instead that arms control regulations (e.g., transparency and verification regimes, confidence-building measures, and international treaties) be opted for as a more relevant tool of conflict prevention. At the same time, however, his remarks on Russia's current modus operandi, as long as such an international regime does not yet exist, are in perfect sync with deterrence logic, including his figure of speech about two cowboys pointing their "cyber Colts" at each other. Elena Chernenko, "Nam ne nado borotosia za reputatsiiu," *Kommersant*, April 23, 2018.

113. For example, while Western commentators qualify RT activities as offensive, their Russian counterparts see them as a countermeasure to the Voice of America or any other organ of CP influence on Russia. The typology lies in the eyes of the beholder; one can equally qualify the Russian threat to close certain foreign media operating on Russian territory (in order to restrict malign influence on Russian audiences), in response to sanctions and restrictions of Russian channels, as either an offensive or defensive measure.

114. For the intellectual history of the term *cumulative deterrence* and its original application beyond the Russian case, see Adamsky, "From Israel with Deterrence," *Security Studies*, 2017. For its application in the informational sphere, see: Lucas Kello, *The Virtual Weapon and International Order* (New Haven, CT: Yale University Press, 2017); Uri Tor, "Cumulative Deterrence as a New Paradigm for Cyber Deterrence," *Journal of Strategic Studies* 40, no. 1 (2017): 92–117; also see Doron Almog, "Cumulative Deterrence and the War on Terrorism," *Parameters* 34, no. 4 (2004); Amos Malka, "Israel and Asymmetrical Deterrence," *Comparative Strategy* 27, no. 1 (2008): 1–19.

115. Wirtz, Morgan, and Paul, *Complex Deterrence*.

116. A majority of Russian strategists perceive their interaction with the collective West as a protracted, almost civilizational, conflict, rather than a short-term military campaign confined in space and time. Thus, there is a constant, somewhat cyclical transition from one state of deterrence to another (i.e., from general to specific and back again). For how the "protracted conflict perception" shapes the approach to deterrence, see Efraim Inbar and Eithan Shamir, "Mowing the Grass," *International Affairs*, 2018.

117. For example, since 2017 the Russian Center for Reconciliation of Belligerent Sides in Syria has been issuing daily updates about the positive dynamic and Russian humanitarian missions in five foreign languages that are then replicated, recited, and spun by the Russian international and foreign media. This produces an informational splash, an echo that is disproportionally louder than actual reality and developments on the ground. This persistent informational pressure creates an informational agenda and potentials, which can be exploited and leveraged, for example during negotiations on the political-economic settlement in Syria during and following the civil war. On paper this body deals with real problems, but in reality it only produces such papers. For example, see "Mezhvedomstvennye koordinatsionnye shtaby RF I SAR sdelali sovmestnoe zaiavlenie o problemakh vozvrashceniia siriiskikh bezhentsev v rodnye mesta v usloviiakh santsionnogo davleniia stran zapada," mil.ru, April 5, 2020; "Billiuteni RBPD Tsentra Po Primereniiu Vrazhduiuschikh Storon," mil.ru. This favorable informational background (*infofon*) is a potential prepared in advance (*zagotovki*), which creates more room for maneuvering at the moment of need. Several entities are part of the same endeavor and have their own channels of disseminating information from several different directions to the same international audience or to different audiences, further multiplying the effect; for example, the ROC's ecclesiastical diplomacy uninterruptedly escorted and enhanced military-diplomatic informational potentials during the operation in Syria. Dmitry (Dima) Adamsky, "Christ-loving Diplomats: Russian Ecclesiastical Diplomacy in Syria," *Survival* 61, no. 6 (2019): 49–68.

118. For example, consider the Russian informational coercion operations related to the Naama Issaschkahr and Zecharia Baumel episodes. See Vera Michlin-Shapir and Daniel Rakov, "Pray for Naama—an RT Informational Influence Operation in Israel" (forthcoming).

119. For example, see Lilly and Cheravitch, 2020. A historical analogy that well illustrates this mix of learning and shaping logics through operational friction would be the continuous probing raids of the U.S. Air Force and Navy around the perimeter of the Soviet borders, constant friction with the Soviet Air Defense, and deep-penetration raids by U.S. strategic bombers within the Soviet hinterland throughout the Cold War, and especially in its late period, in frames of the U.S. countervailing strategy. Also similar are the psyops conducted in tandem with these raids to produce a mutually reinforcing signaling effect. For example, see Gordon Barrass, *The Great Cold War* (Stanford, CA: Stanford University Press, 2008).

120. The notion somewhat parallels the Western concept of "cyber hygiene." For example, see Eviatar Matania, Lior Yoffe, and Michael Mashkautsan, "A Three-Layer

Framework for a Comprehensive National Cyber-security Strategy," *Georgetown Journal of International Affairs* 17, no. 3 (2016): 77–84.

121. For example, see Marlene Laruelle, *Russia's Niche Soft Power: Sources, Targets and Channels of Influence* (Paris, IFRI, 2021).

122. For example, see Bilyana Lilly and Joe Cheravitch, "The Past, Present and Future of Russia's Cyber Strategy and Forces," *International Conference on Cyber Conflict* (Tallinn, 2020): 129–55.

123. For example, see S. A. Modestov, "Strategicheskoe sderzhivanie na teatre informatsionnogo protivoborstva," *Vestnik AVN* 26, no. 1 (2009): 33–36; Burenok, 2008; Vasilii Burenok, "Informatsionnoe protivoborstvo I neiadernoe sderzhivanie," *Zaschita I Bezopasnost'*, no. 3 (2008).

124. For example see *Complex Deterrence*.

125. Apparently, due to how Russia qualifies IW, this is also how it sees itself as a target of foreign influence (there is mental war being waged against it) and only responding in kind.

126. John Arquilla, *Bitskreig: The New Challenge of Cyberwarfare* (London: Wiley, 2021).

127. David Ronfeldt and John Arquilla, *Whose Story Wins: Rise of the Noosphere, Noopolitik and Information-Age Statecraft* (Santa Monica, CA: RAND, 2020).

128. Richard Harknett and Michael Fischerkeller, "Deterrence Is Not a Credible Strategy for Cyberspace," *ORBIS* 61 (2017): 381–93; Soesanto and Smeets.

129. Richard Harknett and Emily Goldman, "The Search for Cyber Fundamentals," *Journal of Information Warfare* (2016); Richard Harknett and Michael Fischerkeller, "Persistent Engagement and Cost Imposition," *Lawfare*, February 6, 2020; Soesanto and Smeets.

130. Command Vision for USCYBERCOM: Achieve and Maintain Cyberspace Superiority (US CYBERCOM, 2018).

131. Soesanto and Smeets.

CHAPTER 3

1. The literature suggests that this has been the case over history worldwide and more recently in the informational (cyber) sphere, as illustrated by cyber innovations in the U.S. in particular. See Stephen Rosen, *Wining the Next War: Innovation and the Modern Military* (Ithaca, NY: Cornell University Press, 1995); Sally White, 2019; Jon Lindsay, *Information Technology and Military Power* (Ithaca, NY: Cornell University Press, 2020).

2. For example, see Nathan Leitis, *The Operational Code of Politburo* (New York: McGraw-Hill, 1951); Nathan Leites, *Soviet Style in Management* (New York: Crane Russak, 1985); Jack Snyder, *The Soviet Strategic Culture: Implications for Nuclear Operations* (Santa Monica, CA: RAND, 1977); Matthew Evangelista, *Innovation and the Arms Race: How the US and the USSR Develop New Military Technologies* (Ithaca, NY: Cornell University Press, 1993); Kimberly Marten, *Engaging the Enemy: Organizational Theory and Soviet Military Innovation* (Princeton, NJ: Princeton University Press, 1993); Robert Bathurst, *Intelligence and the Mirror* (New York: Sage, 1993).

3. For example, see Fritz W. Ermarth, *Russia's Strategic Culture: Past, Present and Transition?* (Fort Belvoir, VA: DTRA Press, 2006); Norbet Eitelhuber, "The Russian Strategic Culture and What It Implies for the West," *Connections* 9, no. 1 (Winter 2009): 1–28; Lyudmila Igumnova, "Russia's Strategic Culture Between American and European Worldviews," *Journal of Slavic Military Studies* 24, no. 2 (2011): 253–73.

4. For example, see Graeme Herd, *Understanding Russian Strategic Behavior: Imperial Strategic Culture and Putin's Operational Code* (London: Routledge, 2022); Lawrence Freedman, *Ukraine and the Art of Strategy* (Oxford: Oxford University Press, 2019); Stephen Covington, "The Culture of Strategic Thought Behind Russia's Modern Approaches to Warfare," *Harvard Belfer Papers*, October 2016; Ofer Fridman, "Russian Mindset and War: Between Westernizing the East and Easternizing the West," *Journal of Advanced Military Studies*, Special Issue on Strategic Culture, no. 1 (2022): 24–35; Kerrane Evan, "Moscow's Strategic Culture: Russian Militarism in an Era of Great Power Competition," *Journal of Advanced Military Studies* 1 (2022): 69–87.

5. For example, see Amund Osflaten, "Russian Strategic Culture after the Cold War: The Primacy of Conventional Force," *Journal of Military and Strategic Studies* 20, no. 2 (2021); Dmitry (Dima) Adamsky, "Russian Campaign in Syria—Change and Continuity in Strategic Culture," *Journal of Strategic Studies* 43, no. 1 (2019): 104–25; Martti Kari and Katri Pynnoniemi, "Theory of Strategic Culture: An Analytical Framework for Russian Cyber Threat Perception," *Journal of Strategic Studies*, September 11, 2019; Tracey German, "Harnessing Protest Potential: Russian Strategic Culture and the Colored Revolutions," *Contemporary Security Policy* 41, no. 4 (2020): 541–63.

6. Yaacov Falkov, "Intelligence-Exalting Strategic Cultures: A Case Study of the Russian Approach," *Intelligence and National Security* 37, no. 1 (2022): 90–108; Mette Skak, "Russian Strategic Culture: The Generational approach and the Counterintelligence State Thesis," in Roger Kanet, ed., *Routledge Handbook of Russian Security* (London: Routledge, 2019).

7. For example, see Katalin Miklossy and Hanna Smith, eds., *Strategic Culture in Russia's Neighborhood* (London: Routledge, 2020); Pavel Baev, "Threat Assessments and Strategic Objectives in Russia's Arctic Policy," *Journal of Slavic Military Studies* 31, no. 1 (2019); Dmitry Gorenburg, "Russian Strategic Culture in a Baltic Crisis," *Marshall Centre Security Insights*, no. 25 (March 2019); Dogachan Dagi, "The Russian Stand on the Responsibility to Protect: Does Strategic Culture Matter?" *Journal of Asian Security and International Affairs* 7, no. 3 (2020): 370–86; David Lewis, "Strategic Culture and Russia's Pivot to East," *Security Insights*, no. 34 (July 2019).

8. For example, see "Change and Continuity in Russian Strategic Culture," in Angela Borozna, ed., *The Sources of Russian Foreign Policy Assertiveness* (London: Palgrave Macmillan, 2022); Isabelle Facon, "Russian Strategic Culture in the 21 Century," *Strategic Asia 2016–2017*, November 8, 2016; Polina Sinovets, "From Stalin to Putin, Russian Strategic Culture in the 21 Century," *Philosophy Study* 6, no. 7 (2016); Polina Sinovets and Mykyta Nerez, "The Essence of Russian Strategic Culture: From the Third Rome to the Russian World," *International and Political Studies* 34, no. 1 (2021): 123–36; Roger Kanet, "Russian Strategic Culture, Domestic Politics and Cold War 2.0," *European Politics and Society* 20,

no. 2 (2018): 190–206; Eugene Rumer and Richard Sokolosky, *Etched in Stone: Russian Strategic Culture and the Future of Transatlantic Security* (Washington, DC: Carnegie Endowment for International Peace, 2021); Pavel Baev, *Transformation of Russian Strategic Culture: Impact from Local Wars and Global Confrontation* (Paris: IFRI, 2020); Anna Antczak, "Russian Strategic Culture: Prisoner of Imperial History?" *Polish Political Science Studies* 60 (2018): 233–42; Jørgen Staun, "At War with the West—Russian Military-Strategic Culture," in Niels Bo Poulsen and Jørgen Staun, eds., *Russia's Military Might: A Portrait of Its Armed Forces* (Copenhagen: Djøf, 2021).

9. Expert discourse usually associates these elements with the Soviet era; however, they have deep cultural underpinnings and derive from the older Tsarist organizational cultures and traditions, predating the USSR. Exploration of the latter could be a separate avenue of research, which is beyond the scope of this book. Here the discussion utilizes them as a given variable.

10. For a literature review and elaboration, see Adamsky, 2010, chapters 2, 4, and 5. Also see Theo Farrell, *Sources of Military Change: Culture, Politics, Technology* (London: Lynne Rienner, 2002); Emily Goldman and Leslie Eliason, *Diffusion of Military Technology and Ideas* (Stanford, CA: Stanford University Press, 2003).

11. For example, see Sterlin, Protasov, and Kreidin; Ponomarev, Poddubnyi, and Polegaev; D. G. Evstaf'ev and A. M. Il'nitsky, "Prioritety upravleniia natsionalnoi bezopasnost'iu v usloviiakh postglobalnogo mira," *VM*, no. 3 (2021): 6–24.

12. Adamsky, 2010; *JSS*, 2019.

13. Isaiah Berlin, *The Soviet Mind* (Washington, DC: Brookings Institution, 2004); Lawrence Graham, *Science in Russia* (Cambridge: Cambridge University Press, 1993); *Science, Philosophy and Human Behavior in the Soviet Union* (New York: Columbia University Press, 1987); Lev Gumilevskii, *Russkie Inzhinery* (Moscow: Molodaia Gvardiia, 1953); V. F. Shapavolov, *Istoki I Smysl Rossiiskoi Tsivilizatsii* (Moscow: Fair Press, 2003); and V. Solov'ev, *Natsional'nyi Vopros v Rossii* (Moscow: AST, 1988).

14. D. G. Evstaf'ev and A. M. Il'nitsky, "Prioritety upravleniia natsionalnoi bezopasnost'iu v usloviiakh postglobalnogo mira," *VM*, no. 3 (2021): 6–24; Shimon Naveh, *In Pursuit of Military Excellence* (London: Routledge, 1997); Leitis, *The Operational Code of Politburo*; Bathurst, *Intelligence and the Mirror*; and Christopher Donnelly, *Red Banner* (London: Jane's Information Group, 1988).

15. For instance, in Syria the holistic approach applied to both the political-strategic and the operational-tactical aspects of the campaign. Adamsky, *JSS*, 2019.

16. In reference to this phenomenon, Stalin argued that the Party must combine the broad outlook of the Russian revolutionary with American practicality. Leites, *Operational Code*, 30; and Adamsky, 2010; Graham, *Science in Russia*; *Science, Philosophy and Human Behavior in the Soviet Union*.

17. For example, see Graham, *Science in Russia*; *Science, Philosophy and Human Behavior in the Soviet Union*; Donnelly; Bathurst, *Intelligence and the Mirror*; Vadim Kozhinov, *O russkom nacional'nom soznanii* (Moscow: Algoritm, 2002); Mikhail Epstein, *Na granitzakh kultur* (New York: Slovo, 1995); Leites, *Soviet Style in Management*; and A. Kokoshin, *Inovatsionnye vooruzhennye sily* (Moscow: URSS, 2009).

18. Andrew Monaghan, *How Moscow Understands War and Military Strategy* (Washington, DC: Center for Naval Analysis, 2020).

19. N. A. Dobroliubov, "Chto takoe oblomovschina?" *Otechestvennye Zapiski*, nos. 1–4 (1895): 59–68; I. A. Goncharov, *Oblomov* (Moscow: Izdatelstvo Detskaia Literatura, 1967). Lenin, Stalin, and other Soviet leaders saw *oblomovschina* as one of the primary indigenous Russian evils, which could constrain the realization of communist ideals in Russia, threatening to turn the whole Soviet enterprise into an unfeasible utopia. For example, see V. Arkhangelskii, "Oblomovschina," *Literaturnaia Entsiklopedia* (Moscow: Sovetskaia Entsiklopedia, 1934), 165–72; V. I. Lenin, "O mezhdunarodnom I vnutrennem polozhenii Sovetskoi respubliki," *Polnoe Sobranie Sochenenii* 45 (Moscow: Politizdat, 1970), 1–16; Viktor Mazin, "Nelenivye Zametki o Leni: Oblomov, Lenin and kapitalizatsiia leni," *LOGOS* 29, no. 1 (2019): 243–58.

20. For elaboration, see Adamsky, 2010.

21. One cultural constraint has been the inclination to stage events for show (*pokazukha*), to embellish reality (*priukrashivanie deistvitel'nosti*), as epitomized by the Potemkin villages figure of speech. Adamsky, 2010. Also see Editorial, "Komanduiuschego I nachshtab Balflota sniali za priukrashivenie deistvitel'nosti" Lenta.ru, June 29, 2016.

22. For example, see Ronald Hingley, *The Russian Mind* (New York: Scribners, 1977); *Novaya Gazeta*, "My podarili protivniku preimuschestvo v 15 let," December 3, 2018; Pavel Baev, "Russia Absent from North Korean Crisis," *EDM*, April 24, 2017. For the "endemic bardak" in the Russian planning system and for the personal qualities of the commanders, see Roger McDermott, "The Brain of the Russian Army: Futuristic Visions Tethered by the Past," *Journal of Slavic Military Studies* 27 (2014): 4–35; Valerriy Zamulin, "To Defeat the Enemy Was Less a Problem than the Laziness and Indolence of Our Own Commanders," *Journal of Slavic Military Studies* 29, no. 4 (2016): 707–26; Adamsky, *JSS*, 2019.

23. For example see Robert Dalsjo, Michael Jonsson, and Johan Norberg, "A Brutal Examination: Russian Military Capability in Light of the Ukraine War," *Survival* 64, no. 3 (2022): 7–28.

24. In part, however, this incoherence reflects the state of the strategic community in the midst of conceptual learning, innovation, and modernization, and is thus not entirely irreversible pathology. Dmitry (Dima) Adamsky, "Nuclear Incoherence: Deterrence Theory and Non-Strategic Nuclear Weapons in Russia," *Journal of Strategic Studies* 37, no. 1 (2014): 91–134.

25. Adamsky, 2010. This claim goes beyond military affairs and has deeper metaphysical meaning. Russian sources deliberating the phenomenon of *oblomovshina* through dialectical lenses see an aptitude for sophisticated abstract thinking and strategizing as enabled by practical laziness, apathy toward practice, and procrastination. One might therefore speculate that the unity of negations encapsulated in *oblomovschina* enables a holistic perception of reality, which accounts in turn for the sophistication of Russian strategic thought. For example, see Valerii Pankrashin, "Iubilei oblomovschiny," *BBC News Russkaia Sluzhba*, October 15, 2009.

26. For elaboration and sources, see Adamsky, 2010, 42–45. Also see V. B. Zarudnitsky, "Vtoraia Mirovaia I Velikaia Otechestvennaia Voina: Uroki I Vyvody," *VM*, no. 3 (2021): 102–17.

27. Ibid.

28. Epitomized, for example, in the notion of *informational strike*, which by the psychological-cognitive-informational suppression of the adversary's decision-makers and operators aims at breaking the internal coherence of the enemy system, and not its integral physical annihilation.

29. Epitomized, for example, by the reestablishment in 2018 of the Main Military Political Directorate.

30. Adamksy, *Russian Nuclear Orthodoxy*, 2019.

31. M. D. Ionov, "O Refliksivnom Upravlenii Protivnikom v Boiu," *Voennaia Mysl'*, no. 1 (1995); Fedor Chausov, "Osnovy Refleksivnogo Upravleniia," *Morskoi Sbornik*, no. 9 (1999); N. I. Turko and S. A. Modestvov, "Refleksivnoe Upravelenie Razvitiem Strategicheskikh Sil Gosudarstva," in *Sistemnyi Analiz na Poroge 21 Veka*, Conference Proceedings, Moscow, 1996; S. Leonenko, "Refleksivnoe Upravlenie Protivnikom," *Armeiskii Sbornik*, no. 8 (1995).

32. Adamsky, *IFRI*, 2015.

33. Mason Clark, 25, the definition of RC.

34. Andrei A. Kokoshin, one of the leading Russian contemporary defense intellectuals, is the one who introduced the term *strategic gesture* into the Russian professional discourse. Kokoshin has borrowed this term from A. Svechin, the Soviet military theoretician from the prewar period, whose work Kokoshin has been steadily popularizing within the Russian military milieu, since his tenure as head of the NSC and deputy minister of defense and until today. Kokoshin has been referring readers to Svechin, whom he sees as a luminary of contemporary Russian military thought, on many themes related to the character of war, military innovations, RMA, and forecasting in military affairs. In the 1990s, when Russia officially introduced nuclear deterrence as state policy, a period that coincided with the second wave of Russian deterrence exploration, Kokoshin doubled down on Svechin's references to the art of force demonstration, which he dubbed "the art of strategic gesture," as it was exactly the Russian, pre-nuclear duplicate of the Western notion of deterrence that was immediately relevant then, especially for expanding options on the escalation ladder. Kokoshin thoughtfully and thoroughly adapted Svechin's work to the needs of the moment, and in an effort to popularize his legacy, referred to him in almost each of his works, whether or not related to deterrence. Arguably, this piece of Svechin's work is indeed the most valuable indigenous Russian scholarship on the subject per se, as opposed, for example, to Ogarkov's work, which left an imprint indirectly. Kokoshin argued that Russian military science had insufficiently elaborated on the subject of *strategic gesture*, and repeatedly called for investing intellectual energy into this. That said, it is unclear to what extent Kokoshin succeeded in his effort. Since the author has been unable to trace the process in detail and to establish the exact impact of Svechin's legacy within the Russian community of practice, this monograph relates to Svechin in a footnote rather than in a separate section, which does

justice neither to this most rigorous Russian-Soviet military-strategic thinker, nor to Kokoshin, who is in many regards his contemporary intellectual equivalent. A. A. Kokoshin, "Voenno-Politicheskoe Predvideinie," *NVO*, August 5, 1998; "Voina I Voennoe iskusstvo," *Sotsiologicehskie Isledovaniia* 372, no. 3 (2015): 97–106; "Asimetrichnyi otvet nomer odin," *NVO*, August 1, 2007; *Armiia I Politika* (Moscow: IMO, 1995); Aleksei Fenenko, "Kakimi budut voiny budushcego?" *RSMD*, July 19, 2017; C. K. Oznobischev, V. Ia. Potapov, and V. V. Skokov, *Kak Gotovilsia Asummetrichnyi Otvet na Strategicheskuiu Initsiativu Reigana* (Moscow: URSS, 2010).

35. "Khitrost' voennaia," in S. B. Ivanov, *Voennaia enciklopedia* (Moscow: Voennoe izdatel'stvo, 2004); V. N. Lobov, *Voennaia khitrost'* (Moscow: Moskovskoe voenno-istoricheskoe obshestvo, 2001).

36. For example, see Herr von Zinger, *Strategemy. O Kitaiskom iskusstve zhit' I vizhivat'* (Moscow: Eksmo, 2004); V. Voevodin, *Strategii voiny, biznessa, manipuliatsii, obmana* (Moscow: Et setera, 2004).

37. G. Leer, *Metod voennykh nauk* (Moscow: SPB, 1894), 53; N. P. Michenic, *Strategiia* (Moscow: SPB, 1898), 203–4; V. Lobov, *Voennaia Khitrost'* (Moscow: Logos, 2001). See also I. Vorob'ev and V. Kiselev, "Strategiia nepriamykh desitvii v novom oblike," *Voennaya Mysl'* 9 (2006); and "Voennaia Khitrsot," in *Voenno-Entsiklopedicheskii Slovar'* (Moscow: Voenizdat, 2007).

38. M. Gareev, "Voennaia nauka na sovremennom etape," *VPK* 13, no. 481 (April 2013).

39. For example, see S. K. Oznobishev, V. Ia. Potapov, and V. V. Skokov, *Kak Gotovilsia Asimetrichnyi Otvet SOI* (Moscow: URSS, 2010); Andrei Kokoshin, "Asimetrichnyi otvet na SOI," *Mezhdunarodnaia Zhizn'*, no. 2 (2007).

40. Glantz, 1989; V. N. Lobov, *Voennaia khitrost'* (Moscow: Moskovskoe voenno-istoricheskoe obshestvo, 2001); Krym Nash.

41. For example, consider the Soviet dispatch of forces to Cuba (1962), Soviet military interventions in Czechoslovakia (1968) and Egypt (1969), and the recent Russian interventions in Crimea (2014) and Syria (2015). Tom Cubbage, "Strategic and Operational Deception," in Michael Handel, ed., *War, Strategy and Intelligence* (London: Routledge, 2012); Uri Bar-Joseph, *The Watchman Fell Asleep* (Albany: SUNY Press, 2012); Dima Adamsky, *Operation Kavkaz* (Tel Aviv: Maarachot, 2006), *IFRI*, 2015, and *IFRI*, 2018. *Maskirovka* could acquire formidable dimensions, especially toward kinetic war and in wartime, when it might turn into a stand-alone combined arms operation with massive deployment of decoy forces and weaponry, misleading maneuvers (*otvlekaiuschii manevr*), the spread of disinformation, operational radio-games staging false communication traffic between dummy formations, and even false attacks (from the battalion to the division levels) to simulate concentrations of forces and to disguise the main direction of the strategic offense. For the sake of *maskirovka*, designed to ensure strategic success in the longer run, Soviet commanders were ready to sacrifice considerable forces and weaponry in battle. For example, see Georgii Zhukov, *Vospominania I Razmyshleniia* (Moscow: Voenizdat, 1980); David Glantz, *Soviet Military Deception in the Second World War* (London: Routledge, 1989); Antony Beevor, *Stalingrad* (London:

Penguin, 1999); Paul Adair, *Maskirovka (Deception): Hitler's Greatest Defeat* (London: Rigel and Cassell, 2004).

42. D. Prokhorov and A. Kolpakidi, *Vneshniaia Razvedka Rossii* (Moscow: Olma Press, 2001), 77–80; L. V. Shebarshin, *Ruka Moskvy* (Moscow: Tsentr Press, 1992); Ion Mihai Pacepa and Ronald Rychlak, *Disinformation* (London: WND Books, 2013); Christopher Andrew and Vasilly Mitrokhin, *The World Was Going Our Way* (New York: Basic Books, 2005); *The KGB in Europe and in the West* (Basic Books, 2000); Dominique Poirier, *DGSE: The French Spy Machine* (independently published, 2019).

43. "Meropriiatiia aktivnye," in *Kontrrazvedovatel'nyi slovar'* (Moscow: Vysschaia Krasnozmanennaia Shkola KGB pri SOVMINe SSSR im. F.E.Dzerzhinskogo, 1972).

44. Shebarshi; Kolpakidi and Prokhorov; Andrew and Mitrokhin; Poirier; Pacepa and Rychlak.

45. For the historical and current usage of the term and its relationship to other features of operational art, see Dmitry (Dima) Adamsky, "Discontinuity in Russian Strategic Culture? A Case Study of Mission Command Practice," *Marshall Center Security Insight* no. 49 (February 2020); "Aktivnost' Oborony," in *Voenno-Entsiklopedicheskii Slovar'* (mil.ru); V. E. Savkin, *Osnovnue printsipy operativnogo isskusstva I taktiki* (Moscow: Voenizdat, 1972); A. Karaiani and I. Syromiatova, *Prikladnaia voennaia psikhologia* (St. Petersburg: Izdatel'stvo Piter, 2006); A. Kuleba, "Psikhologicheskaia podgotovka voennosluzhaschikh k vedeniiu aktivnykh boevykh desitvii," *Armeiskii Sbornik*, no. 8 (2019): 78–94; Vladimir Kriuchkov, "Trundye mili k ratnomu masterstvu," *KZ*, October 30, 2020; Rod Thornton, "Soviet Principle of Aktivnost' in Warfare," Russia Seminar, February 2, 2021, https://www.youtube.com/watch?v=kuN41R7h7Cw.

46. V. A. Anokhin, D. V. Kholuenko, and N. M. Gromyko, "Otsenka effektivnosti dezorganizattsii informatsionno-upravliaiuschikh system operativnykh I takticheksikh formirovanii protivnika," *Vestnik AVN*, no. 3 (2019): 69–73; "Otsenka boesposobnosti VF s uchetom effektivnosti dezorganizatsii upravleniia," *VM*, no. 12 (2019): 48–56. Combat dynamism also makes it possible to avoid and inflict surprises, as seizure of the initiative (*zahvat iniciativi*) is linked in Russian operational art to surprising the enemy (*dostizhenie vnezapnosti*). Reconnaissance by fighting (*razvdeka boem*) is one of the tools to achieve this. The organizing logic is simple: to avoid surprise one needs to prescribe (*zadat'*) the operational tempo, impose (*naviazat*) the course of events, and be in constant combat friction with the adversary (*bespokoit boevye poriadki protivnika*). As such, *aktivnost'* and active measures during the threatening period make it possible to seize the initiative in the initial stage of war or prior to a major engagement (*srazhenie*), to shape the enemy toward it, or, on the strategic level and if executed systematically, to influence the correlation of forces in one's favor.

47. Dmitry Rogozin, "Deistviia sistematicheskie boevye," *Voina I Mir v Terminakh I Opredeleniiakh* (Moscow: Veche, 2014). Also see "SBD," in A. M. Plekhov and S. G. Shapkin, *Slovar' Voennykh Terminov* (Moscow: Voenizdat, 1988).

48. "Sistematicheskie boevye destviia," *Voennyei Entsiklopedicheskii Slovar'*, mil.ru.

49. For example, see A. Romanov and Iu. Blinkov, "Vzgliady Rukovodstva NATO na Podgotovku I Priminenie OVVS alianssa v buduschikh operatsiiakh," *ZVO*, no. 9

(2009): 46–53. When conceptualizing the hybrid war that the West has been waging against Russia, Russian experts argue that the adversary seeks victory by possessing an implicit grand strategic goal that serves as guidance (*tselepologanie*) for the general plan (*obschii plan*), and "systematic influence" on the weak spots of the adversary by the complex of hybrid threats. The author's lexicon reveals the thinking traits and cognitive style characteristic of the products of the Russian strategic culture and professional milieu. Aleksandr Bartosh, "Novoe izmerenie gibtidnoi voiny," *NVO*, no. 18 (2020); "Strategiia I kontrstagiia gibridnoi voiny," *VM*, no. 10 (2018).

50. "A type of operational activity of the state security organs aimed at preventing adversarial subversion . . . by the following means: (i) deterrence (*uderzhanie*) from subversion—covert influence on adversarial cognition and will to incite the adversary to refuse realization of subversion; (ii) distraction to irrelevant object—covertly influencing adversarial cognition, disorienting and channeling adversarial effort to the object, interaction with which will not result in a desired outcome; (iii) hindering subversion—creation of obstacles, which hamper the adversary from establishing contact with the object of actions; (iv) depriving him of the means of subversion—preventing the adversary from acquiring means of subversion, their extraction or damage, precluding the adversary from the capacity to realize his plot." "Operativnoe preduprezhdenie podryvnoi deiatelnosti protivnika," and "operativnoe presechenie podruvnoi deiatelnosti protivnika," in *Kontrrazvedovatel'nyi slovar'*.

51. *Operational seizure* rests on the following methods: "inducement to halt subversive activities, compromising (*komprometatsia*), organizational decomposition (*razlozhenie*) and exposure (*razoblachenie*)."

52. The academization of Soviet intelligence studies within the KGB started much later than in the military, mainly under Andropov, from the late 1960s to early 1970s and onward. Falkov defines the state of intelligence theory development during the Andropov era as an "explosion of intellectual the creativity." Yaacov (Kobi) Falkov, "Soviet Intelligence Culture" (forthcoming).

53. "Profilaktika," in *Kontrrazvedovatelnyi Slovar*, 238–39.

54. The term prevention, *presechenie* in Russian, is widely used in the Russian criminology lexicon, especially the rubric of "measures of prevention" in the Russian legal criminal code. Wikipedia translates the term *presechenie* to English as "deterrence" (in the penology context). https://en.wikipedia.org/wiki/Deterrence_(penology).

55. "Also, inducement to halt subversive activities could be based on ideological re-education of personalities engaged in subversion, as a result of which they change their political convictions and halt hostile activities towards the Soviet state. "A desire not to hurt the interests of the Soviet state will be a motivation for halting subversion." "Sklonenie k prekrascheniiu podryvnoi deiatel'nosti," *Kontrrazvedovatel'nye Slovar'*.

56. For example, see Thomas Rid, "Deterrence Beyond the State," *Comparative Security Policy* 33, no. 1 (2012): 124–47.

57. Moreover, the above operations even had a combat planning expression—"operational combination"—referring to concrete procedures for the employment of means and measures aimed at creating operational conditions and a configuration to

coerce the adversary into particular actions. "Kombinatsiia operativnaia," *Kontrra-zvedovatel'nye Slovar'*.

58. RMA is a radical military innovation in which new organizational structures together with novel concepts of operations, usually (although not necessarily) driven by new weaponry (enabled by novel technologies), fundamentally change the conduct of warfare. The RMA/MTR terminology was part of the broader analytical methodology within Soviet military science for diagnosing shifts in the character of war. Adamsky, 2010.

59. Ogarkov promoted three interrelated arguments about the character of future war: that the prowess of advanced conventional RSCs would be comparable to the combat potentials of tactical-operational nuclear weapons; that these complexes blur the dividing line between the offensive and defensive modes of war, making this distinction obsolete; and that on the battlefield the precision strike into the entire operational-strategic depth underscores the maneuvering of fires and effects rather than of platforms and forces. Adamsky, *The Culture of Military Innovation*.

60. In modified form, the methodology and anthology of Ogarkov's works turned into one of the linchpins of the U.S. military innovations during the 2000s. The Soviet MTR ideas became a precursor to and source of inspiration for such notions of the U.S. defense transformation as network-centric warfare (NCW), informational superiority, jointness, and effect-based operations (EBO). Dmitry (Dima) Adamsky, "Through the Looking Glass: The Soviet MTR and the American RMA," *Journal of Strategic Studies* 31, no. 2 (2008): 257–94; Dmitry (Dima) Adamsky, "Vliianie idei marshala Ograkova na Zapadnuiu voennuiu mysl," *Annual Ogarkov Readings* (Moscow: CAST, 2019), https://www.youtube.com/watch?v=EJ3orZ2-UUU&t=222s.

61. Reforms under Baluevsky, Makarov, Gerasimov, Serdiukov and Shoigu.

62. Michael Kofman, "The Ogarkov Reforms: The Soviet Inheritance Behind Russia's Military Transformation," *Russia Military Analysis Blog*, July 2019; Adamsky, "Vliianie"; Adamsky, *IFRI*, 2018.

63. The author owes the original idea to Michael Kofman and builds on it here and in earlier publications. See Adamsky, "Vliianie"; Kofman, "The Ogarkov Reforms"; "The Ogarkov Period: Soviet Origins of the Russian Views of Deterrence," *Russian Seminar*, February 2, 2021, https://www.youtube.com/watch?v=3vouTxigJ_c&t=695s.

64. For example, see the impact of a hypersonic arsenal as an enabler of nonnuclear, Zysk, 2020.

65. Obviously, Ogarkov rejected limited nuclear war, as there was no conceptual place and empirical need to differentiate between regional and global nuclear engagements (a demand that would emerge in Russia in the 1990s). However, his vision of conventional battle alone achieving the political goals of war, and the notion of a strike into the entire operational-strategic depth without capturing the territory were precursors to several aspects of the SO for Destruction of Critical Objects, one of the main operational expressions of the Russian operational art of deterrence. Adamsky, "Vliianie"; Kofman, 2021.

66. Kofman, 2021.

67. For example, see V. A. Zhurkin, S. A. Karaganov, and A. V. Kortunov, *Razumnaia dostatochnost' I novoe politicheskoe myshlenie* (Moscow: Obschestvennye nauki I sovremennost', 1989); S. A. Tiushkevich, "Razumnaia dostatochnost' dlia oborony: parametry I kriterii," *VM*, no. 5 (1989): 53–61; A. G. Arbatov, "Oboronnaia dostatochnost' I bezopasnsot'," *Znanie*, no. 4 (1990).

68. For example, see A. A. Marchenko, "Razumnaia dostatochnost' kak strategiia reagirovaniia respondentov v veb oprosakh," *Monitoring Obshestvennogo Mneniia: Ekonomicheskie I Sotsialnye Peremeny* 5 (2016): 31–40.

69. In the current Russian economics and business discourse it is a general principle of administration, an alternative to "management by optimization." The Russian dictionary of economic terms states that business "subjects operating in accordance with the RS principle, change their rules of conduct only in case of the changing circumstances, when these rules do not produce satisfying results. This is not about optimization [of the existing rules], but a search for more appropriate [new] rules by trial and error. Once [decision-makers] find appropriate rules, they calm down and continue to stick to the principle of reasonable sufficiency." I. M. Osadchaia, ed., *Ekonomika. Tolkovyi Slovar'* (Moscow: Izdatel'stvo Ves' Mir, 2000).

70. Adamsky, *IFRI*, 2018; *JSS*, 2019; Michael Kofman, *Syria and the Russian Armed Forces* (Philadelphia: FPRI, 2020).

71. For example, see Sergei Riabkov, "Iadernyi arsenal Rossii nakhoditsia na urovne razumnoi dostatochnsoti," TV Zvezda, July 4, 2014; Dmitry Suslov, "Ot Pariteta k Razumnoi Dostatochnosti," *Rossiia v Global'noi Politike*, no. 6 (November/December 2010); Alexey Arbatov, "Iadernyi Potolok," *VPK*, July 21, 2014; Iurii Solomov and Igor' Korotechko, "Ot Intelekta profesionalizma politicheskoi eliti zavisit sostoianie gosudarstva," *Natsional'naia Oborona*, no. 10 (2020): 34–41.

72. "Defensive sufficiency is a measure of adequacy of the state's defense potential to the level of external military danger (threat) and to the state of one's economy. In the broader sense, the term reasonable defense sufficiency is used to characterize high effectiveness of political and economic means of the state, coupled with the art of diplomacy to utilize peacemaking efforts aimed at maintaining national security (goals) and decreasing the pressure of military expenditures on the economy. Employment of principles of deterrence makes it possible to find a systemic approach to solving the problem of the adequacy of the state's defense potential to the demands of reasonable sufficiency. Principles of deterrence establish qualitative-quantitative criteria for armed forces potential in peacetime, in the threatening period, and in the initial and subsequent periods of war, if it turns into a protracted one." Dmitry Rogozin, ed., *Voina I Mir v Terminakh I Opredeleniiakh* (Moscow: Veche, 2014). *Sufficiency* of *nuclear means and forces* stands for "a state's minimal nuclear combat potential, ensuring active deterrence of an aggressor from unleashing war." The dictionary article on *sufficiency of regular* (i.e., conventional) *means and forces* conveys a similar logic and literally calls for the utilization of "the principle of reasonable defensive sufficiency" when defining the arsenal's size and shape.

73. For example, see Edward Geist, "Before Sderzhivanie: Soviet Nuclear Strategy and Its Legacy," Russia Seminar, January 26, 2021, https://www.youtube.com/watch?v=A2RunPOtLkw; Anya Fink, "On the Evolution of Damage in Russian Military Thought," Russia Seminar, January 26, 2021, https://www.youtube.com/watch?v=pzTm8Gh3wbo. Also see Kofman and Fink, July 2020. It would probably be an oversimplification to designate RS as a default option, deriving from Moscow's objective material limitations. This was indeed the case in the original historical setting during *Perestroika*. It may be true as well of the Russian operation in Syria, when scholars analyze the logic of the Russian campaign design there through the lens of RS. However, even when the correlation of forces starts moving in Moscow's favor, for example, as was the case in Syria from a certain point of the intervention, Russian military planners stuck to this unwritten stratagem, which, if applied correctly, ensures what Western strategic studies dub "utility of force." See Adamsky, *IFRI*, 2019; Kofman, FPRI, 2020.

74. Clint Reach, Vikram Kilmbi, and Mark Cozad, *Russian Assessments and Applications of the Correlation of Forces and Means* (Washington, DC: RAND, 2020). This section builds on their work and on Adamsky, 2010; Adamsky, 2013; Adamsky, *JSS*, 2020.

75. The current reincarnation of the Soviet COFM in contemporary Russian military science often features under the name *qualimetry* (named after the use of formal mathematical methods to quantify the qualitative characteristics of weapons, forces, and doctrines). For the Soviet COFM, see S. Tyushkevich, "Metdologiia sootnosheniia sil storon v voine," *VM*, no. 6 (1969); B. I. Strelchenko and E. A. Ivanov, "Nekotorye Aspekti Otsenki Sootnosheniia Sil v Operatsiiakh," *VM*, no. 10 (1987); V. I. Tsugichko and F. Stoili, "Metod Boevykh potentsialov," *VM*, no. 4 (1997): 23–28; S. A. Bogdanov and L. V. Zakharov, "O vyrabotke edinykh podkhodov k otsenke boevykh potentsialov vooruzhenii," *VM*, nos. 8–9 (1992). For the contemporary applications of this methodology in the Russian military, see "Sootneshenie sil I sredstv," *Russian Military Dictionary*, mil.ru; V. I. Ostankov and P. S. Kazarin, "Metodologiia Sravnitelnogo Analiza Boevykh Potentsialov," *VM*, no. 11 (2012); V. N. Tsugichko, "O Kategorii Sootnoshenie Sil v Potentsial'nykh Voennykh Konfliktakh," *VM*, no. 3 (2002); *Prognozirovanie sotsial'no-ekonomicheskikh protsessov* (Moscow: URSS, 2017); V. S. Brezgin and A. I. Buravlev, "O metodologii otsenki boevykh potentsialov tekhniki i voinskikh formirovanii," *VM*, no. 8 (2010); V. V. Shumov, "Uchet psukhologicheskikh faktroov v modeliakh boia," *Kompiuternye Isssledovaniia I Modelirovanie* 8, no. 6 (2016): 951–64; A. S. Bonin and G. I. Gorchitsa, "O boevykh potentsialakh obraztsov VVT, formirovanii i sootnosheniiakh sil gruppirovok storon," *VM*, no. 4 (2010); V. V. Shumov and V. O. Korepanov, "Matematicheskie modeli boevykh I voennykh deistvii," *Kompiuternye Issledovaniia I Modelirovanie* 12, no. 1 (2020): 217–42; Iu. N. Pavlovskii, "O Faktore L.N. Tolstogo V Vooruzhennoi Bor'be," *Matematicheskoe Modelirovanie* 5, no. 1 (1993). For qualimetry, see Yu. M. Andrianov and A. I. Subetto, *Kvalimietriia v priborostroenii i mashinostrenii* (Leningrad: Mashinostroenie, 1990).

76. Dmitry (Dima) Adamsky, "The Art of Net Assessment an Uncovering Foreign Military Innovations: Learning from Andrew Marshall's Legacy," *Journal of Strategic Studies*, June 2020.

77. Clint Reach, "Russian Views on COFM and Nuclear Deterrence," Russia Semi-nar, February 2, 2021, https://www.youtube.com/watch?v=1ocLOhA9icw. Also see Reach, Kilmbi, and Cozad, 2020.

CHAPTER 4

1. Ideally, stand-alone intelligence collection and analysis efforts are required that are intended exclusively for deterrence operation planning. Without "essential elements of information" for the needs of deterrence, any argument about which values of oppo-nents should be exploited within the frames of a deterrence program becomes more in-tuitive than systematic.

2. Another difficulty related to the signaling stage is the ambiguity dilemma. On the one hand, a "subject of coercion" seeks to communicate to an "object" what it considers to be unacceptable behavior that will come at a cost. On the other hand, red lines may be deliberately left ambiguous out of fear that specification may be counterproductive. Clear designation of red lines enables the challenger to operate very close to, but still below, the unacceptable level of violence, thus avoiding retaliation.

3. Department of Defense, Deterrence Operations, 52–56; Larkin, "The Limits of Tailored Deterrence"; Payne, "Understanding Deterrence."

4. Samuel Charap, "Moscow's Calibrated Coercion in Ukraine and Russian Strate-gic Culture," *Marshall Center Security Insights*, no. 63 (September 2020).

5. For the argument and supporting theoretical and empirical literature, see Adam-sky, "From Israel with Deterrence."

6. Ibid.

7. Milevski, 2014.

8. Michael Howard and Peter Paret, *On War* (Princeton, NJ: Princeton University Press, 1984), 527–30, 566–73; Michael Handel, *Masters of War* (London: Frank Cass, 2001), 185; Edward Luttwak, *Strategy* (Cambridge, MA: Harvard University Press, 2003), 32–50.

9. Also, crossing the culmination point may provoke an opponent to embark on dangerous military innovations undesired by the initiator of coercion.

10. These claims are particularly applicable to the informational domain, where ac-tors employ forceful coercive signaling more readily than in the nuclear-conventional realms. Uri Tor, *JSS*; Gaycken and Martellini, 2013.

11. "Steps to bolster credibility can be irrational in terms of deterrence stability. If the point is to deter an attack, and stability rests on each side being confident it can deter, then one side's determined effort to gain the capacity to fight and win for the sake of credibility will breed deterrence instability." Patrick M. Morgan, *Deterrence Now* (Cambridge: Cambridge University Press, 2003), 52, cited in Milevski, 2014. Also see Austin Long, *Deterrence—From Cold War to Long War* (Washington, DC: RAND, 2008); Michael Mazarr, *Understanding Deterrence* (Washington, DC: RAND, 2018); Dmitry (Dima) Adamsky, "Unintended Escalation: Five Lessons from Israel for the Russia-NATO Standoff," *Harvard Russia Matters*, February 14, 2018.

12. Uri Bar-Joseph, "ISSR Article Review 82: 'From Israel with Deterrence: Strategic Culture, Intra-war Coercion and Brute Force," *ISSF H-Diplo*, June 16, 2017.

13. Lukas Milevski, "Deterring Able Archer," *Journal of Strategic Studies* 37, nos. 6–7 (2014): 1050–65.

14. Kristin Ven Bruusgaard, "Russian Concept of Deterrence" Russia Seminar, Finnish National Defense University, January 2021, https://www.youtube.com/watch?v=Kl-v5SJjKuw; Anya Fink, "On the Evolution of Damage in Russian Military Thought," Russia Seminar, Finnish National Defense University, January 2021, https://www.youtube.com/watch?v=nzKbfMXr9Do&t=12s; Nora Vanaga and Toms Rostoks, *Deterring Russia in Europe* (London: Routledge, 2019).

15. Kofman, Fink, and Edmonds, 2020.

16. Kofman, Fink, and Edmonds, 2020. Also see Bruusgaard, January 2021; Charap, 2020. For examples illustrating this solid theoretical-methodological foundation, see V. M. Burenok and Iu. A. Pechatnov, "O kriterial'nykh osnovakh iadernogo sderzhivaniia," *Vooruzhenie I Ekonomika* 22, no. 1 (2013); Iu. A. Pechatnov, "Analiz otechestvennykh I zarubezhnykh podkhodov k razrabotke kontseptual'nykh modelei silovogo strategicheskogo sderzhivaniia," *Vooruzhenia I Ekonomika* 14, no. 2 (2011).

17. Bruusgaard, January 2021; Adamsky, 2017.

18. Charap et al., 2022.

19. For the major systematic effort in the West to deal with the question as a stand-alone subject matter, see Samuel Charap, Andrew Stravers, John Drennan, Dara Massicot, Sean Zeigler, Gregory Weider Fauerbach, Mark Stalczynski, and Melissa Shostak, *Understanding Russian Coercive Signaling* (Santa Monica, CA: RAND, 2022). Also see Andrew Bowen, "Coercive Diplomacy and the Donbas," *Journal of Strategic Studies* 42, no. 3 (2019). For the same question in a broader context, see Charles Ziegler, "A Crisis of Diverging Perspectives: US-Russian Relations and the Security Dilemma," *Texas National Security Review* 4, no. 1 (Winter 2021).

20. Bruusgaard and Fink, January 2021; Adamsky, 2017; Charap et al., 2022.

21. According to this view, Western strategic establishments perfectly realize the drivers and essence of Moscow's coercive signals, but publicly, officials intentionally twist their perception of Russia for political purposes, and only naïve pundits, the general public, and "useful idiots" fed with NATO agitprop misdiagnose Russian coercive signals and intentions. Interviews with Russian experts, 2020–21. Andrei Sushentsov's comments on William Burns's memoirs well illustrate this view, which is widespread in the Russian expert community. "Piat' vyvodov ob otnosheniiakh Rossii I SShA iz knigi Billa Bernsa," February 13, 2021, https://www.youtube.com/watch?v=vafxfAE83pk&t=462s. Others believe that elements within the U.S. strategic community and think-tank industry get things right when interpreting the Kremlin's signals for U.S. decision-makers, but distort them driven by competition for resources and bureaucratic power. Interviews with Russian experts, 2020–21. For the Russian take on the U.S. think-tank industry that supports policymaking, see Ilnitskii, *VM*, 2021.

22. Bruusgaard, January 2021; Adamsky, 2015.

23. Giles, 2019; Monaghan, 2019.

24. For the intellectual history of these views and their evolution since the late 1990s see Andrew Monaghan, *Dealing with the Russians* (London: Polity, 2019).

25. For example, see Dmitry (Dima) Adamsky, "Unintended Escalation: Five Lessons from Israel for the Russia-NATO Standoff," *Harvard Russia Matters*, February 14, 2018.

26. For the intellectual history of the Western study of the subject matter, see Kristin Ven Bruusgaard, "Russian Nuclear Strategy and Conventional Inferiority," *Journal of Strategic Studies* 44, no. 1 (2021); Adamsky, 2017. Western strategists assume that once at war, Moscow may de-escalate or terminate hostilities by gradually increasing the deployment and employment of dual-use systems.

27. How exactly would the West not misdiagnose coercion as brute force aimed at "control" (i.e., all-out war) rather than "influence" (i.e., to coerce by the limited use of force)? How do Russian strategists expect their Western counterparts to deduce correctly from Moscow's signaling that in the next step the Russian military will (or will not) move from the conventional to the nuclear stage? Bruusgaard, January 2021. Also see Adamsky, 2014, 2017.

28. Variations on the theme of coercive signaling feature in the Russian theoretical discourse under the rubric of the "art of strategic gesture," a topic, in the words of leading Russian defense intellectuals, traditionally underexplored in the Russian IR literature. Koka in *JSS*, 2017 and first report.

29. While in nuclear deterrence force is demonstrated but not used, cross-domain coercive signaling may involve a certain level of actual engagement. Thus, in the eyes of the opponent the line between *coercion* and *warfighting* becomes blurred, and deterrence may be indistinguishable from the use of brute force. In any given episode, especially in the initial phase, for any actor experiencing forceful signaling, it is objectively puzzling to establish whether the competitor is employing a "strategy of influence" (i.e., coercion) or a "strategy of control" (i.e., war).

30. For a thorough Western analysis of the Russian views in this matter, see Keir Giles, "Assessing Russian Success and Failure," in Viljar Veebel and Sandis Sraders, eds., *The Russia Conference Papers 2021* (Tartu: Tartu University Press, 2021).

31. For elaboration, see Jeffrey Mankoff, *Russian Foreign Policy: The Return of Great Power Politics* (New York: Rowman & Littlefield, 2009); *Empires of Eurasia: How Imperial Legacies Shape International Security* (New Haven, CT: Yale University Press, 2021).

32. Since 2008 the Russian armed forces have been in the midst of a major military innovation, unlike anything since the Soviet MTR modernization under Marshall Nikolai Ogarkov in the late 1970s. Certain segments of the Russian strategic community assume that coercive engagements have generated valuable benefits, in terms of knowledge, testing, and experimentation opportunities for the modernization of weapon systems, ConOps, and organizations. These "learning" benefits, in their view, suffice to qualify episodes of coercive engagement as valuable. One could also argue that the image of an effective power broker and provider of security to Middle Eastern actors, another derivative of Russian coercion activities, created more room for geopolitical maneuvering as well as political-military-economic opportunities for the Kremlin.

Kofman, *Syria and Russian Armed Forces*; *Grand Strategy*; Matthew Rojansky and Amos Gilead, eds., *Russia in the Middle East* (Washington, DC: Kennan Institute, 2021).

33. Bruusgaard, January 2021.

34. Bruusgaard, January 2021.

35. Bruusgaard, January 2021. For the broad historical context in which the current Russian leadership situates its interaction with the collective West, and for the Kremlin's self-perception of waging a long-term counterdeterrence (*kontr-sderzhivanie*) endeavor, see Andrew Monaghan, *Dealing with the Russians* (London: Polity Press, 2019). Also see Keir Giles, *Moscow Rules: What Drives Russia to Confront the West* (London; Chatham House, 2019); Vanaga and Rostoks, *Deterring Russia*.

36. Bruusgaard, January 2021.

37. Bruusgaard, January 2021; Lawerence Freedman, *Ukraine and the Art of Strategy* (Oxford: Oxford University Press, 2019); Charap, 2020. Samuel Charap has convincingly shown that all the parties to the confrontation have been worse off since the crisis erupted in 2014 and eventually realized the dead end of their coercion techniques. Building on Charap's claim, one could argue that both actors crossed the culmination point of coercion and found themselves in an inadvertent escalation, leading to a lose-lose state of affairs. Samuel Charap, *Everyone Loses: The Ukraine Crisis and the Ruinous Contest for Post-Soviet Eurasia* (London: Routledge, 2017). For Charap's recent variation on the theme, see Samuel Charap, "Expanding the Scope for Statecraft in U.S. Russia Policy," *WOTR*, May 2021.

38. Monaghan (2019) and Giles (2019) unpack in detail the genealogy and consequences of Western misperceptions of Russia. For the Russian reading of the interaction, see Bartosh, *VM*, x2.

39. Andrew Bowen and Cory Welt, *Russia: Foreign Policy and U.S. Relations* (Washington, DC: CRS, 2021), 33–39.

40. Coercion in the DT realm apparently demands more dedicated investments, including a willingness to use force to earn and maintain a strategic reputation for the purposes of prospective coercion. This situation is not unique to Russia, and has been observed across various strategic communities. For example, see Keren Yarhi-Milo, *Who Fights for Reputation? The Psychology of Leaders in International Conflict* (Princeton, NJ: Princeton University Press, 2018); T. V. Paul, Patrick Morgan, and James Wirtz, *Complex Deterrence: Strategy in the Global Age* (Chicago: University of Chicago Press, 2009).

41. For example see: Stefan Soestano and Max Smeets, "Cyber Deterrence: The Past, Present and Future" in Osinga and Swejis.

42. Il'nitskii, "Mental'nye voiny."

43. Michael Kofman, *Russian Analytical Digest*.

44. For example, see Charap, *WOTR*, May 2021.

45. A much longer historical perspective is needed to estimate the impact of sanctions and isolation. However, as of this writing, such a geopolitical climate is apparently tremendously damaging to the Kremlin's quest for digitalization and transition to the AI era. Seen as the path to a bright national future, it is currently curtailed in terms of business, scientific-technological, and industrial opportunities. Russian IT and AI

products, competitive by international standards, have been limited by geopolitical regulations. Max Suchkov; Katarzyna Zysk, *JSS*, 2021.

46. For failures, see Luttwak, *Strategy*, 47–49; Dmitry (Dima) Adamsky, "The 1983 Nuclear Crisis—Lessons for Deterrence Theory and Practice," *Journal of Strategic Studies* 36, no. 1 (January 2013): 4–41; Scott Sagan and Kenneth Waltz, "Political Scientists and Historians in Search of the Bomb," *Journal of Strategic Studies* 36, no. 1 (March 2013): 149; Yaacov Falkov, "Tried and Trusted Patriots for the CIA: Latvian Case Study of the KGB Operativnaia Igra Theory," *International Journal of Intelligence and Counter Intelligence* (2021). For successes, see Uri Bar-Joseph, "A Chance Not Taken: Sadat's Peace Initiative of February 1973 and Its Rejection by Israel," *Journal of Contemporary History* 41, no. 3 (July 2006): 545–56, esp. 552; Yaacov Falkov, "To Read Clausewitz in the KGB: Discovering Russian Concept of Culmination in Intelligence Operations" (2021). Computer simulations suggest that informational coercion, either alone or as part of a cross-domain scheme, increases the risk of crossing the culmination point. Christopher Gerritzen, "The End of Interventions? Simulating Cyber Weapons as Deterrence Against Humanitarian Interventions," Discussion Paper No. 6, Rhine-Waal University of Applied Sciences, January 2020.

47. Carl von Clausewitz leaves this task to "intuition of military genius." Echoing him, Handel argues that culmination "is not a theoretically fixed, but a fluctuating point," and that its correct identification depends on constantly changing circumstances. Handel, *Masters of War*, 184–90. Identifying the culmination point requires "meticulous calculation of the current relative strength of both sides as well as the careful projection of anticipated trends in their relative strength." Handel, *Masters of War*, 185. Western practitioners therefore sometimes turn to the net-assessment method, which they see as a tool well suited to serving this goal. The net-assessment method is an analytical technique that enables the exploration, diagnosis, and evaluation of protracted strategic interactions. Net-assessment models a dynamic and multidimensional strategic competition between oneself and an antagonist and attempts to diagnose intended and unintended consequences over time. Mahnken, 2020.

48. For example, see Stephanie Pezard and Ahsley Rhoades, *What Provokes Putin's Russia? Deterring Without Unintended Escalation* (Washington, DC: RAND, 2020); Dmitry (Dima) Adamsky, "From Israel with Deterrence: Strategic Culture, Intra-war Coercion and Brute Force," *Security Studies* 26, no. 1 (2017): 157–84. Eran Ortal x2 *Eshtonon*; Itai Brun on Culmination, in Itai Shapira, *Small Wars*.

49. V. M. Burenok and Iu. A. Pechatnov, *Strategicheskoe Sderzhivanie* (Moscow: Granitsa, 2010), esp. chapter 4. Iu. A. Pechatnov, "Nauchno-metodicheskii podkhod k formirovaniiu pokazatelia effektivnosti mekhanizma silovogo neiadernogo sderzhivaniia," *Strategicheskaia Stabil'nost'*, no. 1 58 (2012): 67–75. Avodto shel otam mekabrim al oto nose. Burenok and Pechatnov, senior officials from the 46th TsNII, and for more than two decades among the leading nonacademic scholars of deterrence strategy and operations in the Russian military, have been setting the tone in the field. The intellectual sources of their work can be traced to the conceptualization of nonnuclear strategic deterrence and predate the post-2014 phase of confrontation. However, the latter

probably further stimulated their research agenda, as this type of coercion became handier than ever before.

50. At least in 2015 the military saw the models for the latter task as relatively underexplored. For example, in 2015 Russian military experts still lacked criteria for defining or calculating unacceptable damage, prospective and actual, to critical social-military-economic infrastructure or to political-military command-and-control systems, by means of conventional aggression inflicted on Russia. In theory, such a codified procedure makes it possible to estimate the conditions under which the military would recommend to senior leadership that nonnuclear aggression be de-escalated by nuclear means. O. Aksenov, Iu. Tret'jakov, and E. Filin, "Osnovnye principi sozdaniia sistemy ocenki tekucshego I prognoziruemoga uscherba," *VM*, no. 6 (2015): 68–74.

51. Charap, 2020.

52. In contrast to the BDA discipline, which is largely a tactical-operational endeavor, here the focus is at a higher level and of broader scope, dealing mainly with the political-strategic effects of the operation. In a way, the challenge is comparable to producing BDA methodology for Effect Based Operations (EBO) and "operational net-assessment," topics that resulted in several professional confusions and controversial debates. For the intellectual history of the original concepts, see Thomas Mahnken, ed., *Net Assessment and Military Strategy: Retrospective and Prospective Essays* (New York: Cambria Press, 2020); Paul Davis, *Effects Based Operations* (Washington, DC. RAND, 2002); James Mattis, "USJFCOM Commander's Guidance for EBO," *Parameters* 37 (Autumn 2008): 18–25.

53. Burenok and Pechatnov, 2010; Pechatnov, 2012.

54. Iu. A. Pechatnov, "K Voprosy o dalneishem sovershenstvovanii teorii silovogo strategicheskogo sderzhivaniia," *Izvestiia Rossiiskoi Akademii Raketnykh I Artilleriiskikh Nauk* 81, no. 1 (2014): 27–31.

55. Bruusgard, January 2021.

56. For the Soviet and Russian works on operations analysis that Russian practitioners are apparently utilizing, see Iu. B. Germeir, *Vvedenie v teoriiu issledovaniia operatsii* (Moscow: Nauka, 1971); B. Radvik, *Voennoe planirovanie I analiz sistem* (Moscow: Voenizdat, 1972); S. F. Vikulov and G. P. Zhukov, *Voenno-ekonomicheskii analiz I issledovanie operatsii* (Moscow: Voenizdat, 1987); V. I., *Teoreticheskie osnovy sistemnogo analiza* (Moscow: Maior, 2006).

57. For elaboration, see the first part of this research on the ideational-cultural sources of deterrence *à la Russe*.

58. As the thorough genealogy of the concept offered by Clint Reach, Vikram Kilambi, and Mark Cozad indicates, *qualimetry*, once a subdiscipline in the Soviet military methodology of COFM, has turned into a euphemism for the latter in the Russian military. COFM (*sootnoshenie sil I sredstv*) is a sophisticated Soviet, and now Russian, evaluation method for estimating the superiority-inferiority relationship of adversarial groupings of forces in a given theater of operations or in strategic competition as a whole (in which case it includes both military and nonmilitary factors). The evaluation

includes analysis of qualitative and quantitative factors and their first- and second-order effects in dynamic interaction. Clint Reach, Vikram Kilmbi, and Mark Cozad, *Russian Assessments and Applications of the Correlation of Forces and Means* (Washington, DC: RAND, 2020). For elaboration on the Russian and Soviet theory and practice of COFM and its relevance to deterrence *à la Russe,* see the first part of this research.

59. "Operativnye igry," in *Kontrrazvedovatel'nyi slovar'* (Moscow: Vysschaia Krasnozmanennaia Shkola KGB pri SOVMINe SSSR im. F.E.Dzerzhinskogo, 1972).

60. See the previous part of this work on the intellectual sources of informational deterrence.

61. Falkov, 2021. It is not accidental that theoreticians of Russian *operational games* (in intelligence affairs) and *reflexive control* (in military affairs) have been inspired by, and often utilize, principles and models from Russian and foreign game theory (*teoria igr*), to develop applied knowledge for combat operations.

62. Guided by the principle of reasonable sufficiency (*razumnaia dostatochnost'*) and a holistic approach (*kompleksnyi podkhod*), among several other strategic dictums, the operation's designers found the golden range between overshooting and undershooting. Primary sources indicate that the Russian military deliberately, rather than impulsively or intuitively, calibrated the volume of operational energy injected into the theater according to the dynamic strategic circumstances. Systematic application of this approach, whatever the procedural-organizational mechanism that supports it, enabled Russian strategists and operators not to cross the Clausewitzian culmination point throughout the campaign. For elaboration, see Michael Kofman, *Syria and Russian Armed Forces* (Philadelphia: FPRI, 2020); Dmitry (Dima) Adamksy, *Moscow's Syria Campaign: Russian Lessons for the Art of Strategy* (Paris: IFRI, 2018). For elaboration on reasonable sufficiency and a holistic approach, see the first part of this work. For Russian military analysis of the campaign elaborating on these matters, see A. E. Savinkin, "Rossiiskaia Nauka Pobezhdat': Uroki Siriiskogo Uregulirovaniia," *Voennyi Akademicheskii Zhurnal* 22, no. 2 (2019): 15–44.

63. For the lengthier discussion of this challenge, and specifically in the context of the Russian-Ukraine war, including the failure of the Russian supreme command in the initial stage of the campaign, see Lawrence Freedman, *The Politics of Command* (Oxford: Oxford University Press, 2022). Also see Eliot Cohen, *Supreme Command: Soldiers, Statesmen, and Leadership in Wartime* (New York: Anchor, 2003).

CHAPTER 5

1. "For too long, people in Western Europe have been lulled into thinking that a new war on the continent was impossible. For Mr. Putin, that point of view needs to be changed, Mr. Sushentsov said, to compel the West to accept Russia's demands." Anton Troianovski, "Putin is operating on his own Timetable, and It May be a Long One," *New York Times,* 8 February 2022.

2. "People are spoiled by an overly long peace. They think of security as a given, as something that is attained for free, rather than something that must be negotiated. This is a mistake. . . . Russia has departed from the tactic of simply asking to be listened

to. . . . Russian leaders have seen that this does not work and that it is necessary to make clear the risks of the Russian position being ignored." Anton Troianovski, "Putin is operating on his own Timetable, and It May be a Long One," *New York Times*, 8 February 2022.

3. As opposed to the massive use of brute force to dominate and control, routine *mabam* does not have an end state and its goal is to constantly preserve the balance of regional trends in Israel's favor—which eventually results, in the view of Israeli experts, in deterrence. *Mabam*, an acronym of "campaign between the wars," seeks to leave a psychological imprint on the adversary, exacerbate his feeling of vulnerability, and dissuade him from the next round of warfare, either due to lack of self-confidence or due to lack of capabilities. If these efforts fail, then *mabam* facilitates better opening conditions for the next massive military clash and a better correlation of forces on the battlefield. Strikes on various targets across the Middle East and Africa that have been attributed to Israel during the last decade constitute particular examples of *mabam* in action. Adamsky, "From Israel with Deterrence"; Inbar and Shamir, "Mowing the Grass."

4. David Rothkopf, "Current and Former U.S. Officials Say the U.S. and NATO Have Plenty of Resources at Their Disposal Without Having to Resort to the Nuclear Option," Daily Beast, April 19, 2022.

5. Western experts took notice of additional activities aimed at increasing the survivability and readiness of the Russian nuclear triad, qualifying them as standard wartime operational procedures. For examples see Kristin Ven Bruusgaard, "Understanding Putin's Nuclear Decision-Making," *War on the Rocks*, March 22, 2022.

6. An inclination to deter by ambiguity is evident in Putin's figure of speech about the red lines being defined ad hoc in every strategic episode. Such an approach lets competitors know that a tripwire triggering an explosion exists, but makes them guess about its exact whereabouts in each situation. "Poslanie Prezidenta Federalnomu Sobraniiu," kremlin.ru, April 21, 2021.

7. Similarly, no consensus seems to exist in the West on Russian deterring damage criteria (*sderzhivaiuschii ushcerb*). If Moscow crosses the nuclear threshold, what extent of damage infliction does it see as sufficing to de-escalate aggression and shape Western strategic choices? Apparently, the Russian defense and military communities are debating this as well.

8. https://www.youtube.com/watch?v=T6mw9U62ZJU; https://www.youtube.com/watch?app=desktop&v=VlMLBlEKS6c.

9. For example, see V. V. Kruglov and A. S. Shubin, "O vozrastaiuschem znachenii uprezhdeniia v deistviiakh," *VM*, no. 12 (December 2021): 27–34; V. V. Selivanov and Iu. D. Il'in, "Kontesptsiia voenno-tekhnicheskogo assimetrichnogo otveta po sderzhivaniiu veroiatnogo protivnika ot razviazivaniia voennykh konfliktov," *VM*, no. 2 (February 2022): 31–47; V. B. Zarudnitskii, "Faktory dostizheniia pobedy v voennykh konfliktah budusschego," *VM*, no. 8 (August 2021): 34–47; A. A. Bartosh, "Sderzhivanie I prinuzhdenie v strategii gibridnoi voiny," *VM*, no. 9 (September 2021).

10. It also has intellectual sources in the Tsarist and Soviet traditions, often under the rubric of surprise strike (*vnezapnoe napadenie/udar*). Russian experts who popularize

prevention in contemporary operations acknowledge that it corresponds with such "principles of military art" as "seizure of initiative, decisiveness, activism and continuity of action, surprise and military cunningness (deceit of adversary)." Kruglov and Shubin, *VM*, December 2021.

11. Kruglov and Shubin, *VM*, December 2021.

12. Selivanov and Il'in, *VM*, February 2022.

13. Military experts designate hypersonic air- and naval-based precision-guided missiles as the most effective tool for preventive strikes (*oruzhie uprezhdaiuschikh udarov*) and call for establishing a new form of operations—preventive strategic strike (*strategicheskii udar*) (i.e., missile air-naval preventive strike). Authors refer to the Avantgard, Sarmat, Tsikron, Kinzhal, and Paseidon hypersonic cruise and ballistic missiles as the main tools of such a strike. Selivanov and Il'in, *VM*, February 2022.

14. Kruglov and Shubin, *VM*, December 2021.

15. Selivanov and Il'in, *VM*, February 2022.

16. In particular, this refers to "repulsion of aero-space aggression," "strike on critical infrastructure," and "unified strategic operation on the theater of military operations."

17. Kruglov and Shubin, *VM*, 2021; Selivanov and Il'in, *VM*, February 2022.

18. Apparently, this refers to warning about adversarial preparations for attack, rather than an alarm to enable "launch on warning" when the enemy strike is on its way.

19. The notion of a *tekhnosfera* appears to be a general rubric under which ideas on the impact of emerging technologies on strategy have been discussed. A. A. Kokoshin, "Perspektivy razvtiia nauchnoi tekhnosfery I budushee voin I neboevogo primenenia voennoi sily," *Vestnik AVN* 67, no. 2 (2019): 26–29.

20. For example see V. A. Kovtun, D. P. Supotnitskii, and N. I. Shilo, "Siriiskaia Khimicheskaia Voina," *Vestnik RKhBZ* 2, no. 3 (2018): 7–39; V. A. Kovtun, A. N. Golipal, and A. V. Melnikov, "Khimicheskii terrorizm kak silovoi instrument provedeniia vneshnei politiki SShA I stran Zapada," *Vestnik Voisk RHBZ* 1, no. 2 (2017): 12–13; A. Ordin, "Rossiiskaia diplomatiia I problema khimicheskogo oruzhiia," *Vestnik uchenykh mezhdunarodnikov* 3, no. 17 (2021): 22–32; S. Koshelev and V. Sumenkov, "Napravleniia sovershenstvovaniia radiatsionnoi, khimicheskoi I biologicheskoi zaschiti v sovremennykh usloviiakh," *Voennaia Mysl'*, no. 1 (2022): 108–20; R. P. Koshkin, "Ugroza primeneniia khimicheskogo I biologicheskogo oruzhiia," *Strategicheskie Prioritety* 18, no. 2 (2018): 25–39.

21. For example see V. Moiseev, "Oruzhie neletal'nogo deistviia kak sredstvo voenno-silovogo vozdeistviia (kompleksnogo porazheniia protivnika), *Voennaia Mysl'*, no. 11 (2021): 41–48; A. Zaitsev, "Novyi mirovoi poriadok kak istoricheskaia neobkhodimost' I ispol'zvonaie oruzhiia neletal'nogo deistviia," *Trudy BGTU: Istoriia I Filosophia* 1, no. 245 (2012): 107–11; D. V. Zaitsev, A. V. Kozlov, and V. M. Moiseev, "Rol' i mesto oruzhiia neletal'nogo deistviia v konflitkah nizkoi intensivnosti," *Strategicheskaia Stabil'nost'* 4, no. 61 (2012): 27–35; L. N. Il'in and V. V. Rylin, "O nekotorykh aspektakh primimenniia otravliaiuschikh veschestv neletal'nogo deistviia," *Voennaia Mysl'*, no. 12 (2018): 87–91; D. Iu. Soskov, S. F. Sergeev, and D. V. Zaitsev, "Primenenie oruzhiia neletal'nogo deistviia v usloviiakh vnutrennego vooruzhennogo konflikta," *Voennaia*

Mysl', no. 4 (2018): 55–61; D. Soskov, D. Zaitsev, V. Kornilov, and E. Lozhkin, "Oruzhie neletelnogo deistviia," *Arsenal Otechestva* 55, no. 5 (2021): 70–74; V. V. Selivanov, D. P Levin, and Iu. D. Il'in, "Metodologicheskie voprosy razvitiia oruzhiia neletalnogo deistviia," *Voennaia Mysl'*, no. 2 (2015): 10–22; L. N. Il'in and V. V. Rylin, "Inkapasitanty kak oruzhie neletalnogo deistviia," *Voennaia Mysl'*, no. 9 (2014): 37–42; A. A. Kuz'min, E. V. Ivchenko, and A. B Seleznev, "Irritanty: sovremennoe pereosmyslenie aktual'nosti dlia VS I perspektivy sozdaniia medetsinskih sredstv zaschiti," *Vestnik Rossiiskoi Voenno-Medetsinskoi Akademii* 3, no. 71 (2020): 188–93; N. V. Kurdil' and A. V. Ivaschenko, "Sovremennye boevye khimicheskie sredstva nesmertel'nogo deistviia: toksikologicheskie I klinicheskie aspekty," *Medetsina neotlozhnykh sostoianii* 1, no. 64 (2015): 11–19; V. B. Antipov, and S. V. Novichkov, "Otsenka normativno-pravovoi bazy primeneniia VS RF neletal'nykh sredstv porazheniia na khimicheskoi osnove," *Voennaia Mysl'*, no. 5 (2012): 56–60.

22. "Zasedanie Soveta Bezopasnosti," kremlin.ru, March 26, 2021.

23. Bartosh, 2018; Podberezkin, 2017; A. I. Vladimirov, *Osnovy obschei teorii voiny* (Moscow: Sinergiia, 2013), 1, 49. This framing is somewhat similar to the Western notion of "great-power competition." However, the Russian expression is deeper and broader than the Western term, which implicitly refers to the current geopolitical competition of the U.S. with the incumbent regimes in Moscow and Beijing. This term is usually absent from the lexicon of the Russian practitioners. See "Why Isn't Russia Talking About the Great Power Competition?" Carnegie Endowment for International Peace, May 27, 2021; Bartosh, 2018, 8. Russian defense experts emphasize the work of Samuel Huntington to illustrate the essence of the current great-power competition and to justify adjustments in the art of military strategy. For example, see Vladimirov, 2019; Podberezkin, 2017, 412–13. See similar assertions on the societal aspect of modern warfare in Suchkov and Teck, 23.

24. Bartosh, *Strategicheskaia kul'tura*.

25. Bartosh, 2018, 15–17. For an illustration of this approach in the Middle East, see E. O. Savchenko, "Specifika primeneniia isntrumentov vneshnepoliticheskoi strategii SShA na Blizhnem Vostoke," *VM* (December 2018): 5–17.

26. A. I. Podberezkin, *Sovremennaia Voennaia Politika Rossii* (Moscow: MGIMO, 2017), 373–588.

27. I. M. Popov and M. M. Khazmatov, *Voina Buduschego: Kontseptual'nye Osnovy I Prakticjhecheskie Vovody* (Moscow: Kuchkovo Pole, 2016), 832–33; Podberzkin, 2017, 386–87. For the "moral-spiritual" decomposition of the armed forces, see Maxim Suchkov and Seam Teck, *Buduschie Voiny* (Moscow: Valdaiskii Kluv, 2019), 10; V. T. Dotsenko, "Psihologicheskaia gotovnsot' voennosluzhaschikh," *VM*, no. 1 (2019): 87–99; L. A. Kolosova, A. A. Tomilov, R. B. Beliaev, and A. E. Sergienko, "Moral'no-psihologicheskoe obespechenie deiatel'nosti voisk v boevykh usloviiakh kak sistema," *VM*, no. 2 (2019): 79–86; Bartosh, "Strategiia i kontr-strategiia."

28. *Doktrina informatzionnoi bezopasnosti RF*, December 5, 2016; A. V. Skrypnik, "O Vozmozhnom Podkhode k Opredeleniyu i Mesta Oruzhiya Napravlennoi Elektromagnitnoi Energii v Mekhanizme Silovogo Strategicheskogo Sderzhivanya,"

Vooruzhenia I Ekonomika 3, no. 19 (2012), cited in Dave Johnson, "Russia's Deceptive Nuclear Policy," *Survival* 63, no. 3 (July 2021): 123–42; Dave Johnson, correspondence, June 2021. Also see Maxim Suchkov, "Whose Hybrid Warfare?" *Small Wars and Insurgencies* 32, no. 3 (2021).

29. Editorial, "Sovetnik Shoigu zaiavil o mental'oi voine SShA protiv Rossii," *Kommersant*, March 25, 2021; Editorial, "Psikhologicheskaia Oborona: informatsionnoe protivoborstvo v usliikh mental'noi voiny," *Forum Army 2021*, MO RF, August 2021.

30. Dmitry (Dima) Adamsky, *Russian Nuclear Orthodoxy: Religion, Politics and Strategy* (Stanford, CA: Stanford University Press, 2019); Michael Kofman, "Blessed Be Thy Nuclear Weapons: The Rise of Russian Nuclear Orthodoxy," *War on the Rocks*, June 21, 2019; Nikolas Gvosdev, "How the ROC Influences Russia's Behavior," *National Interest*, July 8, 2019; Suchkov, 2021.

31. The ROC is providing moral support and justification for the Kremlin's strategy and operations and boosting the troops' morale. Dmitry Adamsky, "Russia Botched Its Early Propaganda Campaign," *Foreign Policy*, April 30, 2022.

32. Dmitry (Dima) Adamsky, "Russian Orthodox Church and Nuclear Command and Control: A Hypothesis," *Security Studies* 28, no. 5 (2019). Also see Boris Knorre and Aleksei Zygmont, "Military Piety in the 21st Century Orthodox Christianity: Return to Classical Traditions of Formation of a New Theology of War?" *Religions* 11, no. 2 (2020): 1–17.

33. Mihail Suslov, "The Utopia of Holy Rus' in Today's Geopolitical Imagination," *Plural* 2, no. 1 (2014): 81–97; Dmitrii Sidorov, "Post-Imperial Third Rome," *Geopolitics* 1 (2006): 317–47; Jardar Ostbo, *The New Third Rome* (Stuttgart: Ibidem Press, 2016).

34. Zhanna Neigebaur, "Korni Rossiiskogo Atomnogo Pravoslaviia," *Discourse*, August 20, 2019; Marlene Laruelle, *Russian Nationalism* (New York: Routledge, 2019); Maria Engstrom, "Contemporary Russian Messianism," *Contemporary Security Policy* 35, no. 3, (2014): 365–79; "Contemporary Russian Messianism," in Lena Jonson and Andrei Erofeev, eds., *Russia-Art Resistance and the Conservative-Authoritarian Zeitgeist* (New York: Routledge, 2017); Nadezhda Arbatova, "Three Faces of Russia's Neo-Eurasianism," *Survival* 61, no. 6 (2019).

35. Editorial, "Aggressors Will Be Annihilated," *Moscow Times*, October 19, 2018; "Putin otvetil na vopros o blizosti k raiu," *RIA Novosti*, October 3, 2019. Milena Faustova and Andrei Mel'nikov, "Torzhestvo Iadernogo Pravolsaviia Otkladivaiut na Osen'," *NG Religii*, May 31, 2021. Also see Pavel Korobov, "Miry Miro: V RPTs Razrabotiali Dokument o Blagoslovlenii Voennykh I Ikh Oruzhiia," *Kommersant*, June 1, 2021.

36. "Krym imeet dlia Rossii sakral'noe znachenie," *RIA Novosti*, December 4, 2014.

37. Marlene Laruelle, "Russia's Mediterranean Call," *ODR*, November 9, 2018; Curanovic, 2018; "Pravo pervim podniatsia v ataku."

38. David Lewis, *Russia's New Authoritarianism: Putin and the Politics of Order* (Edinburgh: Edinburgh University Press, 2020).

39. Marlene Laruelle, *Is Russia Fascist? Unraveling Propaganda East and West* (Ithaca, NY: Cornell University Press, 2021); Paul Robinson, *Russian Conservatism* (DeKalb:

Northern Illinois University Press, 2019); Glenn Diesen, *Russian Conservatism: Managing Change under Permanent Revolution* (Lanham, MD: Rowman and Littlefield, 2021).

40. Jeffrey Mankoff, *Empires of Eurasia: How Imperial Legacies Shape International Security* (New Haven, CT: Yale University Press, 2021).

41. Alicija Curanovic, *The Sense of Mission in Russian Foreign Policy* (London: Routledge, 2021); Maria Engstrom, "Contemporary Russian Messianism and New Russian Foreign Policy," *Contemporary Security Policy* 35, no. 3 (2014): 356–79.

42. Maria Engstrom argues that "Russia's eschatological mission, as expressed through the concept of Russia as katechon/restrainer," was formulated in neoconservative circles in the early 2000s by Aleksandr Dugin and Egor Kholmogorov. According to this doctrine, Russia's mission to protect the world from evil must be carried out by any means—military, spiritual, and cultural. Maria Engstrom, "Daughter-Land: Contemporary Russian Messianism and Neo-conservative Visually," in Lena Jonson and Andrei Eorfeev, eds., *Russia-Art Resistance and the Conservative-Authoritarian Zeitgeist* (London: Routledge, 2017), 84–103. Also see Engstrom, 2014. One indication of the omnipresence of religion in politics may be the fact that church-state relations have turned into one of the most serious cleavages and deepest dividing lines in Russian society. Dmitry Uzlaner, "Konets pravolsavnogo konsensusa: religiia kak novyo raskol rossiiskogo obschestva," *Novoe literaturnoe obozrenie* 3, no. 163 (2020).

43. Some of the sources of this activism have been unrelated to national security. Driven by an internal social-political interest to increase the numbers of practicing males (over the diminishing but still female majority of the ROC congregations), the ROC during the last decades has been intentionally emphasizing "normative masculinity in the Orthodox environment." Boris Knorre, "Masculine Strategies in Russian Orthodoxy: From Asceticism to Militarization," in K. Bluhm, G. Pickhan, J. Stypesnka, and A. Wierzchloska, eds., *Gender and Power in Eastern Europe* (London: Springer, 2020).

44. Scholars attribute this martyrdom fetish to "the post-atheist vacuum," which the depoliticized and de-ideologized military has been seeking to fill. For example, see Elina Kahla, "Why Did the Seamen Have to Die? The Kursk Tragedy and the Evoking of Old Testament Blood Sacrifice," in Katri Pynnoniemi, ed., *Nexus of Patriotism and Militarism in Russia* (Helsinki: Helsinki University Press, 2021). Dmitry (Dima) Adamsky, "Christ-Loving Warriors: Ecclesiastical Dimension of the Russian Military Campaign in Syria," *Problems of Post-Communism* (2019); "Christ-Loving Diplomats: Russian Ecclesiastical Diplomacy in Syria," *Survival* 61, no. 6 (January 2020): 49–68.

45. Adamsky, 2022.

46. Jacub Grygiel, "Russia's Orthodox Grand Strategy," *American Interest*, April 2020; Govsdev, 2019; Brad Roberts, "The Bishops and the Bomb, Take Two," Jon Askonas, "The ROC and the Russian Nuclear Complex," Irina do Quenoy, "Getting Comfortable with Russian Nuclear Orthodoxy," and Anya Fink, "Rhinestone Covered Icons at Russia's Los Alamos," in *Book Review Roundtable, TNSR*, September 18, 2019; James Sher and Kaarel Kullamaa, "The Russian Orthodox Church: Faith, Power, and Conquest," Estonian Foreign Policy Institute, 2019; Alicja Curanovic, *The Religious Factor in Russia's Foreign Policy* (London: Routledge, 2012).

47. Olga Oliker, "Moving Beyond Russian Nuclear Orthodoxy," in *Book Review Roundtable, TNSR*, September 18, 2019.

48. Clint Reach, Russia Seminar, Finnish National Defense University, February 2, 2021, https://www.youtube.com/watch?v=3vouTxigJ_c&t=695s.

49. Maxim Suchkov, "Iadernoe Pravoslavie v voine buduschego," *Rossiia V Global'noi Politike*, July 5, 2019.

50. Andreas Wenger and Alex Wilner, *Deterring Terrorism: Theory and Practice* (Stanford, CA: Stanford University Press, 2012); Alex Wilner, "Deterring the Undeterrable," *Journal of Strategic Studies* 34, no. 1 (2011): 3–37; Emanuel Adler, "Complex Deterrence in the Asymmetric-Warfare Era," in Paul, Morgan, and Wirtz, eds., *Complex Deterrence*; Shmuel Barr, "Religion in War in the 21st Century," *Comparative Strategy* 39, no. 5 (2020): 443–74; "God, Nations, and Deterrence: The Impact of Religion on Deterrence," *Comparative Strategy* 30, no. 5 (2011): 428–52.

51. Roseanne W. McManus, "Revisiting the Madman Theory," *Security Studies* 28, no. 5 (2019): 976–1009.

52. Thomas Mahnken and Gillian Evans, "Ambiguity, Risk and Limited Great Power Conflict," *Strategic Studies Quarterly* (Winter 2019): 57–76; Dave Johnson, 2021.

53. There have been outbreaks of wartime and peacetime brutality in Russian, Soviet, and Tsarist military history. In some of these cases the political leadership and military command initiated the atrocities. In other cases they deliberately utilized the incipient brutality to intimidate and coerce. Early Soviet experiences include the Red and White Terrors during the Civil War, the suppression of peasants' anti-Bolshevik rebellions, followed by deportations and massive repression toward, during, and after the Great Patriotic War. These were acts of deliberate coercion. Innumerable incidents of rape and looting were reported, especially when the Red Army crossed the border into German territory. These were grassroots outbreaks, which the commanders decided not to stop. In more recent times, there have been documented examples of Russian brutality in Afghanistan, the Caucasus, and Chechnya. However, the extent to which these were ordered from above or rather originated on the ground is a matter of debate. Similarly, there is a debate whether or not the leadership exploited this for coercive purposes. Nazi Germany possessed separate doctrines and separate military organizations for fighting and for punitive operations. It was the Wehrmacht that mainly executed the fighting, and it was the Einsatzgruppen that mainly conducted atrocities, although the missions of both organizations at times were interchangeable.

54. See for example Trenin and Lukianov, *Russia in Global Affairs*, April 2022.

55. The taxonomy of approaches usually features in the Russian discourse according to the archetypes, which they dub Anglo-Saxon (mainly equated with the U.S.), East-Asian (mainly equated with the Chinese), Roman-German (mainly that of continental Europe), and Islamic. A. V. Manoilo, *Rol' Kul'turno-Tsivilizatsionnykh Modelei I Tekhnologii Informatsionno-Psikhologicheskogo Vozdeistviia v Razreshenii Mezhdunarodnykh Konfliktov* (PhD diss., MGU, 2009).

56. For example, see Timoti Tomas,"Kontseptsia kiber/informatsionnogo sderzhivaniia KNR: Mnenie iz SShA," *Digital Report*, July 27, 2015. For the Western take on the

Chinese approach, see Dean Cheng, "An Overview of Chinese Thinking about Deterrence," in *Deterrence in the 21ˢᵗ Century*.

57. According to the Russian sources, *veishe*, as a term referring to coercion in all of its forms, is much older and richer than the Western analogue in terms of practical experience. S. A. Sebekin and A. V. Kostrov, "Voennaia filosofia Kitaia I kibervoina: traditsionnaia kontseptual'naia osnova dlia netraditsionnykh operatsii," *Mezhdunarodnye Ontosheniia* 17, no. 3 (2019).

58. In the Russian conceptualization of informational deterrence, the focus is shifting away from the political leadership to political elites and society, its culture, values, and mentality. "Denial and resilience" are attributed the same importance as "punishment." Finally, "deterrence of everything," a buzzword associated with this wave, somewhat corresponds with the Russian concept of "strategic deterrence." The latter is holistic, as it seeks to encompass the widest range of domains and tools of influence.

59. Amr Yussuf, "Military Doctrines in Israel and Iran: A Doctrinal Hybridity," *Middle Eastern Journal* (forthcoming). Also see Guy Freedman, "Iranian Approach to Deterrence: Theory and Practice," *Comparative Strategy* 36, no. 5 (2017): 400–412; Shamir and Inbar, "Mowing the Grass," 2017; Adamsky, "From Israel with Deterrence," 2017.

60. S. A. Sebekin and A. V. Kostrov, "Voennaia filosofia Kitaia I kibervoina: traditsionnaia kontseptual'naia osnova dlia netraditsionnykh operatsii," *Mezhdunarodnye Ontosheniia* 17, no. 3 (2019.

CONCLUSION

1. For the recent caveats, uncertainties, and relative incoherence in the Russian deterrence theory and escalation management doctrine, see Lukas Milevski, "Russia's Escalation Management and a Baltic Nuclear-Weapon Free Zone," *Orbis* (Winter 2022): 95–110.

2. Bartosh, *VM*, September 2021. There have been Russian references to "compellence to peace" (*prinuzhdenie k miru*) since the 2008 Georgia war.

3. At times, deterrence *à la Russe* comes across as what Moscow does to be respected. This at once resembles "general deterrence" and the scholarship on "prestige" and "honor," which views the latter as the main currency in world politics. For example, see Andrei P. Tsygankov, *Russia and the West from Alexander to Putin: Honor in International Relations* (Cambridge: Cambridge University Press, 2012); Jonathan Mercer, "The Illusion of International Prestige," *International Security* 41, no. 4 (2017): 133–68. For the examples of Russian academic works that illustrate this "deterrence of everything" inclination and "prestige" and "honor" tendency, see Podberezkin, *Strategicheskoe Sderzhivanie: Novii Trend* (Moscow: MGIMO, 2019 and 2017). I am thankful to the anonymous reviewer for drawing my attention to this argument.

BIBLIOGRAPHY

Adair, Paul. *Maskirovka (Deception): Hitler's Greatest Defeat*. London: Rigel and Cassell, 2004.

Adamsky, Dmitry (Dima). "The Art of Net Assessment and Uncovering Foreign Military Innovations: Learning from Andrew Marshall's Legacy." *Journal of Strategic Studies* 43, no. 5 (2020): 611–44.

———. "Christ-Loving Diplomats: Russian Ecclesiastical Diplomacy in Syria." *Survival* 61, no. 6 (2019): 49–68.

———. "Christ-Loving Warriors: Ecclesiastical Dimension of the Russian Military Campaign in Syria." *Problems of Post-Communism* 67, no. 6 (2019): 433–45.

———. *Cross-Domain Coercion: The Current Russian Art of Strategy*. Paris: IFRI, 2015.

———. *The Culture of Military Innovation: The Impact of Cultural Factors on Revolution in Military Affairs in Russia, the US and Israel*. Stanford, CA: Stanford University Press, 2010.

———. "Discontinuity in Russian Strategic Culture? A Case Study of Mission Command Practice." *Marshall Center Security Insight*, no. 49 (February 2020).

———. "From Israel with Deterrence: Strategic Culture, Intra-war Coercion and Brute Force." *Security Studies* 26, no. 1 (2017): 157–84.

———. "From Moscow with Coercion: Russian Deterrence Theory and Strategic Culture." *Journal of Strategic Studies* 41, no. 1–2 (2018): 33–60.

———. *Moscow's Syria Campaign: Russian Lessons for the Art of Strategy*. Paris: IFRI, 2018.

———. "The 1983 Nuclear Crisis–Lessons for Deterrence Theory and Practice." *Journal of Strategic Studies* 36, no. 1 (2013): 4–41.

———. "Nuclear Incoherence: Deterrence Theory and Non-Strategic Nuclear Weapons in Russia." *Journal of Strategic Studies* 37, no. 1 (2014): 91–134.

———. *Operation Kavkaz*. Tel Aviv: Maarachot, 2006.

———. "Russia Botched Its Early War Propaganda Campaign, but Now It's Doubling Down." *Foreign Policy*, April 30, 2022.

———. "Russian Campaign in Syria: Change and Continuity in Strategic Culture." *Journal of Strategic Studies* 43, no. 1 (2019): 104–25.

———. *Russian Nuclear Orthodoxy: Religion, Politics and Strategy*. Stanford, CA: Stanford University Press, 2019.

———. "Russian Orthodox Church and Nuclear Command and Control: A Hypothesis." *Security Studies* 28, no. 5 (2019): 1010–39.

———. "Strategic Culture." In John Baylis, James Wirtz, and Jeannie Johnson, eds., *Strategy in the Contemporary World.* Oxford: Oxford University Press, 2022.

———. "Through the Looking Glass: The Soviet MTR and the American RMA." *Journal of Strategic Studies* 31, no. 2 (2008): 257–94.

———. "Unintended Escalation: Five Lessons from Israel for the Russia-NATO Standoff." *Harvard Russia Matters*, February 14, 2018.

———. "Vliianie Idei Marshala Ograkova na Zapadnuiu Voennuiu Mysl." *Annual Ogarkov Readings.* Moscow: CAST, 2019. https://www.youtube.com/watch?v=EJ3orZ2-UUU&t=222s.

Adler, Emanuel. "Complex Deterrence in the Asymmetric-Warfare Era." In T. V. Paul, Patrick M. Morgan, and James J. Wirtz, eds., *Complex Deterrence: Strategy in the Global Age.* Chicago: University of Chicago Press, 2009.

Ahmadian, Hassan, and Payam Mohseni. "Iran's Syria Strategy: The Evolution of Deterrence." In Frans Osinga and Tim Swejis, eds., *Deterrence in the 21st Century: Insights from Theory and Practice.* The Hague: Springer and Asser Press, 2021.

Aksenov, O., Iu Tret'jakov, and E. Filin. "Osnovnye Principi Sozdaniia Sistemy Ocenki Tekucshego I Prognoziruemogo Uscherba." *Voennaia Mysl'*, no. 6 (2015): 68–74.

Almog, Doron. "Cumulative Deterrence and the War on Terrorism." *Parameters* 34, no. 4 (2004): 4–19.

Andrew, Christopher, and Vasilly Mitrokhin. *The KGB in Europe and in the West.* New York: Basic Books, 2000.

———. *The World Was Going Our Way: The KGB and the Battle for the Third World.* New York: Basic Books, 2005.

Andrianov, Yu. M., and A. I. Subetto. *Kvalimietriia v Priborostroenii i Mashinostrenii.* Leningrad: Mashinostroenie, 1990.

Anokhin, V. A., D. V. Kholuenko, and N. M. Gromyko. "Otsenka Effektivnosti Dezorganizattsii Informatsionno-upravliaiuschikh System Operativnykh I Taktichek-sikh Formirovanii Protivnika." *Vestnik AVN*, no. 3 (2019): 69–73.

Antipov, V. B., and S. V. Novichkov. "Otsenka normativno-pravovoi bazy primeneniia VS RF neletal'nykh sredstv porazheniia na khimicheskoi osnove." *Voennaia Mysl'*, no. 5 (2012): 56–60.

Anokhin, V. A., G. D. Vistorobskii, D. V. Kholuenko, and N. M. Gromyko. "Otsenka Boesposobnosti VF s uchetom effektivnosti dezorganizatsii upravleniia." *Voennaia Mysl'*, no. 12 (2019): 48–56.

Antczak, Anna. "Russian Strategic Culture: Prisoner of Imperial History?" *Polish Political Science Studies* 60 (2018): 233–42.

Arbatov, A. G. "Oboronnaia Dostatochnost' i Bezopasnsot'." *Znanie*, no. 4 (1990).

Alexey Arbatov. "Iadernyi Potolok." *VPK*, July 21, 2014.

———. "Zdravyi Smysl i Razoryzhenie." *Rossiia v Global'noi Politike*, no. 4 (July/August 2010).

Arbatova, Nadezhda. "Three Faces of Russia's Neo-Eurasianism." *Survival* 61, no. 6 (2019): 7–24.

Arkhangelskii, V. "Oblomovschina." In *Literaturnaia Entsiklopedia* (Moscow: Sovets-kaia Entsiklopedia, 1934), 165–72.

Arquilla, John. *Bitskreig: The New Challenge of Cyberwarfare.* London: Wiley, 2021.

Askonas, Jon. "The ROC and the Russian Nuclear Complex." In *Book Review Round-table: Russian Nuclear Orthodoxy.* TNSR, 2019.

Baev, Pavel. "Russia Absent from North Korean Crisis." *EDM* 14, no. 53 (April 24, 2017).

———. "Threat Assessments and Strategic Objectives in Russia's Arctic Policy." *Journal of Slavic Military Studies* 32, no. 1 (2019): 25–40.

———. *Transformation of Russian Strategic Culture: Impact from Local Wars and Global Confrontation.* Paris: IFRI, 2020.

Balybin, V. A. "Zavoevanie Prevoskhodstva nad Protivnikom v Upravlenii Primenitel'no k Operatsii (boiu)." *Voennaia Mysl'*, no. 3 (2016): 3–8.

Bar-Joseph, Uri. "A Chance Not Taken: Sadat's Peace Initiative of February 1973 and Its Rejection by Israel." *Journal of Contemporary History* 41, no. 3 (2006): 545–56.

———. *The Watchman Fell Asleep.* Albany: SUNY Press, 2012.

Barr, Shmuel. "God, Nations, and Deterrence: The Impact of Religion on Deterrence." *Comparative Strategy* 30, no. 5 (2011): 428–52.

———. "Religion in War in the 21st Century." *Comparative Strategy* 39, no. 5 (2020): 443–74.

Barrass, Gordon. *The Great Cold War.* Stanford, CA: Stanford University Press, 2008.

Bartosh, A. A. "Novoe Izmerenie Gibtidnoi Voiny." *Nezavisimoye Voyennoye Obozreniye*, no. 18 (2020).

———. "Sderzhivanie I Prinuzhdenie v Strategii Gibridnoi Voiny." *Voennaia Mysl'*, no. 9 (2021): 18–34.

———. "Strategiia I Kontrstrategiia Gibridnoi Voiny." *Voennaia Mysl'*, no. 10 (2018): 5–21.

Bathurst, Robert. *Intelligence and the Mirror: On Creating an Enemy.* New York: Sage, 1993.

Becker, Jordan, and Edmund Malesky. "The Continent of the Grand Large? Strategic Culture and Operational Burden Sharing in NATO." *International Studies Quarterly* 61, no. 1 (2017): 163–80.

Beevor, Antony. *Stalingrad.* London: Penguin, 1999.

Bekkevold, Jo Inge, Ian Bowers, and Michael Raska, eds. *Security Strategy and Military Change in the 21st Century: Cross-Regional Perspectives.* London: Routeldge, 2015.

Berger, Thomas. *Cultures of Antimilitarism: National Security in Germany and Japan.* Baltimore: Johns Hopkins University Press, 1998.

Berlin, Isaiah. *The Soviet Mind.* Washington, DC: Brookings Institution, 2004.

Biehl, Heiko, Bastian Giegerich, and Alexandra Jonas, eds. *Strategic Cultures in Europe.* Berlin: Springer, 2013.

Bloomfield, Alan. "Time to Move On: Re-conceptualizing the Strategic Culture Debate." *Comparative Security Policy* 33. no. 3 (2012): 437–61.

Bogdanov, S. A., and V. N. Gorbunov. "O Kharaktere Vooruzhennoi Bor'by v XXI Veke." *Voennaia Mysl'*, no. 3 (2009): 2–15.

Bogdanov, S. A., and L. V. Zakharov. "O Vyrabotke Edinykh Podkhodov k Otsenke Boevykh Potentsialov Vooruzhenii." *Voennaia Mysl'*, nos. 8–9 (1992): 42–49.

Bonin, A. S., and G. I. Gorchitsa. "Eche Raz o Boevykh Potentsialakh Obraztsov VVT, Formirovanii i Sootnosheniiakh Sil Gruppirovok Storon." *Voennaia Mysl'*, no. 4 (2010): 61–67.

Borozna, Angela. *The Sources of Russian Foreign Policy Assertiveness*. Basingstoke, UK: Palgrave Macmillan, 2022.

Bowen, Andrew. "Coercive Diplomacy and the Donbas: Explaining Russian Strategy in Eastern Ukraine." *Journal of Strategic Studies* 42, nos. 3–4 (2019): 312–43.

Bowen, Andrew, and Cory Welt. *Russia: Foreign Policy and U.S. Relations*. Washington, DC: CRS, 2021.

Bracken, Paul. *The Second Nuclear Age: Strategy, Danger, and the New Power Politics*. New York: St. Martin's Griffin, 2013.

Brezgin, V. S., and A. I. Buravlev. "O Metodologii Otsenki Boevykh Potentsialov Tekhniki i Voinskikh Formirovanii." *Voennaia Mysl'*, no. 8 (2010).

Bruusgaard, Kristin Ven. "Russian Concept of Deterrence." In *Russia Seminar*, Finnish National Defense University, January 2021. https://www.youtube.com/watch?v=Kl-v5SJjKuw.

———. "Russian Nuclear Strategy and Conventional Inferiority." *Journal of Strategic Studies* 44, no. 1 (2021): 3–35.

———. "Russian Strategic Deterrence." *Survival* 58, no. 4 (2016): 7–26.

———. "Understanding Putin's Nuclear Decision-Making." *War on the Rocks*, March 22, 2022.

Bunn, Elaine. *Can Deterrence Be Tailored?* Strategic Forum no. 225. Institute for National Strategic Studies, National Defense University, February 2007.

Burenok, V. M. "Informatsionnoe Protivoborstvo I Neiadernoe Sderzhivanie." *Zaschita I Bezopasnost'*, no. 3 (2008).

Burenok, V. M., and O. B. Achasov. "Neiadernoe Sderzhivanie." *Voennaia Mysl'*, no. 12 (2007): 12–16.

Burenok, V. M., and Iu. A. Pechatnov. "O Kriterial'nykh Osnovakh Iadernogo Sderzhivaniia." *Vooruzhenie I Ekonomika* 1, no. 22 (2013).

———. *Strategicheskoe Sderzhivanie*. Moscow: Granitsa, 2010.

Burenok, V. M., Iu. A. Pechatnov, and R. G. Tagirov. "K Voprosu ob Opredelenii Urovnei Nepriemlemosti Posledstvij pri Reshenii Zadachi Silovogo Strategicheskogo Sderzhivanija." *Vestnik AVN* 26, no. 1 (2009): 44–49.

Charap, Samuel. *Everyone Loses: The Ukraine Crisis and the Ruinous Contest for Post-Soviet Eurasia*. London: Routledge, 2017.

———. "Expanding the Scope for Statecraft in U.S. Russia Policy." *WOTR*, May 2021.

———. "Moscow's Calibrated Coercion in Ukraine and Russian Strategic Culture." *Marshall Center Security Insights*, no. 63 (September 2020).

———. "Strategic Sderzhivanie: Understanding the Contemporary Russian Approach to Deterrence." *Marshall Center Security Insight*, no. 62 (September 2020).

Charap, Samuel, Andrew Stravers, John J. Drennan, Dara Massicot, Sean M. Zeigler, Gregory Weider Fauerbach, Mark Stalczynski, and Melissa Shostak. *Understanding Russian Coercive Signaling.* Santa Monica, CA: RAND, 2022.

Chausov, Fedor. "Osnovy Refleksivnogo Upravleniia." *Morskoi Sbornik*, no. 9 (1999).

Chekinov, S. G., and S. A. Bogdanov. "Vliianie Neprjamyh Dejstvij na Harakter Sovremennoj Vojny Nachal"nogo Perioda XXI Stoletija." *Voennaia Mysl'*, no. 6 (2011): 3–13.

Cheng, Dean. "An Overview of Chinese Thinking about Deterrence." In Frans Osinga and Tim Swejis, eds., *Deterrence in the 21st Century: Insights from Theory and Practice.* The Hague: Springer and Asser Press, 2021.

Chernenko, Elena. "Nam ne Nado Borotosia za Reputatsiiu." *Kommersant*, April 23, 2018.

———. "Vmesto Vstrechi Izmenit Nelzia: kak Sorvalis Rossiisko-Amerikanskie Peregovori po Kiberbezopasnosti." *Kommersant*, March 3, 2018.

Cohen, Eliot. *Supreme Command: Soldiers, Statesmen, and Leadership in Wartime.* New York: Anchor, 2003.

Covington, Stephen. "The Culture of Strategic Thought behind Russia's Modern Approaches to Warfare." *Harvard Belfer Papers*, October 2016.

Cubbage, Tom. "Strategic and Operational Deception." In Michael Handel, *War, Strategy and Intelligence.* London: Routledge, 2012.

Curanovic, Alicja. *The Religious Factor in Russia's Foreign Policy.* London: Routledge, 2012.

———. *The Sense of Mission in Russian Foreign Policy.* London: Routledge, 2021.

Dagi, Dogachan. "The Russian Stand on the Responsibility to Protect: Does Strategic Culture Matter?" *Journal of Asian Security and International Affairs* 7, no. 3 (2020): 370–86.

Dalgaard-Nielsen, Anja. "The Test of Strategic Culture: Germany, Pacifism and Preemptive Strikes." *Security Dialogue* 36, no. 3 (2005): 339–59.

Dalsjo, Robert, Michael Jonsson, and Johan Norberg. "A Brutal Examination: Russian Military Capability in Light of the Ukraine War." *Survival* 64, no. 3 (2022): 7–28.

Davis, Paul. *Effects Based Operations.* Washington, DC: RAND, 2002.

Deal, Jacqueline Newmyer. "China's Approach to Strategy and Long-Term Competition." In Thomas Mahnken, ed., *Competitive Strategies for the 21st Century.* Stanford, CA: Stanford University Press, 2012.

Diesen, Glenn. *Russian Conservatism: Managing Change under Permanent Revolution.* Lanham, MD: Rowman and Littlefield, 2021.

Dobroliubov, N. A. "Chto Takoe Oblomovschina?" *Otechestvennye Zapiski*, nos. I–IV (1895): 59–68.

Donnelly, Christopher N. *Red Banner: The Soviet Military System in Peace and War.* London: Jane's Information Group, 1988.

Donskov, Iu. E., and A. L. Moraresku. "K Voprosu o Formakh Primenenia Chastie I Podrazdezelenii REB." *Voennaia Mysl'*, no. 7 (2018): 101–8.

Dotsenko, V. T. "Psihologicheskaia Gotovnsot' Voennosluzhaschikh." *Voennaia Mysl'*, no. 1 (2019): 87–99.

Dylevskii, I. N., V. O. Zapivakhin, S. A. Komov, and A. A. Krivchenko. "O Dialektike Sderzhivaniia." *Voennaia Mysl'*, no. 7 (2016): 6–8.

Editorial. "Aggressors will be Annihilated." *Moscow Times*, October 19, 2018.

Editorial. "Komanduiuschego I Nachshtab Balflota Sniali za Priukrashivenie Deistvitel'nosti." *Lenta.ru*, June 29, 2016.

Editorial. "Krym Imeet Dlia Rossii Sakral'noe Znachenie." *RIA Novosti*, December 4, 2014.

Editorial. "My Podarili Protivniku Preimuschestvo v 15 Let." *Novaya Gazeta*, December 3, 2018.

Editorial. "Psikhologicheskaia Oborona: Informatsionnoe Protivoborstvo v Uslovijah Mental'noi Voiny." *Forum Army 2021*, MO RF, August 2021.

Editorial. "Putin Otvetil na Vopros o Blizosti k Raiu." *RIA Novosti*, October 3, 2019.

Editorial. "Sovetnik Shoigu Zaiavil o Mental'oi Voine SShA Protiv Rossii." *Kommersant*, March 25, 2021.

Eisenstadt, Michael. *The Strategic Culture of the Islamic Republic of Iran.* Washington, DC: Washington Institute, 2015.

Eitelhuber, Norbet. "The Russian Strategic Culture and What It Implies for the West." *Connections* 9, no. 1 (2009): 1–28.

Engstrom, Maria. "Contemporary Russian Messianism and New Russian Foreign Policy." *Contemporary Security Policy* 35, no. 3 (2014): 365–79.

———. "Contemporary Russian Messianism and Neo-conservative Visuality." In Lena Jonson and Andrei Erofeev, eds., *Russia-Art Resistance and the Conservative-Authoritarian Zeitgeist.* New York: Routledge, 2017.

Epstein, Mikhail. *Na Granitzakh Kultur.* New York: Slovo, 1995.

Ermarth, Fritz W. *Russia's Strategic Culture: Past, Present and Transition?* Fort Belvoir, VA: DTRA Press, 2006.

———. "Russian Strategic Culture in Flux: Back to the Future?" In Jeannie L. Johnson, Kerry M. Kartchner, and Jeffrey A. Larsen, eds., *Strategic Culture and Weapons of Mass Destruction: Culturally Based Insights into Comparative National Security Policymaking.* New York: Palgrave Macmillan, 2009.

Evan, Kerrane. "Moscow's Strategic Culture: Russian Militarism in an Era of Great Power Competition." *Journal of Advanced Military Studies* 1 (2022): 69–87.

Evangelista, Matthew. *Innovation and the Arms Race: How the US and the USSR Develop New Military Technologies.* Ithaca, NY: Cornell University Press, 1993.

Evsiukov, A. V., and A. L. Khriapin. "Rol' Novykh System Strategicheskih Vooruzhenii v Obespechenii Strategicheskogo Sderzhivaniia." *Voennaia Mysl'*, no. 12 (2020): 26–30.

Evstaf'ev, D. G., and A. M. Il'nitsky. "Prioritety Upravleniia Natsionalnoi Bezopasnost'iu v Usloviiakh Postglobalnogo Mira." *Voennaia Mysl'*, no. 3 (2021): 6–24.

Facon, Isabelle. "Russian Strategic Culture in the 21 Century." *Strategic Asia 2016–2017*, November 8, 2016.

Falkov, Yaacov. "Intelligence-Exalting Strategic Cultures: A Case Study of the Russian Approach." *Intelligence and National Security* 37, no. 1 (2022): 90–108.

———. "To Read Clausewitz in the KGB: Discovering Russian Concept of Culmination in Intelligence Operations." *Journal of Slavic Military Studies* 35, no. 1 (2022): 94–114.

———. "'Tried and Trusted Patriots for the CIA': Latvian Case Study of the KGB *Operativnaia Igra* Theory." *International Journal of Intelligence and CounterIntelligence* 36, no. 2 (2022): 41–62.

Farrell, Theo, and Terry Terriff, eds. *Sources of Military Change: Culture, Politics, Technology*. London: Lynne Rienner, 2002.

Farrell, Theo, Terry Terriff, and Frans Osinga, eds. *A Transformation Gap: American Innovations and European Military Change*. Stanford, CA: Stanford University Press, 2010.

Faustova, Milena, and Andrei Mel'nikov. "Torzhestvo Iadernogo Pravolsaviia Otkladivaiut na Osen'." *NG Religii*, May 31, 2021.

Fenenko, Aleksei. "Anti-miagkaia Sila v Politicheskoi Teorii." *Mezhdunarodnye Processy* 18, no. 1 (2020): 40–71.

———. "Between MAD and Flexible Response." *Russia in Global Affairs*, no. 2 (April/June 2011).

———. "Kakimi Budut Voiny Budushcego?" *RSMD*, July 19, 2017.

Fenenko, A. V., and V. A. Veselov. "Protivovozdushnaia Mosch' v Mirovoi Politike." *Mezhdunarodnie Processi* 17, no. 2 (2019): 47–69.

Fink, Anya. "On the Evolution of Damage in Russian Military Thought." *Russia Seminar*, January 26, 2021. https://www.youtube.com/watch?v=pzTm8Gh3wbo.

———. "Rhinestone Covered Icons at Russia's Los Alamos." In *Book Review Roundtable: Russian Nuclear Orthodoxy*. Austin, TX: TNSR, 2019.

Fink, Anya, and Michael Kofman. *Russian Strategy for Escalation Management: Key Debates and Players in Military Thought*. Washington, DC, 2020.

Freedman, Guy. "Iranian Approach to Deterrence: Theory and Practice." *Comparative Strategy* 36, no. 5 (2017): 400–412.

Freedman, Lawrence. *Deterrence*. Cambridge: Policy Press, 2004.

———. *The Politics of Command*. Oxford: Oxford University Press, 2022.

———. *Ukraine and the Art of Strategy*. Oxford: Oxford University Press, 2019.

Fridman, Ofer. "Russian Mindset and War: Between Westernizing the East and Easternizing the West." *Journal of Advanced Military Studies*, Special Issue on Strategic Culture, no. 1 (2022): 24–35.

Galeotti, Mark. *The Weaponizaiton of Everything: A Field Guide to the New Way of War*. New Haven, CT: Yale University Press, 2022.

Gareev, M. A. "Itogi Deiatel'nsoti AVN za 2008 i Zadachi Akademii na 2009 god." *Vestnik AVN* 26, no. 1 (2009).

———. "Strategicheskoe Sderzhivanie." *Strategicheskaia Stabil'nost'* 46, no. 1 (2009): 2–13.

———. "Voennaia Nauka na Sovremennom Etape." *VPK* 13, no. 481 (April 2013).

Gartzke, Erik, and Jon Lindsay, eds. *Cross-Domain Deterrence: Strategy in an Era of Complexity.* Oxford University Press, 2019.

Geist, Edward. "Before Sderzhivanie: Soviet Nuclear Strategy and Its Legacy." *Russia Seminar,* January 26, 2021. https://www.youtube.com/watch?v=A2RunPOtLkw.

George, Alexander L. "The Need for Influence Theory and Actor-Specific Behavioral Models of Adversaries." In Barry R. Schneider and Jerrold M. Post, eds., *Know Thy Enemy: Profiles of Adversary Leaders and Their Strategic Cultures.* Maxwell, AL: USAF Counterproliferation Center, 2003.

Geraschenko, Konstantin. "Chasovye Runeta." *VPK,* no. 19 (May 21, 2019).

Gerasimov, V. "Vektory Razvitiia Voennoi Strategii." *KZ,* March 4, 2019.

German, Tracey. "Harnessing Protest Potential: Russian Strategic Culture and the Colored Revolutions." *Contemporary Security Policy* 41, no. 4 (2020): 541–63.

Germeir, Iu. B. *Vvedenie v Teoriiu Issledovaniia Operatsii.* Moscow: Nauka, 1971.

Gerritzen, Christopher. "The End of Interventions? Simulating Cyber Weapons as Deterrence against Humanitarian Interventions." *Discussion Paper No. 6,* Rhine-Waal University of Applied Sciences, January 2020.

Giles, Keir. "Assessing Russian Success and Failure." In Viljar Veebel and Sandis Sraders, eds., *The Russia Conference Papers 2021.* Tartu: Tartu University Press, 2021.

———. *Moscow Rules: What Drives Russia to Confront the West.* London: Chatham House, 2019.

———. "Russian Information War: Construct and Purpose." In Timothy Clack and Robert Johnson, eds., *The World Information War.* London: Routledge, 2021.

Glantz, David. *Soviet Military Deception in the Second World War.* London: Routledge, 1989.

Goldman, Emily, and Leslie Eliason, eds. *The Diffusion of Military Technology and Ideas.* Stanford, CA: Stanford University Press, 2003.

Goncharov, I. A. *Oblomov.* Moscow: Izdatelstvo Detskaia Literatura, 1967.

Gorenburg, Dmitry. "Russian Strategic Culture in a Baltic Crisis." *Marshall Centre Security Insights,* no. 25 (March 2019).

Graaff, Bob de, ed. *Intelligence Communities and Cultures in Asia and the Middle East.* New York: Lynne Reinner, 2020.

Graham, Lawrence. *Science in Russia.* Cambridge: Cambridge University Press, 1993.

———. *Science, Philosophy, and Human Behavior in the Soviet Union.* New York: Columbia University Press, 1988.

Gray, Colin. *Out of the Wilderness: Prime Time for Strategic Culture.* Fort Belvoir, VA: Defense Threat Reduction Agency, 2006.

———. "Out of the Wilderness: Prime Time for Strategic Culture." *Comparative Strategy* 26, no.1 (2007): 1–20.

———. "Strategic Culture as Context: The First Generation of Theory Strikes Back." *Review of International Studies* 25, no. 1 (1999): 49–69.

Gricenko, S. A., L. B. Rezancev, O. N. Skliarova, and I. Iu. Cherednekov. "Dezoragnaizacii Upravelniia Nezakonnimi Voennimi Formirovaniiami v Khode Kontrterroristicheskoi Operatsii." *Voennaia Mysl'*, no. 5 (2016): 22–27.

Grin'ko, V. L., and S. I. Kohan. "Kontseptsiia Sderzhivaniia: Strategicheskai Stabil'nsot' v Sovremmenukh Usloviiakh." *Voennaia Mysl'*, no. 4 (1993).

Grishin, V. P., and S. V. Udaltsov. "Iadernoe Sderzhivanie." *Vestnik AVN*, no. 1 (2008).

Grygiel, Jacub. "Russia's Orthodox Grand Strategy." *American Interest*, April 2020.

Gumilevskii, Lev. *Russkie Inzhinery*. Moscow: Molodaia Gvardiia, 1953.

Gvosdev, Nikolas. "How the ROC Influences Russia's Behavior." *National Interest*, July 8, 2019.

Haglund, David. "What Can Strategic Culture Contribute to Our Understanding of Security Policies in the Asia Pacific Region?" *Contemporary Security Policy* 35, no. 2 (2014): 310–28.

Handel, Michael. *Masters of War: Classical Strategic Thought*. London: Frank Cass, 2001.

Harknett, Richard, and Michael Fischerkeller. "Deterrence Is Not a Credible Strategy for Cyberspace." *ORBIS* 61 (2017): 381–93.

———. "Persistent Engagement and Cost Imposition." *Lawfare*, February 6, 2020.

Harknett, Richard, and Emily Goldman. "The Search for Cyber Fundamentals." *Journal of Information Warfare* 15, no. 2 (2016): 81–89.

Hashim, Ahmed. *Iranian Ways of War*. Oxford: Oxford University Press, 2021.

Herd, Graeme. *Understanding Russian Strategic Behavior: Imperial Strategic Culture and Putin's Operational Code*. London: Routledge, 2022.

Heuser, Beatrice. "Victory in a Nuclear War? Comparison of NATO and WTO War Aims and Strategies." *Contemporary European History* 7, no. 3 (1998): 311–27.

Heuser, Beatrice, and Eitan Shamir, eds. *Insurgencies and Counterinsurgencies: National Styles and Strategic Cultures*. Cambridge: Cambridge University Press, 2016.

Hines, John G., Ellis M. Mishulovich, and John F. Shull. *Soviet Intentions, 1965–1985*. Germantown, MD: BMD Federal, 1995.

Hingley, Ronald. *The Russian Mind*. New York: Scribners and Sons, 1977.

Hobson, Rolf. "Blitzkrieg, the RMA and Defense Intellectuals." In Dmitry (Dima) Adamsky and Kjell Inge Bjerga, eds., *Contemporary Military Innovation: Between Anticipation and Adaptation*. London: Routledge, 2012.

Howard, Michael, and Peter Paret. *On War*. Princeton, NJ: Princeton University Press, 1984.

Howlett, Darryl, and John Glenn. "Nordic Strategic Culture." *Cooperation and Conflict* 40, no. 1 (2005): 121–40.

Igumnova, Lyudmila. "Russia's Strategic Culture between American and European Worldviews." *Journal of Slavic Military Studies* 24, no. 2 (2011): 253–73.

Inbar, Efraim, and Eitan Shamir. "'Mowing the Grass': Israel's Strategy for Protracted Intractable Conflict." *Journal of Strategic Studies* 37, no. 1 (2014): 65–90.

Il'in, L. N., and V. V. Rylin. "Inkapasitanty kak oruzhie neletalnogo deistviia." *Voennaia Mysl'*, no. 9 (2014): 37–42.

———. "O nekotorykh aspektakh primimenniia otravliaiuschikh veschestv neletal'nogo deistviia." *Voennaia Mysl'*, no. 12 (2018): 87–91.

Ionov, M. D. "O Refliksivnom Upravlenii Protivnikom v Boiu." *Voennaia Mysl'*, no. 1 (1995).

Jackson, Van. *On the Brink: Trump, Kim, and the Threat of Nuclear War.* Cambridge: Cambridge University Press, 2018.

Jervis, Robert. "Deterrence Theory Revised." *World Politics* 31, no. 2 (1979): 289–324.

Johnson, Dave. *Russia's Conventional Precision Strike Capabilities, Regional Crisis, and Nuclear Threshold.* Livermore, CA: CGSR, 2018.

———. "Russia's Deceptive Nuclear Policy." *Survival* 63, no. 3 (July 2021): 123–42.

Johnson, Jeannie L. *The Marines, Counterinsurgency, and Strategic Culture: Lessons Learned and Lost in America's Wars.* Washington, DC: Georgetown University Press, 2018.

Johnson, Jeannie L., Kerry Kartchner, and Jeffrey Larsen, eds. *Strategic Culture and Weapons of Mass Destruction.* London: Palgrave Macmillan, 2009.

Johnson, Jeannie L., Kerry M. Kartchner, and Marilyn J. Maines, eds. *Crossing Nuclear Thresholds: Leveraging Sociocultural Insights into Nuclear Decision-making.* London: Palgrave Macmillan, 2018.

Kahla, Elina. "Why Did the Seamen Have to Die? The Kursk Tragedy and the Evoking of Old Testament Blood Sacrifice." In Katri Pynnoniemi, ed., *Nexus of Patriotism and Militarism in Russia.* Helsinki: Helsinki University Press, 2021.

Kam, Ephraim. "Iran's Deterrence Concept." *INSS Strategic Assessment* 24, no. 3 (July 2021).

Kanet, Roger. "Russian Strategic Culture, Domestic Politics and Cold War 2.0." *European Politics and Society* 20, no. 2 (2018): 190–206.

Karaganov, Sergei "Preodolet' Sderzhivanie." *Rossiiskaia Gazeta*, April 6, 2011.

Karaiani, A., and I. Syromiatova. *Prikladnaia Voennaia Psikhologia.* St. Petersburg: Izdatel'stvo Piter, 2006.

Karasek, Tomas. "Tracking Shifts in Strategic Culture: Analyzing Counterinsurgency as a Rise of a Strategic Subculture." *Obrana A Stratgie* 16, no. 1 (2016): 113–42.

Kari, Martti, and Katri Pynnoniemi. "Theory of Strategic Culture: An Analytical Framework for Russian Cyber Threat Perception." *Journal of Strategic Studies*, September 11, 2019.

Katagiri, Nori. "Japanese Concepts of Deterrence." In Frans Osinga and Tim Swejis, eds., *Deterrence in the 21st Century: Insights from Theory and Practice.* The Hague: Springer and Asser Press, 2021.

Kazennov, Sergei, and Vladimir Kumachev. "Khochesh Mira—Gotovsia k Chemu?" *Nezavisimoye Voyennoye Obozreniye*, May 29, 2015.

Kello, Lucas. *The Virtual Weapon and International Order.* New Haven, CT: Yale University Press, 2017.

Kholunenko, D.V., V. A. Anokhin, A. S. Korobeinikov, and A. A. Lakhin. "Radioelektonnyi i Radio-Ognevoi Udary: Osnovnye Formy Primenenia Chastei REB." *Voennaia Mysl'*, no. 11 (2019): 21–27.

Khudoleev, Viktor. "Strazhniki Efira na Pravilnom Puti." *KZ*, April 15, 2020.

Knopf, Jeffrey W. "The Fourth Wave in Deterrence Research." *Contemporary Security Policy* 31, no. 1 (2010): 1–33.

Knorre, Boris. "Masculine Strategies in Russian Orthodoxy: from Asceticism to Militarization." In Katharina Bluhm, Gertrud Pickhan, Justyna Stypinska, and Agnieszka Wierzcholska, eds., *Gender and Power in Eastern Europe: Changing Concepts of Femininity and Masculinity in Power Relations.* London: Springer, 2020.

Knorre, Boris, and Aleksei Zygmont. "Military Piety in the 21st Century Orthodox Christianity: Return to Classical Traditions of Formation of a New Theology of War?" *Religions* 11, no. 2 (2020): 1–17.

Kofman, Michael. "Assessing Russian Fait Accompli Strategy." *Russian Analytical Digest*, November 2020.

———. "Blessed Be Thy Nuclear Weapons: The Rise of Russian Nuclear Orthodoxy." *WOTR*, June 21, 2019.

———. "Drivers of Russian Grand Strategy." *FRIVARLD Briefing*, no. 6 (2019).

———. "The Ogarkov Period: Soviet Origins of the Russian Views of Deterrence." *Russian Seminar*, February 2, 2021. https://www.youtube.com/watch?v=3vouTxigJ_c&t=695s.

———. "The Ogarkov Reforms: the Soviet Inheritance behind Russia's Military Transformation." *Russia Military Analysis Blog*, July 2019.

———. *Syria and the Russian Armed Forces: An Evaluation of Moscow's Military Strategy and Operational Performance.* Philadelphia: FPRI, 2020.

Kofman, Michael, and Anna Loukianova Fink. "Escalation Management and Nuclear Employment in Russian Military Strategy." *WOTR*, June 23, 2020.

Kofman, Michael, Anya Fink, and Jeffrey Edmonds. *Russian Strategy for Escalation Management: Evolution of Key Concepts.* Washington, DC, 2020.

Kokoshin, A. A. *Armiia I Politika.* Moscow: IMO, 1995.

———. "Asimetrichnyi Otvet na SOI." *Mezhdunarodnaia Zhizn'*, no. 2 (2007).

———. "Asimetrichnyi Otvet Nomer Odin." *Nezavisimoye Voyennoye Obozreniye*, August 1, 2007.

———. "Bomba Spravljaet Jubilej: k 55-letiju so Dnja Otechestvennoj Termojadernoj RDS -37." *Nezavisimoye Voyennoye Obozreniye*, 44, November 2010.

———. *Iadernye Konflikty v XXI Veke.* Media Press, 2003.

———. *Inovatsionnye Vooruzhennye Sily i Revoljucija v Voennom Dele.* Moscow: URSS, 2009.

———. *Obespechenie Strategicheskoi Stabilnosti v Proshlom i Nastojashhem: Teoreticheskie i Prikladnye Voprosy.* Moscow: URSS, 2009.

———. "Perspektivy Razvtiia Nauchnoi Tekhnosfery i Budushee Voin i Neboevogo Primenenia Voennoi Sily." *Vestnik AVN* 2, no. 67 (2019): 26–29.

———. "Strategicheskoe Iadernoe i Neiadernoe Sderzhivanie: Prioreitety Sovremennoi Epokhi." *Vestnik Rossiiskoi Akademii Nauk* 84, no. 3 (2014): 195–205.

———. "Voenno-Politicheskoe Predvideinie." *Nezavisimoye Voyennoye Obozreniye*, August 5, 1998.

———. "Voina I Voennoe Iskusstvo: Politologicheskoe i Sociologicheskoe Izmerenija." *Sotsiologicehskie Isledovaniia* 372, no. 3 (2015): 97–106.

Kokoshin, A. A., Iu. N. Baluevskii, and V. Ia. Potapov. "Vliianie Noveishikh Teknologii i Sredstv Vooruzhennoi Bor'by na Voennoe Iskusstvo." *Mezdhunarodye Otnosheniia i Mirovaia Politika*, no. 4 (2015).

Kolesova, N. A., and I. G. Nasenkova, eds. *Radioelektronnaia Bor'ba: ot Eksperimentov Proshlogo do Reshajushhego Fronta Budushhego*. Moscow: CAST, 2015.

Kolosova, L. A., A. A. Tomilov, R. B. Beliaev, and A. E. Sergienko. "Moral'no-psihologicheskoe Obespechenie Deiatel'nosti Voisk v Boevykh Usloviiakh kak Sistema." *Voennaia Mysl'*, no. 2 (2019): 79–86.

Komov, S. A., S. V. Korotkov, and I. N. Dydelvskii. "Ob Evolutsii Aovremennoi Ameri-kanksoi Doktriny." *Voennaia Mysl'*, no. 6 (2008): 54–61.

Koniakhin, B. A., and V. I. Kovalev. "Mekhanism Realizatsii Strategicheskogo Sderzhivaniya Potencial'nyh Protivnikov ot Razvyazyvaniya Agressii." *Strategicheskaia Stabil'nost'* 1, no. 46 (2009): 27–31.

Korn, Erik Benjamin, Daniel Nicholas Boccio, Scott Scher, Rashide Assad Atala, Ab-dulrahman Yaaqob Al-Hamadi, and Steven Jun Sic Park. *Strategic Culture and Cyberwarfare Strategies: Four Case Studies*. SIPA Capstone Workshop, 2018.

Korobeinikov, A. S., and S. I. Pasichnik. "Osobennosti Metodicheskogo Obespecheniia Otzenki Effektivnsoti REB pri Modelirovanii Kompleksnogo Porazheniia Informatsionno-upravliaiuschih System Protivnika." *Voennaia Mysl'*, no. 11 (2015): 58–64.

Korobov, Pavel. "Miry Miro: V RPTs Razrabotiali Dokument o Blagoslovlenii Voennykh I Ikh Oruzhiia." *Kommersant*, June 1, 2021.

Korobushin, V. V. "Nadezhnoe Strategicheskoe Iadernoe Sderzhivanie." *Strategicheskaia Stabil'nost'*, 46, no. 1 (2009): 14–18.

Korobushin, V. V., V. I. Kovalev, and G. N. Vinokurov. "Predel Sokrascheniia SIaS." *Vestnik AVN* 28, no. 3 (2009).

Korolev, I., V. Pavlov, and V. Petrov. "REB v Voinakh Buduschego." *Armeiskii Sbornik*, no. 8 (2016): 39–48.

Koshelev, S., and V. Sumenkov. "Napravleniia sovershenstvovaniia radiatsionnoi, khimicheskoi I biologicheskoi zaschiti v sovremennykh usloviiakh." *Voennaia Mysl'*, no. 1 (2022): 108–20.

Koshkin, R. P. "Ugroza primeneniia khimicheskogo I biologicheskogo oruzhiia." *Strategicheskie Prioritety* 18, no. 2 (2018): 25–39.

Kovachich, Leonid, Kinolai Markotkin, and Elena Chernenko. *Gonka Tekhnologii: perspektivy II v Rossii I Kitae*. Moscow: Carnegie Moscow Center, 2020.

Kovtun, V. A., A. N. Golipal, and A. V. Melnikov. "Khimicheskii terrorism kak silovoi instrument provedeniia vneshnei politiki SShA I stran Zapada." *Vestnik Voisk RHBZ* 1, no. 2 (2017): 12–13.

Kovtun, V. A., D. P. Supotnitskii, and N. I. Shilo. "Siriiskaia Khimicheskaia Voina." *Vestnik RKhBZ* 2, no. 3 (2018): 7–39.

Kozhinov, Vadim. *O Russkom Nacional'nom Soznanii*. Moscow: Algoritm, 2002.

Krebs, Ronald, and Jennifer Lobasz. "Fixing the Meaning of 9/11." *Security Studies* 16, no. 3 (2007): 409–51.

Kreidin, S. V. "Global'noe i Regional'noe Sderzhivanie." *Voennaia Mysl'*, no. 4 (1999).

———. "O Problemakh Global'nogo i Regional'nogo Sderzhivaniia." *Voennaia Mysl'*, no. 5 (1998).

Kriuchkov, Vladimir. "Trundye Mili k Ratnomu Masterstvu." *KZ*, October 30, 2020.

Kroenig, Matthew. *The Logic of American Nuclear Strategy: Why Strategic Superiority Matters*. Oxford: Oxford University Press, 2020.

Kruglov, V. V., and A. S. Shubin. "O Vozrastaiuschem Znachenii Uprezhdeniia v Deistviiakh." *Voennaia Mysl'*, no. 12 (December 2021): 27–34.

Krutskikh, A. "O Kiberugrozakh i Sposobakh Protivodeistviia Im." *Mezhdunarodnaia Zhyzn'*, April 23, 2019.

Kuleba, A. "Psikhologicheskaia Podgotovka Voennosluzhaschikh k Vedeniiu Aktivnykh Boevykh Desitvii." *Armeiskii Sbronik*, no. 8 (2019): 78–94.

Kurdil', N. V., and A. V. Ivaschenko. "Sovremennye boevye khimicheskie sredstva nesmertel'nogo deistviia: toksikologicheskie I klinicheskie aspekty." *Medetsina neotlozhnykh sostoianii* 1, no. 64 (2015): 11–19.

Kuz'min, A. A., E. V. Ivchenko, and A. B Seleznev. "Irritanty: sovremennoe pereosmyslenie aktual'nosti dlia VS I perspektivy sozdaniia medetsinskih sredstv zaschiti." *Vestnik Rossiiskoi Voenno-Medetsinskoi Akademii* 3, no. 71 (2020): 188–93.

Kuznetsov, V. I., Y. Y. Donskov, and O. G. Nikitin. "K Voprosu o Roli i Meste Kiberprostranstva v Sovremennyh Boevyh Dejstvijah." *Voennaia Mysl'*, no. 3 (2014): 13–17.

Lantis, Jeffrey. "Strategic Culture and Tailored Deterrence: Bridging the Gap Between Theory and Practice." *Contemporary Security Policy* 30, no. 3 (2009): 467–85.

———. "Strategic Cultures and Security Policies in the Asia-Pacific." *Contemporary Security Policy* 35, no. 2 (2014): 166–86.

Larkin, Sean P. "The Limits of Tailored Deterrence." *Joint Force Quarterly* 63 (4th Quarter 2011): 47–57.

Laruelle, Marlene. *Is Russia Fascist? Unraveling Propaganda East and West*. Ithaca, NY: Cornell University Press, 2021.

———. *Russian Nationalism: Imaginaries, Doctrines, and Political Battlefields*. New York: Routledge, 2019.

———. "Russia's Mediterranean Call: From Kerch to Palmyra, but without Constantinople?" *ODR*, November 9, 2018.

———. *Russia's Niche Soft Power: Sources, Targets and Channels of Influence*. Paris: IFRI, 2021.

Last, Edward. *Strategic Culture and Violent Non-State Actors: A Comparative Study of Salafi-Jihadist Groups*. London: Routledge, 2020.

Lastochkin, I. Iu. "Perspektivy Razvitija Vojsk Radiojelektronnoj Bor''by Vooruzhennyh Sil Rossijskoj Federacii." *Voennaia Mysl'*, no. 12 (2020): 86–87.

———. "Rol' I Mesto Radioelektronoi Bor'by v Sovremennyh i Budushhih Boevyh Dejstvijah." *Voennaia Mysl'*, no. 12 (2015): 14–19.

Lazarevich, E. G., S. K. Kolganov, and A. N. Semashko. "Tekhnologicheskaia Osnova Obespecheniia Voennoi Bezopasnosti Gosudarstva." *Nauka i Voennaia Bezopasnost'*, no. 2 (2007).

Lazukin, V. F., N. I. Korolev, and V. N. Pavlov. "Bazovye Element Taktiki Voisk REB." *Voennaia Mysl'*, no. 11 (2017): 15–20.

Leer, G. *Metod Voennykh Nauk*. Moscow: SPB, 1894.

Leitis, Nathan. *The Operational Code of Politburo*. New York: McGraw-Hill, 1951.

———. *Soviet Style in Management*. New York: Crane Russak, 1985.

Lenin, V. I. "O mezhdunarodnom I vnutrennem polozhenii Sovetskoi respubliki." *Polnoe Sobranie Sochenenii* 45 (1970): 1–16.

Leonenko, S. "Refleksivnoe Upravlenie Protivnikom." *Armeiskii Sbornik*, no. 8 (1995).

Lewis, David. *Russia's New Authoritarianism: Putin and the Politics of Order*. Edinburgh: Edinburgh University Press, 2020.

———. "Strategic Culture and Russia's 'Pivot to the East': Russia, China, and 'Greater Eurasia.'" *Security Insights*, no. 34 (July 2019).

Libben, Joshua. "Am I My Brother's Peacekeeper? Strategic Cultures and Change among Major Troop Contributors to UN." *Canadian Foreign Policy Journal* 23, no. 3 (2017): 324–39.

Libel, Tamir. *European Military Culture and Security Governance: Soldiers, Scholars and National Defence Universities*. London: Routledge, 2016.

———. "Explaining the Security Paradigm Shift: Strategic Culture, Epistemic Communities, and Israel's Changing National Security Policy." *Defense Studies* 16, no. 2 (2016): 137–56.

———. "Rethinking Strategic Culture: A Computational (Social Science) Discursive-Institutionalist Approach." *Journal of Strategic Studies* 43, no. 5 (2020): 686–709.

Lilly, Bilyana, and Joe Cheravitch. "The Past, Present and Future of Russia's Cyber Strategy and Forces." *International Conference on Cyber Conflict*. Tallinn, 2020.

Lindsay, Jon. *Information Technology and Military Power*. Ithaca, NY: Cornell University Press, 2020.

Lobov, V. N. *Voennaia khitrost'*. Moscow: Logos, 2001.

Long, Austin. *Deterrence—From Cold War to Long War*. Washington, DC: RAND, 2008.

———. *The Soul of Militaries: Counterinsurgency Doctrine and Military Culture in the US and UK*. Ithaca, NY: Cornell University Press, 2016.

Lupovici, Amir. "The Emerging Fourth Wave of Deterrence Theory—Toward a New Research Agenda." *International Studies Quarterly* 54, no. 3 (2010): 705–32.

———. "Toward a Securitization Theory of Deterrence." *International Studies Quarterly* 63, no. 1 (2019): 177–86.

Luttwak, Edward. *Strategy*. Cambridge, MA: Harvard University Press, 2003.

Mahnken, Thomas, ed. *Net Assessment and Military Strategy: Retrospective and Prospective Essays*. New York: Cambria Press, 2020.

———. *Secrecy and Stratagem: Understanding Chinese Strategic Culture*. Washington, DC: Lowy Institute for International Policy, 2011.

———. *Technology and the American Way of War.* New York: Columbia University Press, 2008.

Mahnken, Thomas, and Gillian Evans. "Ambiguity, Risk and Limited Great Power Conflict." *Strategic Studies Quarterly* (Winter 2019): 57–76.

Malka, Amos. "Israel and Asymmetrical Deterrence." *Comparative Strategy* 27, no. 1 (2008): 1–19.

Mallory, King. *New Challenges in Cross-Domain Deterrence.* Santa Monica, CA: RAND, 2018.

Mankoff, Jeffrey. *Empires of Eurasia: How Imperial Legacies Shape International Security.* New Haven, CT: Yale University Press, 2021.

———. *Russian Foreign Policy: The Return of Great Power Politics.* New York: Rowman & Littlefield, 2009.

Manoilo, A. V. *Gosudarstvennaia Informatsionnaia Poltika v Osobykh Usloviiakh.* Moscow: MIFI, 2003.

———. "Kontseptsii Politicheskogo Regulirovaniia Informatsionno-pshychologicheskoi Voiny." *Nacional'naja Bezopasnost'/Nota Bene,* no. 3/4 (2010): 98–116.

———. "Upravlenie Psikhologicheskoi Voinoi." *Politika I Obschestvo,* no. 2 (2004).

———. *Rol' Kul'turno-Tsivilizatsionnykh Modelei I Tekhnologii Informatsionno-Psikhologicheskogo Vozdeistviia v Razreshenii Mezhdunarodnykh Konfliktov.* PhD diss., MGU, 2009.

Mansoor, Peter, and Williamson Murray, eds. *The Culture of Military Organizations.* Cambridge: Cambridge University Press, 2019.

Marchenko, A. A. "Razumnaia Dostatochnost' kak Strategiia Reagirovaniia Respondentov v Web Oprosah." *Monitoring Obshestvennogo Mneniia: Ekonomicheskie I Sotsialnye Peremeny* 5 (2016): 31–40.

Marten, Kimberly. *Engaging the Enemy: Organizational Theory and Soviet Military Innovation.* Princeton, NJ: Princeton University Press, 1993.

Matania, Eviatar, Lior Yoffe, and Michael Mashkautsan. "A Three-Layer Framework for a Comprehensive National Cyber-security Strategy." *Georgetown Journal of International Affairs* 17, no. 3 (2016): 77–84.

Mattis, James. "USJFCOM Commander's Guidance for EBO." *Parameters* 38, no. 3 (2008): 18–25.

Matvichiuk, V. V., and A. L. Khriapin. "Metodicheskij Podhod k Ocenke Eeffektivnosti Boevogo Primenenija Vysokotochnogo Oruzhija Bol"shoj Dal"nosti." *Strategicheskaia Stabil'nost'* 1, no. 46 (2009): 51–55.

———. "Sistema Strategicheskogo Sderzhivaniia v Novih Uslovijah." *Voennaia Mysl',* no. 1 (2010): 11–16.

Mazarr, Michael. *Understanding Deterrence.* Washington, DC: RAND, 2018.

Mazin, Viktor. "Nelenivye Zametki o Leni: Oblomov, Lenin and Kapitalizatsiia Leni." *LOGOS* 29, no. 1 (2019): 243–58.

McDermott, Roger. "The Brain of the Russian Army: Futuristic Visions Tethered by the Past." *Journal of Slavic Military Studies* 27 (2014): 4–35.

McManus, Roseanne W. "Revisiting the Madman Theory: Evaluating the Impact of Different Forms of Perceived Madness in Coercive Bargaining." *Security Studies* 28, no. 5 (2019): 976–1009.

Mercer, Jonathan. "The Illusion of International Prestige." *International Security* 41, no. 4 (2017): 133–68.

Meyer, Christopher. "The Purpose and Pitfalls of Constructivists Forecasting: Insights from Strategic Culture Research for the EU's Evolution as Military Power." *International Studies Quarterly* 55, no. 3 (2011): 669–90.

Michenic, N. P. *Strategiia.* Moscow: SPB, 1898.

Miklossy, Katalin, and Hanna Smith, eds. *Strategic Culture in Russia's Neighborhood.* London: Routledge, 2020.

Milevski, Lukas. "Deterring Able Archer." *Journal of Strategic Studies* 37, nos. 6–7 (2014): 1050–65.

———. "Russia's Escalation Management and a Baltic Nuclear Weapons Free Zone." *ORBIS* 66, no. 1 (2022): 95–110.

Modestov, S. A. "Strategickeskoe Sderzhivanie na Teatre Informacionnogo Protivoborstva." *Strategicheskaia Stabil'nost'* 1, no. 46 (2009): 33–36.

Moiseev, V. "Oruzhie neletal'nogo deistviia kak sredstvo voenno-silovogo vozdeistviia (kompleksnogo porazheniia protivnika)." *Voennaia Mysl'*, no. 11 (2021): 41–48.

Monaghan, Andrew. *Blitzkrieg and the Russian Art of War.* Manchester: Manchester University Press, 2024.

———. *Dealing with the Russians.* Manchester: Manchester University Press, 2019.

———. *How Moscow Understands War and Military Strategy.* Washington, DC: Center for Naval Analysis, 2020.

———. "Understanding Russia's Measures of War." *Russian Analytical Digest*, November 2020.

Monaghan, Sean. "Deterring Hybrid Threats: Towards a Fifth Wave of Deterrence Theory and Practice." *Hybrid CoE Papers* 12, no. 3 (May 2022).

Montgomery, Evan B. "Posturing for Great Power Competition: Identifying Coercion Problems in U.S. Nuclear Policy." *Journal of Strategic Studies*, February 21, 2021.

Morgan, Patrick M. *Deterrence Now.* Cambridge: Cambridge University Press, 2003.

———. "Evaluating Tailored Deterrence." In Karl Heinz Kamp and David S. Yost, eds., *NATO and 21st Century Deterrence.* Forum Paper No. 8. Rome: NATO Defense College, May 2009.

———. "The State of Deterrence in International Politics Today." *Contemporary Security Policy* 33, no. 1 (2012): 85–107.

Muntianu, A. V., and R. G. Tagirov. "O Nekotorukh Aspektakh Vlianiia Globalizatsii na Mehanizm Strategicheskogo Sderzhivanija." *Strategicheskaia Stabil'nost'* 1, no. 54 (2011): 25–28.

Naveh, Shimon. *In Pursuit of Military Excellence: The Evolution of Operational Theory.* London: Routledge, 1997.

Neigebaur, Zhanna. "Korni Rossiiskogo Atomnogo Pravoslaviia." *Discourse*, August 20, 2019.

Nezhinskii, L. N., and I. A. Chelyshev. "O Doktrinal'nykh Osnovakh Sovetskoi Vneshnei Politiki." *Otechetsvennaia Istoriia*, no. 1 (1995): 5–12.

Novikov, V. K., and S. V. Golubchikov. "Formy Radioelektronnoi Bro'by v Sovremennykh Usloviiakh." *Vestnik AVN*, no. 2 (2019): 139–43.

Novosel'cev, Viktor. *Teoreticheskie Osnovy Sistemnogo Analiza*. Moscow: Maior, 2006.

Nye, Joseph. "Deterrence and Dissuasion in Cyberspace." *International Security* 41, no. 3 (Winter 2016–17): 44–71.

Oliker, Olga. *Between Rhetoric and Reality: Explaining the Russian Federation's Nuclear Force Posture*. PhD diss., Massachusetts Institute of Technology, 2018.

———. "Moving Beyond Russian Nuclear Orthodoxy." In *Book Review Roundtable: Russian Nuclear Orthodoxy*. TNSR, 2019.

Ordin, A. "Rossiiskaia diplomatiia I problema khimicheskogo oruzhiia." *Vestnik uchenykh mezhdunarodnikov* 3, no. 17 (2021): 22–32.

Osadchaia, I. M., ed. *Ekonomika. Tolkovyi Slovar'*. Moscow: Izdatel'stvo Ves' Mir, 2000.

Osflaten, Amund. "Russian Strategic Culture after the Cold War: The Primacy of Conventional Force." *Journal of Military and Strategic Studies* 20, no. 2 (2021): 110–32.

Osinga, Frans, and Tim Swejis, eds. *Deterrence in the 21st Century: Insights from Theory and Practice*. The Hague: Springer and Asser Press, 2021.

Ostankov, V. I., and P. S. Kazarin. "Metodologiia Sravnitelnogo Analiza Boevykh Potentsialov." *Voennaia Mysl'*, no. 11 (2012).

Ostbo, Jardar. *The New Third Rome*. Stuttgart: Ibidem Press, 2016.

Ostovar, Afshon. "The Grand Strategy of Militant Clients: Iran's Way of War." *Security Studies* 28, no. 1 (2018): 159–88.

Ozer, Ayse Irem Aycan. "Iranian Strategic Culture." *Middle Eastern Studies* 8, no. 2 (2016): 44–67.

Oznobischev, C. K., V. Ia. Potapov, and V. V. Skokov. *Kak Gotovilsia Asummetrichnyi Otvet na Strategicheskuiu Initsiativu Reigana*. Moscow: URSS, 2010.

Pacepa, Ion Mihai, and Ronald Rychlak. *Disinformation*. London: WND Books, 2013.

Pankrashin, Valerii. "Iubilei Oblomovschiny." *BBC News Russkaia Sluzhba*, October 15, 2009.

Paul, T. V., Patrick Morgan, and James Wirtz, eds. *Complex Deterrence: Strategy in the Global Age*. Chicago: University of Chicago Press, 2009.

Pavlovskii, Iu. N. "O Faktore L.N. Tolstogo V Vooruzhennoi Bor'be." *Matematicheskoe Modelirovanie* 5, no. 1 (1993).

Payne, Keith B. *The Fallacies of Cold War Deterrence and a New Direction*. Lexington: University Press of Kentucky 2001.

———. "Understanding Deterrence." *Comparative Strategy* 30, no. 5 (2011): 391–92.

Pechatnov, Iu. A. "Analiz Otechestvennykh i Zarubezhnykh Podkhodov k Razrabotke Kontseptual'nykh Modelei Silovogo Strategicheskogo Sderzhivaniia." *Vooruzhenia I Ekonomika* 2, no. 14 (2011).

———. "K Voprosy o Dalneishem Sovershenstvovanii Teorii Silovogo Strategicheskogo Sderzhivaniia." *Izvestiia Rossiiskoi Akademii Raketnykh I Artilleriiskikh Nauk* 81, no. 1 (2014): 27–31.

———. "Nauchno-metodicheskii Podkhod k Formirovaniiu Pokazatelia Effektivnosti Mekhanizma Silovogo Neiadernogo Sderzhivaniia." *Strategicheskaia Stabil'nost'* 58, no. 1 (2012): 67–75.

———. "Retrospektivnyi Analiz Evoliutzii Kontsepsii Sderzhivaniia." *Vooruzhenie I Ekonomika* 9, no. 1 (2010): 11–15.

———. "Teoriia Sderzhivaniia: Genesis." *Vooruzhenie I Ekonomika* 35, no. 2 (2016): 25–32.

Pezard, Stephanie, and Ahsley Rhoades. *What Provokes Putin's Russia? Deterring Without Unintended Escalation.* Washington, DC: RAND, 2020.

Pinchiuk, Aleksandr. "Zdes' Nauchiat Pobezhdat'." *KZ*, September 4, 2019.

Plekhov, A. M., and S. G. Shapkin. *Slovar' Voennykh Terminov.* Moscow: Voenizdat, 1988.

Podberezkin, A. I. *Sovremennaia Voennaia Politika Rossii.* Moscow: MGIMO, 2017.

———. *Strategicheskoe Sderzhivanie: Novii Trend.* Moscow: MGIMO, 2019.

Poirier, Dominique. *DGSE: The French Spy Machine.* Independently published, 2019.

Popov, I. M., and M. M. Khazmatov. *Voina Buduschego: Kontseptual'nye Osnovy I Prakticjhecheskie Vovody.* Moscow: Kuchkovo Pole, 2016.

Prior, Tim. "Resilience: The Fifth Wave in the Evolution of Deterrence." In Oliver Thränert and Martin Zapfe, eds., *Strategic Trends 2018: Key Developments in Global Affairs.* Zurich: ETH Zurich CSS, 2018.

Prokhorov, D., and A. Kolpakidi. *Vneshniaia Razvedka Rossii.* Moscow: Olma Press, 2001.

Protasov, A. A., and S. V. Kreidin. "Sistemy Upravlenia Voiskami." *Strategicheskaia Stabil'nost'* 46, no. 1 (2009): 23–26.

Quenoy, Irina do. "Getting Comfortable with Russian Nuclear Orthodoxy." In *Book Review Roundtable: Russian Nuclear Orthodoxy.* TNSR, 2019.

Radvik, B. *Voennoe Planirovanie I Analiz System.* Moscow: Moscow Voenizdat, 1972.

Rainkhard, Roman. "Novye Formy I Metody Diplomatii." *Mezhdunarodnaia Analitika* 11, no. 4 (2020): 11–19.

Rakov, Daniel, and Yochai Guisky. "Why Joe Biden Should Start a Cybersecurity Dialogue with Russia." *National Interest,* February 18, 2021.

Reach, Clint. "Russian Views on COFM and Nuclear Deterrence." *Russia Seminar,* February 2, 2021. https://www.youtube.com/watch?v=10cLOhA9icw.

Reach, Clint, Vikram Kilmbi, and Mark Cozad. *Russian Assessments and Applications of the Correlation of Forces and Means.* Washington, DC: RAND, 2020.

Riabkov, Sergei. "Iadernyi Arsenal Rossii Nakhoditsia na Urovne Razumnoi Dostatochnsoti." *TV Zvezda,* July 4, 2014.

Rid, Thomas. "Deterrence Beyond the State: the Israeli Experience." *Comparative Security Policy* 33, no. 1 (2012): 124–47.

Roberts, Brad. "The Bishops and the Bomb, Take Two." In *Book Review Roundtable: Russian Nuclear Orthodoxy.* TNSR, 2019.

Robinson, Paul. *Russian Conservatism.* DeKalb: Northern Illinois University Press, 2019.

Rogovskii, E. "Amerikanskaia Srategiia Infromatsionnogo Preobladaniia." *Oko Planety*, December 12, 2009.

Rogozin, Dmitry, ed. *Voina I Mir v Terminakh I Opredeleniiakh*. Moscow: Veche, 2014.

Rojansky, Matthew, and Amos Gilead, eds. *Russia in the Middle East: National Security Challenges for the United States and Israel in the Biden Era*. Washington, DC: Kennan Institute, 2021.

Romanov, A., and Iu. Blinkov. "Vzgliady Rukovodstva NATO na Podgotovku i Priminenie OVVS Alianssa v Buduschikh Operatsiiakh." *ZVO*, no. 9 (2009): 46–53.

Ronfeldt, David, and John Arquilla. *Whose Story Wins: Rise of the Noosphere, Noopolitik, and Information-Age Statecraft*. Santa Monica, CA: RAND, 2020.

Rosen, Stephen. *Winning the Next War: Innovation and the Modern Military*. Ithaca, NY: Cornell University Press, 1995.

Rothkopf, David. "Current and Former U.S. Officials Say the U.S. and NATO Have Plenty of Resources at Their Disposal without Having to Resort to the Nuclear Option." Daily Beast, April 19, 2022.

Ruchkin, Viktor. "Balans Interesov." *KZ*, December 28, 2010.

Ruhle, Michael. *In Defense of Deterrence*. National Institute of Public Policy, April, 2020.

Rumer, Eugene, and Richard Sokolosky. *Etched in Stone: Russian Strategic Culture and the Future of Transatlantic Security*. Washington, DC: Carnegie Endowment for International Peace, 2021.

Sagan, Scott, and Kenneth Waltz. "Political Scientists and Historians in Search of the Bomb." *Journal of Strategic Studies* 36, no. 1 (2013) 143–51.

Savchenko, E. O. "Specifika Primeneniia Isntrumentov Vneshnepoliticheskoi Strategii SShA na Blizhnem Vostoke." *Voennaia Mysl'*, no. 12 (December 2018): 5–17.

Saveliev, A. G. *K Novoi Redaktsii Voennoi Doktriny*. Moscow: URSS, 2009.

Savinkin, A. E. "Rossiiskaia Nauka Pobezhdat': Uroki Siriiskogo Uregulirovaniia." *Voennyi Akademicheskii Zhurnal* 2, no. 22 (2019): 15–44.

Savkin, V. E. *Osnovnue Printsipy Operativnogo Isskusstva I Taktiki*. Moscow: Voenizdat, 1972.

Schelling, Thomas. *Arms and Influence*. New Haven, CT: Yale University Press, 1966.

Sebekin, S. A. *Genezis i Razvitie Strategii Sderzhivaniia Kiberugroz v SShA, KNR, I Rossii*. PhD diss., IGU, 2020.

———. "Neobhodimost' Sovershenstvovaniia Doktriny Sdrzhivaniia v Usloviakh Rosta Kiberugroz." *Problemy Natsional'noi Strategii* 48, no. 3 (2018): 122–36.

Sebekin, S. A., and A. V. Kostrov. "Voennaia Filosofia Kitaia i Kibervoina: Traditsionnaia Kontseptual'naia Osnova Dlia Netraditsionnykh Operatsii." *Mezhdunarodnye Ontosheniia* 17, no. 3 (2019).

Selivanov, V. V., and Iu. D. Il'in. "Kontesptsiia Voenno-teknicheskogo Assimetrichnogo Otveta po Sderzhivaniiu Veroiatnogo Protivnika ot Razviazivaniia Voennykh Konfliktov." *Voennaia Mysl'*, no. 2 (February 2022): 31–47.

Selivanov, V. V., D. P. Levin, and Iu. D. Il'in. "Metodologicheskie voprosy razvitiia oruzhiia neletalnogo deistviia." *Voennaia Mysl'*, no. 2 (2015): 10–22.

Shakirov, O. I. "Kto Pridet s Kibermechem: Podkhody Rossii I SShA k Sderzhivaniiu v Kiberprostranstve." *Mezhdunarodnaia Analitika* 11, no. 4 (2020): 147–69.

Shamir, Eitan. *Transforming Command: The Pursuit of Mission Command in the US, British and Israeli Armies.* Stanford, CA: Stanford University Press, 2011.

Shapira, Itai. "Israeli National Intelligence Culture and the Response to Covid-19." *War on the Rocks*, November 12, 2020.

Shapovalov, V. F. *Istoki I Smysl Rossiiskoi Tsivilizatsii.* Moscow: Fair Press, 2003.

Sharikov, Pavel. "Informacionnoe Sderzhivanie: Transformacija Paradigmy Strategicheskoj Stabil'nosti." *RSMD*, September 5, 2013.

———. "V Boi Idut Kibervoiska." *Nezavisimoye Voyennoye Obozreniye*, April 13, 2012.

Shatokhin, V. Ia. "Iadernaia Sostavliiaiuschaia." *Strategicheskaia Stabil'nsot'* 46, no. 1 (2009): 35–40.

Shebarshin, L. V. *Ruka Moskvy.* Moscow: Tsentr Press, 1992.

Sher, James, and Kaarel Kullamaa. *The Russian Orthodox Church: Faith, Power, and Conquest.* Estonian Foreign Policy Institute, 2019.

Shumov, V. V. "Uchet Psikhologicheskikh Faktroov v Modeliakh Boia." *Kompiuternye Isssledovaniia I Modelirovanie* 8, no. 6 (2016): 951–64.

Shumov, V. V., and V. O. Korepanov. "Matematicheskie Modeli Boevykh i Voennykh Deistvii." *Kompiuternye Issledovaniia I Modelirovanie* 12, no. 1 (2020): 217–42.

Shushkanov, Iu. G., and V. N. Gorbunov. "O Nekotorykh Aspektakh Teorii i Praktiki Priminenia Vooruzhennykh Sil." *Voennaia Mysl'*, no. 1 (January 2010).

Sidorov, Dmitrii. "Post-Imperial Third Rome." *Geopolitics* 1 (2006): 317–47.

Sinovets, Polina. "From Stalin to Putin: Russian Strategic Culture in the XXI Century, Its Continuity, and Change." *Philosophy Study* 6, no. 7 (2016): 417–23.

Sinovets, Polina, and Mykyta Nerez. "The Essence of Russian Strategic Culture: From the Third Rome to the Russian World." *International and Political Studies* 34, no. 1 (2021): 123–36.

Skak, Mette. "Russian Strategic Culture: The Generational Approach and the Counterintelligence State Thesis." In Roger Kanet, ed., *Routledge Handbook of Russian Security.* London: Routledge, 2019.

Smirnov, Anatolii. "Noveishie Kiberstrategii SShA—Preambula Voiny?" *Mezhdunarodnye Protsessy* 16, no. 4 (2018): 181–92.

Snyder, Glen. *Deterrence and Defense: Toward a Theory of National Security.* Princeton, NJ: Princeton University Press, 1961.

Snyder, Jack. *The Soviet Strategic Culture: Implications for Nuclear Operations.* Santa Monica, CA: RAND, 1977.

Solomov, Iurii, and Igor' Korotechko. "Ot Intelekta Profesionalizma Politicheskoi Eliti Zavisit Sostoianie Gosudarstva." *Natsional'naia Oborona*, no. 10 (2020): 34–41.

Solov'ev, V. *Natsional'nyi Vopros v Rossii.* Moscow: AST, 1988.

Soskov, D. Iu., S. F. Sergeev, and D. V. Zaitsev. "Primenenie oruzhiia neletal'nogo deistviia v usloviiakh vnutrennego vooruzhennogo konflikta." *Voennaia Mysl'*, no. 4 (2018): 55–61.

Soskov, D., D. Zaitsev, V. Kornilov, and E. Lozhkin. "Oruzhie neletelnogo deistviia." *Arsenal Otechestva* 55, no. 5 (2021): 70–74.

Starodubtsev, Iu. I., P. V. Zakalkin, and S. A. Ivanov. "Tekhnosfernaia Voina kak Osnovnoi Sposob Razresheniia Konfliktov v Usloviiakh Globalizatsii." *Voennaia Mysl'*, no. 10 (2020): 16–21.

Staun, Jørgen. "At War with the West—Russian Military-Strategic Culture." In Niels Bo Poulsen and Jørgen Staun, eds., *Russia's Military Might: A Portrait of Its Armed Forces.* Copenhagen: Djøf, 2021.

Stratfrod, James. "Strategic Culture and the North Korean Nuclear Crisis." *Security Challenges* 1, no. 1 (2005): 123–33.

Strelchenko, B. I., and E. A. Ivanov. "Nekotorye Aspekti Otsenki Sootnosheniia Sil v Operatsiiakh." *Voennaia Mysl'*, no. 10 (1987).

Stronski, Paul, and Andrew S. Weiss. "Why Isn't Russia Talking About the Great Power Competition?" *Carnegie Endowment for International Peace*, May 27, 2021.

Suchkov, Maxim. "Iadernoe Pravoslavie v Voine Buduschego." *Rossiia V Global'noi Politike*, no. 3 (May/July 2019).

———. "Whose Hybrid Warfare? How 'the Hybrid Warfare' Concept Shapes Russian Discourse, Military, and Political Practice." *Small Wars and Insurgencies* 32, no. 3 (2021).

Suchkov, Maxim, and Seam Teck. *Buduschie Voiny.* Moscow: Valdaiskii Kluv, 2019.

Sukhorutchenko, V. V., A. B. Zelvin, and V. A. Sobolevskii. "Napravlenie Issledovanii Boevykh Vozmozhnostej Vysokotochnogo Oruzhija Bol''shoj Dal''nosti v Obychnom Snarjazhenii." *Voennaia Mysl'*, no. 8 (2009): 32–28.

Suslov, Dmitry. "Ot Pariteta k Razumnoi Dostatochnosti." *Rossiia v Global'noi Politike*, no. 6 (November/December 2010).

Suslov, Mihail. "The Utopia of Holy Rus' in Today's Geopolitical Imagination." *Plural* 2, no. 1 (2014): 81–97.

Sweijs, Tim, and Samuel Zilinick. "The Essence of Cross-Domain Deterrence." In Frans Osinga and Tim Swejis, eds., *Deterrence in the 21st Century: Insights from Theory and Practice.* The Hague: Springer and Asser Press, 2021.

Thornton, Rod. "Soviet Principle of Aktivnost' in Warfare." *Russia Seminar*, February 2, 2021. https://www.youtube.com/watch?v=kuN41R7h7Cw.

Tiushkevich, S. A. "Razumnaia Dostatochnost' Dlia Oborony: Parametry i Kriterii." *Voennaia Mysl'*, no. 5 (1989): 53–61.

Tolstukhina, Anastasiia. "V Garmish-Partenkirkhene Sobralis Veduschie Eksperty Mira po Informatsionnoi Bezopasnosti." *Mezhdunarodnaia Zhyzn'*, April 27, 2018.

Tomas, Timoti. "Kontseptsia Kiber/Informatsionnogo Sderzhivaniia KNR: Mnenie iz SShA." *Digital Report*, July 27, 2015.

Tor, Uri. "Cumulative Deterrence as a New Paradigm for Cyber Deterrence." *Journal of Strategic Studies* 40, no. 1 (2017): 92–117.

Trofimenko, Henry. *Changing Attitudes towards Deterrence.* Los Angeles: University of California Press 1980.

Tsugichko, V. N. "O Kategorii Sootnoshenie Sil v Potentsial'nykh Voennykh Konfliktakh." *Voennaia Mysl'*, no. 3 (2002).

———. *Prognozirovanie Sotsial'no-ekonomicheskikh Protsessov*. Moscow: URSS, 2017.

Tsugichko, V. I., and F. Stoili. "Metod Boevykh potentsialov." *Voennaia Mysl'*, no. 4 (1997): 23–28.

Tsygankov, Andrei P. *Russia and the West from Alexander to Putin: Honor in International Relations*. Cambridge: Cambridge University Press, 2012.

Turko, N. I., and S. A. Modestvov. "Refleksivnoe Upravelenie Razvitiem Strategicheskikh Sil Gosudarstva." *Sistemnyi Analiz na Poroge 21 Veka*. Conference Proceedings, Moscow, 1996.

Twomey, Christopher. *The Military Lens*. Ithaca, NY: Cornell University Press, 2010.

Tyushkevich, S. A. "Metdologiia Sootnosheniia Sil Storon v Voine." *Voennaia Mysl'*, no. 6 (1969).

Uzlaner, Dmitry. "Konets Pravolsavnogo Konsensusa: Religiia kak Novyo Raskol Rossiiskogo Obschestva." *Novoe Literaturnoe Obozrenie* 3, no. 163 (2020).

Vanaga, Nora, and Toms Rostoks, eds. *Deterring Russia in Europe: Defence Strategies for Neighbouring States*. London: Routledge, 2019.

Varfolomeev, Igor'. "Iadernaia Deviatka." *KZ*, May 25, 2011.

Veselov, V. A. "Iaderneyi Faktor v Mirovoi Politike." *Mezhdunarodnye Otnosheniia I Mirovaia Politika*, no. 1 (2010): 68–89.

———. "Programma Kursa Strategicheskaia Stabil'nost'." *Mezhdunarodnye Otnosheniia I Mirovaia Politika*, no. 4 (2010): 135–51.

Vikulov, S. F., and G. P. Zhukov. *Voenno-ekonomicheskii Analiz I Issledovanie Operatsii*. Moscow: Voenizdat, 1987.

Vladimirov, A. I. *Osnovy Obscheii Teorii Voiny*. Moscow: Sinergiia, 2013.

Vladimirov, V. I., and V. I. Stuchinskii. "Obosnovanie Primenenija Avionosnsikh Nositelei Sredstv Radioleletronnoi Bor'bi v Operativnoi Glubine Dlia Zavoevania Informatsionnogo Prevoshodstva." *Voennaia Mysl'*, no. 5 (2016): 15–21.

Voevodin, V. *Strategii Voiny, Biznessa, Manipuliatsii, Obmana*. Moscow: Et setera, 2004.

Volgin, V. A. "Razvitie Form Radioelektronnogo i Ogenvogo Porazheniia Protivnika." *Voennaia Mysl'*, no. 4 (2010): 31–34.

Vorob'ev, I., and V. Kiselev. "Strategiia Nepriamykh Desitvii v Novom Oblike." *Voennaia Mysl'*, no. 9 (2006): 2–10.

Wenger, Andreas, and Alex Wilner, eds. *Deterring Terrorism: Theory and Practice*. Stanford, CA: Stanford University Press, 2012.

White, Sarah P. *Subcultural Influence on Military Innovation: The Development of U.S. Military Cyber Doctrine*. PhD diss., Harvard University, 2019.

Williams, A. M. "Strategic Culture and Cyber Warfare: A Methodology for Comparative Analysis." *Journal of Informational Warfare* 19, no. 1 (2020): 113–27.

Wills, Michael, Ashley J. Tellis, and Alison Szalwinski, eds. *Understanding Strategic Cultures in Asia-Pacific*. National Bureau of Asian Research, 2016.

Wilner, Alex. "Deterring the Undeterrable: Coercion, Denial, and Delegitimization in Counterterrorism." *Journal of Strategic Studies* 34, no. 1 (2011): 3–37.

Wirtz, James J. "Cyber War and Strategic Culture: The Russian Integration of Cyber Power into Grand Strategy." In Kenneth Geers, ed., *Cyber War in Perspective: Russian Aggression against Ukraine*. Tallinn: NATO CCD COE, 2015.

———. *Understanding Intelligence Failure: Warning, Response and Deterrence*. London: Routledge, 2016.

Yarhi-Milo, Keren. *Who Fights for Reputation? The Psychology of Leaders in International Conflict*. Princeton, NJ: Princeton University Press, 2018.

Yossef, Amr. "Military Doctrines in Israel and Iran: A Doctrinal Hybridity." *Middle Eastern Journal* 75, no. 2 (2021): 243–63.

Zabegalin, E. V. "K Voprosy of Opredelenii Termina Informatsionno-tekhnicheskoe Vozdeistvie." *Sistemy Upravleniia, Sviazi I Bezopasnotsti*, no. 2 (2018): 121–50.

Zaitsev, A. "Novyi mirovoi poriadok kak istoricheskaia neobkhodimost' I ispol'zvonaie oruzhiia neletal'nogo deistviia." *Trudy BGTU: Istoriia I Filosophia* 1, no. 245 (2012): 107–11.

Zaitsev, D. V., A. V. Kozlov, and V. M. Moiseev. "Rol' i mesto oruzhiia neletal'nogo deistviia v konflitkah nizkoi intenstivnosti." *Strategicheskaia Stabil'nost'* 4, no. 61 (2012): 27–35.

Zamulin, Valerriy. "To Defeat the Enemy Was Less a Problem than the Laziness and Indolence of Our Own Commanders." *Journal of Slavic Military Studies* 29, no. 4 (2016): 707–26.

Zarudnitskii, V. B. "Faktory Dostizheniia Pobedy v Voennykh Konfliktah Budusschego." *Voennaia Mysl'*, no. 8 (2021): 34–47.

———. "Vtoraia Mirovaia i Velikaia Otechestvennaia Voina: Uroki i Vyvody." *Voennaia Mysl'*, no. 3 (2021): 102–17.

Zelendinova, Vera. "Tsifrovoi Suverinetet Rossii: Missiia Vypolnima." *NG*, August 2020.

Zhang, Shu Guang. *Deterrence and Strategic Culture: Chinese-American Confrontations, 1949–1958*. Ithaca, NY: Cornell University Press, 1993.

Zhukov, Georgii. *Vospominania I Razmyshleniia*. Moscow: Voenizdat, 1980.

Zhurkin, V. A., S. A. Karaganov, and A. V. Kortunov. *Razumnaia Dostatochnost' I Novoe Politicheskoe Myshlenie*. Moscow: Obschestvennye nauki I sovremennost', 1989.

Ziegler, Charles. "A Crisis of Diverging Perspectives: US-Russian Relations and the Security Dilemma." *Texas National Security Review* 4, no. 1 (Winter 2021).

Zimmerman, Rebecca, Kimberly Jackson, Natasha Lander, Colin Roberts, Dan Madden, and Rebeca Orrie. *Movement and Maneuver: Culture and the Competition for Influence among the U.S. Military Services*. Washington, DC: RADN, 2019.

Zinger, Herr von. *Strategemy. O Kitaiskom Iskusstve Zhit' I Vizhivat'*. Moscow: Eksmo, 2004.